The Life & Times of "Himself"... The War Years

A personal story of life during the early Twentieth Century - The Great Depression and Anti- Sub service in World War II by one of those often referred to as the "Greatest Generation

Francis Mahoney

Copyright © 2013 by Francis Mahoney

The Life & Times of "Himself" ... The War Years
A personal story of life during the early Twentieth Century - The Great Depression and Anti- Sub service in World War II by one of those often referred to as the "Greatest Generation

by Francis Mahoney

Printed in the United States of America

ISBN 9781626979505

All rights reserved solely by the author. The author guarantees all contents are original and do not infringe upon the legal rights of any other person or work. No part of this book may be reproduced in any form without the permission of the author. The views expressed in this book are not necessarily those of the publisher.

www.xulonpress.com

In Loving Memory of my Daughter Ellen

This book is dedicated to my daughter Ellen, whose desire was for me to publish this story of my life, Written over many years. I began with a spiral notebook, a manual typewriter, then a Tandy One Thousand computer with only a floppy disk as the hard drive, and eventually a Windows 95 pc. It was a labor of love for the family, thanks in great measure to Ellen's help and persistence. She died of Breast Cancer in 2012 after a nine year battle with the cancer. She spent her life using her God given talents and education to work with non-profit groups, such as Easter Seals, Leukemia, and others. She ended her career with the American Cancer Society working in Advocacy efforts to raise funds for cancer research. She formed her own "Ellen's angels" group to raise funds with the "Making Strides"

annual walk, with great success. Without her this book would not have been published. Thank You Ellen!!

Acknowledgments and Credits

My appreciation to the following for their assistance!!
The great lithograph copies of Jim Kennedy's Patrol Craft from the PCSA Store: The Moonlight Convoy, In Port for R&R, Patrol Craft Underway, and the cover photo "Rough Rider". – These great paintings are gratefully acknowledged in memory of Jim Kennedy.

Thanks to the Patrol Craft Sailors Association for the use of photos and material from its newsletter and files.

Thanks to my grandson, David Mahoney, for his well-done sketches of the Knickers, the Bike etc. from my memories of the past.

Some pictures from my personal files, gleaned from old sources, are of poor quality, but helpful to the story, I apologize!

A personal note: The term "Himself", in the title of the book, derives from the old Irish term for the "Man of the house". Referring to him in the third person. My wife Peggy's immigrant Irish grandmother, Nora (Coyne) Malloy, often asked about me in that manner.

Table of Contents

1	Events leading up to the Orphanage	xi
2	Living in the Orphanage	15
3	After leaving the Orphanage	59
4	Serving in the Navy	137
	Boot camp and Training	
	The Anti-Submarine war in the Atlantic	
	Pacific war in the Solomon's	
	R&R in Australia	
	The Marianas Islands & Iwo Jima	
	Victory in 1945 & Return to the States	
	Duty at Cape May N. J.	
	Discharge from the Navy	
5	Post War	277

Forward to the History

"The Life and Times of Himself"
The "Early Years" and the "War Years"
A Personal History of the life during the Great Depression and
Anti-submarine warfare during World War II – By F.J.Mahoney

"The Early Years," from September 1928 until August 1936. A personal story of what it was like living in an orphanage with five hundred other children during the Great Depression. We lived a life of necessary regimentation while receiving the loving care and support of the people in the community in spite of their own financial difficulties. Recollections of daily life at St. Paul's Orphanage during those difficult years were filled with colorful events, both sad and happy at times, then to experience the joy of living a normal life as a family after eight years in the orphanage. Enjoying the feeling of freedom, being able to come and go with only the rules set down by your parents. The clouds of war were building all through his teen years as Hitler, Mussolini and the Empire of Japan were engaged in world conquest. In America the draft was enacted and boys his age knew they would be involved. Not if, but when war would come to America.

"The War Years," from November 1942 until April 1946, when he served in the U.S. Navy on board an anti-submarine Sub-chaser, the USS PC 606. He relates an interesting account of life on board one of the smallest United States Navy all steel vessels, only 173 feet in length. The ship was originally designed for coastal waters but due to the submarine menace off our shores in the Atlantic, more than 600 of these small vessels, each manned by 60 men and 5 officers, were put into service, escorting convoys of troop and supply ships to the forward areas. Some articles written about these little Sub-chasers called them "The Bucking Bronco's" of the sea. The author tells stories of voyages and invasions throughout the South Pacific, Micronesia and in the Japanese islands. His personal stories tell of the close relationships of the crew. Re-living the boredom of endless days on convoys, the times of stress and humor of life aboard his ship, serving in the war zones until victory was achieved in August 1945.

St. Paul's Orphanage - The Early Years
August 1928 to November 1942

Archival photo of St. Paul's Orphanage, where the author and his two siblings lived for eight years during the Great Depression. From 1928 to 1936. The "Home" as it was called, held over seven hundred children during its peak years. Supported only through the generosity and the good will of the people of Pittsburgh and its Church congregations, and without government regulations.

The Author Francis, Age five, on the right, with his sister Jeannie, Age four and brother Jerry, Age seven.

These were their ages at the time they were placed in St. Paul's Orphanage due to the economic situation of the times, which made it difficult for their father to care for them by himself. The Orphanage was "Home" to abandoned & orphaned children, regardless of race or creed, operated by the Catholic Diocese of Pittsburgh

The Orphanage Years
1928-1936

M y story begins with this account of the circumstances, which led to my siblings and I being placed in the caring environment of St. Paul's orphanage asylum in Crafton, a suburb of Pittsburgh. On the death of our mother, Regina, in 1926, my father was left with three small children to raise. My sister Jeannie was two, I was four, and my brother Jerry was six. With the nation still in recovery from the World War I recession it was difficult for other family members to take us in. Dad made one more attempt to keep us together as a family, renting a small cottage high above the trolley yards on Mt. Washington. The small home was located just across the trolley tracks above the home where Dad's sister, my aunt Margaret and her husband John Patterson lived. They had three boys, Will, John, and Robert. The Patterson family was always close to us, and I have some memories of the house on the side of the steep hill above South Hills junction. We could climb down to the trolley yards where all of the cars were lined up on the sidings and in the barns. The short time we spent at the Patterson home was a happy experience with everyone in the family, so sympathetic to our problems.

How long we lived there, I'm not sure, but I do recall living there on one Fourth of July in 1927, just before we went into the orphanage. My memory of that day is still clear because of a fireworks episode concerning my Dad and me. He had brought home a vegetable box filled with various fireworks to celebrate on the Fourth of July, with stern warnings to us children not to touch them. He put the box under his bed for safety, until it would be time to set them off. How those fire-works were somehow accidentally set off, my memory is not clear, although I do remember being yelled at quite severely for some reason or other shortly after the incident. It couldn't have been my fault, after all I was only five, and the youngest boy at that time. The memory I do have, is Dad pulling out a box of exploding fireworks from under the bed and throwing them, box and all, out the window. Fortunately, they didn't all go off, so there were still many left for a noisy Fourth of July celebration. However the main event didn't even compare to the noise and excitement of that discussion in Dad's room with me, later on.

Our happy days there, near to the Patterson family home, didn't last long. Once again, Dad relied on someone he discovered he couldn't trust. Since he had to go to look for work each day, he hired a housekeeper to look after the house and us. She was also a seamstress, and asked Dad to buy some material so she could make clothes for us. She used up all the material at hand making clothes for her own family, without Dad's knowledge. She continued to ask for more material, but nothing ever seemed to get finished for us. It was one morning after a loud argument over that and some other problem, after Dad had gone to work, she left us alone in the middle of the day, and then made a phone call to notify the Catholic Social workers to report that three young children had been left alone and abandoned, giving them directions on where to find us.

My faint recollections of the event, was these ladies in their big hats coming to the door and telling us we had to go with them, promising that Dad would come to get us later on. I can imagine his shock when poor Dad came home that day only to find his children gone. And in plain view, was a very official notice that we had been taken to St. Gabriel's orphanage until a decision could be made concerning our future care. St. Gabriel's was just a temporary home for short term care of children whose families were having difficulty or who needed time to get a fresh start and to get their affairs in order. It was also a haven for any abandoned children, a common occurrence

The Orphanage Years 1928-1936

during the depression. It was a Catholic Church sponsored program designed to help families in distress to get back on their feet. At that time other Christian and Jewish organizations had similar groups who worked together in the common cause of caring for children, regardless of religion or race.

That evening, when Dad came to see us at St. Gabriel's he explained how it would be best for us to remain there in the care of the orphanage, until he could arrange for us to be together in our own home again. I can remember looking out through the window of the sitting room, through droplets of rain, as Dad slowly walked toward the trolley stop close by. He looked so down and sorrowful to me, with his head bowed, not looking back. Even the room itself, gave an air of gloom to all that was happening to us. That darkened room, with furniture to match, and the formal atmosphere overall didn't provide a very happy feeling in view of what Dad had told us. In my five year old child's mind, and thinking only in the duration of time, I felt sure it would only be a short period, but my older brother Jerry took it much harder, and he fought against the idea for years afterward. Had we known and understood at the time, that our short stay at St. Paul's, would last for eight long years, perhaps Jeannie and I wouldn't have accepted life in the home, so readily either.

Looking back on the events as they occurred, I have often wondered about the impact the orphanage has had on my later life. As fate would have it, consider the fact that riding with us on the bus to St. Paul's from St. Gabriel's, were two boys, Jimmy and Tom. Jimmy was my age and Tom was Jerry's age, so Tom was more a friend of Jerry's in the orphanage, rather than mine. For some reason it was Tom who invited me, out of the blue, to attend his wedding in June 1946, just after my discharge from the Navy, that had such an influence on my future life. His bride, worked at Spears Department store in downtown Pittsburgh. Pa. Among her friends at Spears, was my own future bride, Peggy, who I met at that wedding and married the following year. Details of the whirlwind courtship are told in the "Post War Years", section of my history. As the story happened, after I had left the orphanage in 1936, and served in the Navy until April 1946 and after ten years without any contact with Tom, he invites me to his wedding, and there I meet my wonderful wife. Now I ask you, was it really meant for me to spend those childhood years at St. Paul's orphanage in order to fulfill the plan the Lord had in store for me from the start? Personally, I believe it!

Back to the story: After our bus arrived at the "home", we soon became part of the population, based on our ages. Jean was taken to the girl's kindergarten; I was taken to what was called the Kinders, for those boys five and six. Jerry went to the Minim's, for boys seven and eight years of age. Dad fought so hard to keep us together after our mother died, but here we were, now totally separated and out of contact. Not only did we lose contact with our father, but the close association with our siblings as well. Only on Sundays, when Dad came to visit, were we a family once again, for an hour or two at least. During the eight years, from 1928 to 1936, Dad missed very few of the visitor days. He would bring us fruit and candy, and when he could spare it, he deposited .50¢ with the candy store, so we could enjoy a treat during the week. The candy store was just a small room in the basement, run by one of the Sisters, which was opened for an hour or so after school. Usually, I blew my share of the wealth on cracker-jack; never giving up hoping for the genuine diamond ring they claimed was in some of the boxes.

As I mentioned, my dad always brought us fruit which he bought at a fruit stand in downtown Pittsburgh before getting on the trolley to the orphanage. On one Sunday when we happily opened our bag of goodies, there were carrots and vegetables instead of the long awaited fruit. It seems dad picked up the wrong bag as he left the stand, the carrots were pretty good though and he donated the rest to the kitchen. One thing dad always did for us on his Sunday visits, was to read the Sunday comics, like Tarzan the ape-man, Buck Rodgers, Maggie and Jigg's, Toonerville Trolley, the Katzenjammer kids, Popeye the sailor man, Little Orphan Annie, and many others that were popular at the time. He would start out by reading Tarzan in a scary voice, Tarzan drew his sharp dagger, and he began to battle with the ferocious lion, etc. etc. Those visits lasted for several hours which seemed like minutes, then it was over and we went our separate ways until the next Sunday. Years later, after we left the orphanage, we did have some close father and son talks. He told me of the anguish he always felt having to go back to his rented rooms, leaving us there.

One of my earliest memories of the orphanage was when the doctor at St. Paul's determined that my tonsils were to be removed, and in the conventional medical knowledge of the times, my adenoids were to be removed as well. It seems that adenoids served no visible purpose, and removal was the best thing. Today adenoids are left in for some reason or other. The surgery had to be done at the Mercy hospital in Pittsburgh. The orphanage was only equipped for small emergencies. I can still recall Dad carrying me in my white hospital gown, crying up a storm, mainly because my head had been shaved clean; also fear of the unknown had a strong hand in my bad feelings. Maybe, because everyone kept telling me it would be alright, that just made it worse, even my Dad's promises of lots of ice cream later on, I was suspicious. Finally, when the operation was over, I was awakened with terrible throat pains the operation had caused and the nausea from the ether used to put me to sleep. To make things better, there was my dad just waiting for me to come out of it.

My bed was placed in the men's ward, because of an over-flowing children's ward at the time. It could not have been better, even if I had planned it that way. Because, all the men treated me like a young prince, their wives brought me presents and I was deluged with cookies, candy, and ice cream constantly. I was the poor little orphan kid from St. Paul's who needed TLC and sympathy and I played it to the hilt, just as any fine red-blooded American kid would do! Later, when they rolled my bed out of the men's ward and into the children's ward, my bed was covered with lots of goodies, which I shared with the other kids in the ward. The best part having to get my tonsils out was the one on one time I was able to spend with my dad. Other than on Sunday's, there was little contact between my sister Jeannie, and my brother Jerry. As I recall, there was very little personal communication between us about our friends or our activities at St. Paul's. Sadly, we really didn't have that much in common during our everyday life at the home.

After we had been in the orphanage for a time, and we were both in the main dormitory, Dad requested that I be put in the same division as my brother Jerry. I think his idea was Jerry could look out for his little brother. Unfortunately, the way it worked out I became known as "Peanut", since I was the youngest and smallest kid in "E" division. So, it followed, that Jerry was called "Big Peanut", by juvenile logic. Calling me "Peanut", a nickname that was mine as long as I was in the orphanage, put me in the position of being the one kid little enough for any other guy in the division to beat up. Dad's great theory didn't work very well. Anyway, I thought I could take care of myself and I didn't need any help from my big brother. Later on I was back with my own age group in "F" division, a bigger, tougher, "Peanut" and no longer a punching bag. Especially after my run in with a guy called, Lanky Bill, he was one boy who found great pleasure in picking a fight with me when I was in "E" Division. He was a tall skinny kid, with extra-long arms. Our fights always ended the same, "Peanut" lost!

There was a tough street kid in our division by the name of Nicholas, who just got tired seeing this guy being a bully. So one day he told me I was going into training, and with his help, Lanky Bill would get his! I don't know who taught him how to fight, but he lived on the streets until coming to the home and nobody ever messed with Nick. He worked with me, teaching me all his tricks until he decided I was ready. Early one Saturday we went looking for Bill, little did he know what was in store that day? When we found him he was bending down getting himself a drink at the water fountain. Right then according to my coach's advice, I tapped him on the shoulder and as he turned to see who it was bang, right on the nose, I let him have it. His eyes filled with tears, his nose turned red and as he tried to fight back I pounded on him until he turned tail and ran. All I suffered were a few bruised knuckles, where I had hit the wall instead of Lanky Bill. After that, not only did he lay off me, but a few other potential bullies got the message too. Nick's basic rule for bullies was to avoid conflict if you are able, but if forced into it, hit first hit hard and aim for the nose! It sure worked with my own personal bully then, and a few other occasions in later years.

The Orphanage Years 1928-1936

Vintage sketch of St. Paul's Orphanage and buildings. The main building was for office space. Children's Dining hall, with the church above it. Next, the kitchen and a dining area for staff.

Boys Dormitory
The boy's dormitory was home for over 250 boys. There were six dormitories or Divisions. (A)- for ages 16 & 17 to (F) for ages 5 & 6. Younger boys were housed in another area.

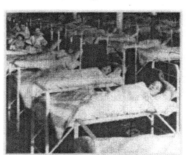

Girls Dormitory
The bed arrangement is much the same as in the boys dormitory's and separated by ages similar to the boys. The girls dormitory was located behind the main group of buildings.

Every kid at the home talked about that wonderful day, when they would be able to leave the home to live with a parent, or a guardian. For many of them, their only hope was to be adopted, but due to the depression there were so many abandoned and homeless children that adoption was rare. During this period Church charitable groups had taken in such large numbers of the homeless kid's, that, "Orphan trains", were organized during the thirties, designed to send older orphans to the western states to be adopted into willing farm families. Older children were especially desired by the farmers who needed help on the farm or in their trade. It was well run by the charitable agencies, which set up homes and adoptions for orphans who accepted the terms. Both the children and their foster parents had recourse to leave the arrangement if it did not work out for whatever reason. I was one of the lucky ones, like my brother Jerry and my sister Jeannie, we had a father who loved us and who wanted, more than anything to prepare a home for us as soon as he was able. One of the stipulations for children living at St. Paul's was the requirement to provide a stable home before the children could leave.

Sometimes Dad would take us away from the home for day's visit to some of our family relatives. One special day I recall, was a train ride to Baden, south of Pittsburgh on the Ohio River. We went to visit my aunt, Sister Mary Paula, my Dad's oldest sister, she was a Catholic nun of the St. Joseph's order who taught first and second grades in the many Parochial schools of the Pittsburgh Diocese. While on that visit in Baden we had a picnic on the convent grounds and the day turned out to be a special treat, because there were several World War One aircraft putting on a show in a nearby town. We could see them in the sky, diving, looping, and performing dangerous rollovers and other aerobatics. The show ended with a parachute jump by one of the flying Dare-devils. Even the sight of a plane in the sky brought out everyone within sight of it, they were so rare in those days. At the orphanage we would all run out and wave when one of the big Ford Tri-motor mail planes flew over, always sure the pilot could see us even if he didn't wave back.

Another trip I recall was to visit one of my mother's sisters, at her home in Beltzhoover not far from where my mother and family grew up. She was my aunt Agnes (Picard) Fitzpatrick, who cared for my grandmother, Catherine Picard. Grandmother was blind and lived in her upstairs bedroom most of the time, until her death in 1938 at age 78. Each of us would take a turn to go up the stairs to visit her. I can remember going into her darkened bedroom and she smiled brightly when I talked to her. As she spoke to me she would run her hands over my face seeming to visualize what I looked like. My cousin Bob Vogel, who is the son of my Aunt Ginny, mother's older sister told me how he would try to tip toe quietly upstairs to surprise her and before he even reached the top, she would somehow recognize his footsteps and call him by name. I don't know when Grandma became blind, but she raised her four children alone after my Grandfather, Nicholas Picard, disappeared. There is a mystery about the disappearance of Grandfather Nicholas. Sometime in 1913 after the family was raised Grandfather just disappeared. He was a carpenter by trade and he went off to work as usual one day and was never heard from again. After his disappearance, grand-mother Catherine and the family had to go on without him.

Uncle Al Fitzpatrick made his own home brew during the prohibition years. It was legal to make an amount of beer for home consumption and a very common thing to do. He had a boxer dog which loved to sample the brew. Uncle Al would put some in a dish saucer for him, then before long the dog was putting on a sideshow, acting quite tipsy. Aunt Agnes would always scold Uncle Al for doing that to the poor dumb animal, but the dog never complained. Dad put a lesson to it, saying too much beer is bad for man or beast. Another memory of Uncle Al was his motorcycle a giant machine with a roomy side car. Uncle Al would give us kids rides up and down the steep hills around Mt. Washington giving us the thrill of our young lives. The hardest thing for me, at the end of those visits, was to say goodbye to our Grandma Catherine. She was so very kind and seemed so lonely and it made me sad to see her all alone like that and I always remembered her in my prayers. When I would find myself feeling sorry for little Peanuts problems I would think of her, unable to see the world around her, living so alone.

On another outing we visited my mother's oldest sister, Aunt Ginny and Uncle Joe Vogel. It was especially memorable, because their home was high above the Monongahela River on Bonifay Street in what was known as Upper St. Clair, looking down on Pittsburgh's South Side, far below with the steel mills pouring their black smoke into the air making steel. I can visualize their house on the upper side of the hill, more like a mountain than a hill to someone as young as I was. It was at their home that I had my first experience listening to popular radio shows like Little Orphan Annie, Tom Mix and Jack Armstrong known on the show as "The All-American boy". We seldom heard any of the daily radio shows while in the orphanage the only radio we had was a large old model with a large horn on top of the unit with several big dials on it. We kept it all shined up at its location on a corner table in the recreation room. The radio was only played on a few special occasions, like Notre Dame Football games, or when the Pitt Panthers played their games at the University of Pittsburgh.

At Aunt Ginny and Uncle Joe's home, there were many cousins to play with their oldest son was Regis, then Joe, Betty, and Rita. The Vogel's had twelve children, but those were the ones I remember best. Especially Rita, who liked to watch me turn red by trying to give me a kiss, causing me to blush from head to toe, she thought that was great fun. Actually, it was fun for me too. Those happy trips away from the home didn't happen, all that often, and I don't have very many recollections of my relatives from those days, but in later years I did meet many of them. They all had a desire to help us at the time, but those were the years of the great depression and it was a struggle for most families just to make ends meet. Aunt Ginny would like to have had my sister Jeannie live with them even though they already had a large family, but Dad had that strong notion that he wanted to keep us together. Perhaps it was something he had promised our mother before she died, but Dad was firm on that idea. In theory we were together there in the orphanage, even though separated for the most part anyway.

It may seem sad to some that I was a poor orphan living in an orphanage, but looking back I didn't think of it that way. Fortunately, I just enjoyed my life as it was with all my many friends, not knowing any other kind of life and accepting the conditions as they were. St. Paul's orphanage was home for over 500 children, a huge complex with had its own church, hospital, school, bakery, laundry, kitchens, mess halls, and dormitories for both boys and girls. St. Paul's had everything necessary to make it self-sufficient. There was a large farm area for growing fresh produce, some fruit trees and labor was never a problem. We all had our chores, depending on age. There was even a coal mine to feed the boilers which provided steam heat and hot water for showers and the laundry. Boys were assigned to dormitories depending on age, starting with Kinder or Kindergarten, and Minim's for 6 year olds. The main boy's dormitory building had (A) through (F) divisions. (F) Division for 6 and 7 year olds, and so on, until (A) division with the oldest boys 17 and 18 years old. Every dormitory had its rows of beds with stool and assigned locker for each boy. Dormitories were equipped with a large washroom; the sinks were back to back in the center, with toilet stalls along both walls. Our hot showers were a bi-weekly group effort as each division made the trip to the main complex basement shower room for a hot shower. During the week sponge baths were taken in the washroom at specific times.

My nose still wears the scar of an incident which happened on one of our weekly shower trips to the main building. When our division had completed its showers, supplied with our clean towel and washcloth for daily use, we put on our clean underwear, shirt and knickers, shoes and socks, for the return trip to our dorm. We had to go down a long hallway to the stairs leading outside. I was assigned to gather any extra loose towels and to put them in the hamper provided. By the time I had performed my task the last of my buddies had left the hallway and were gone up the stairway. I hurried down the hall when someone turned out the lights, leaving me in pitch blackness. I couldn't see my hand in front of my face and I began to feel my way along the wall following the pipes anchored alongside it feeling my way carefully. As I began to gain confidence I started moving faster when suddenly I hit something on the left side of my nose and could feel the blood flowing down my face. I used my wash cloth to hold against my nose and with my finger I could feel the deep cut on my left nostril. I started yelling as loud as I could to get help, but my voice just echoed in the empty hall and nobody answered. Feeling along the wall I found the big valve without a wheel on it. The stem with its sharp end was sticking out from the pipe and had struck my left nostril tearing it open. Deciding it was best to move away from the wall a bit using my hand to guide me along the pipe thus avoiding any other valve stems. Later on I was able to see how fortunate I was that I had only cut my nose. There were other missing wheels that could have just as easily struck me in the eye. When I finally made it back to the dorm I cleaned up in the bathroom sink as best I could, dressing it with some adhesive tape from a first aid kit using it to hold my nostril in place until it healed. Being young, with my body exploding with new cells, it soon healed, but left a scar that is still visible today. Looking back, I know it would have been wiser to turn myself in for first aid in the home hospital, but being such an tough independent kid who would rather do it himself I just let nature take its course. Anyway, the scar has always been an obvious conversation piece over the years.

Every dormitory had what was loosely referred to as the recreation center. Used on only rare occasions of open house or on special visitor's days, each of them had an old radio with attached speaker horn on the top. There were chairs, tables and a small library of children's books, plus assorted games. Except for the times when I was on a work detail to shine up the room, I spent very little time having recreation there. Each dormitory had a room for the Sister in charge, so someone with final authority would be available for emergencies. To help the Sister with her charges one of the older boys from (A) division would stay in the younger dorms to assist in keeping order. With over 40 boys to each division discipline had to be a top priority. Punishment was administered and the rules were always strict. The "Prefect", a nice man and our sports coach, was the man who came around on Saturdays to give the appropriate number of whacks with his strap. All the bad boys who had earned demerits lined up to take their turn bending over the four legged stool placed where all could watch. The limber leather strap was a foot long with a hand grip on the bottom it was thick and had holes several inches apart. Even one whack left its mark on the bottom, something you could show your buddies afterwards, like a special mark or badge of distinction or something we thought was tough, cool in today's lingo. That sort of discipline may sound a bit cruel and today it would be probably be called child abuse, but stern measures had to be taken to keep the foxes from taking over the henhouse. I am sure the girl's had their own lady "Prefect" to maintain discipline, but I don't know how punishment was administered to them my sister Jeannie never mentioned it to me, I guess she never did anything wrong.

Did I ever get the strap? Yes I did, but only a few times. Usually for not being at muster when I should have been. For example; in the summer some of those in our gang liked to sneak out through the thick cemetery hedge fence, which bordered one side of the home. Our purpose was to go for a swim at the "Ice Box" which was a pond formed from a caved in mine that filled up with ice cold spring water from deep underground. The pond was located in the section called Greentree, a few miles away from the home. First we would get a hot coal fire going in order to keep hides from turning blue. Good coal from the old mine was scattered every-where around the mine area for us to use. There was a rope swing which was the only logical way to get into that freezing water. The procedure was to climb up onto the platform nailed to a tree then to swing out and drop into the frigid icy water. The shock would take your breath away and then it was back to the roaring fire to warm up then back to the swing again for another frozen dip. We really did enjoy our "old, cold, swimmin' hole, in spite of turning blue with cold.

We also had to think of the punishment that we knew might follow if we were caught. The problem usually was, back at the home the prefect, a really nice guy in spite of his occupation, was busy taking a muster of the divisions and those who did not answer to their name, were put down to be disciplined. When our turn came up for a paddling we always did our best to act like it wasn't anything, even though our backsides knew better. To be honest, our caretakers had good reason for not wanting us to swim in those mine pit pools. One danger we didn't realize, there were hidden timbers sticking up from down below the water's surface and kids had drowned there from cramps, as well, caused by the frigid water. Perhaps I should not divulge this bit of youthful insanity, but since it is an insight into my personality, here goes. My best friend Joe Fitzgerald and I were the leaders of our small gang of boys who often did everything together, even getting into trouble, so in order to show just how tough we were as leaders, Joe and I, would sometimes be there attending muster and then just refuse to answer when our name was called. Of course, that meant we had to take our punishment later on, but we sure did show that prefect, didn't we? Now don't confuse our little gang of kids who played together and did things as a group, with what a gangs are today, bent on doing unlawful and illegal activities. We were more like the "our gang" of the movies. Actually, as I look back, the only ones we ever harmed were ourselves.

St. Paul's Orphanage - The Early Years
August 1928 to November 1942

St. Paul's Hospital
The hospital was equipped for minor medical emergencies. It was my destination after breaking my arm, when I fell from the roof of the shelter building, and especially the time when I cut my foot in Chartier Creek for a real medical emergency.

A typical scene, similar to St. Paul's farm area. Mainly table vegetables were grown there, with help from all the orphans.

The Orphanage Years 1928-1936

A typical day at St. Paul's began around 6 am. We would take turns at the wash basins. First brushing our teeth with the dampened salt from the containers available for us, no tooth-paste then, it was either the salt or baking soda. No hot water either; we only got that when we got our weekly shower. Then the choice of which clothes to wear would come up. The decision of which pair of knickers trousers should you put on? The pair used for dress or the pair for play? No problem, the dress pair was for church or family visits, so the choice was quite simple. About those knickers trousers, the leg bottoms came to just below the knees with an elastic band around the leg to hold up your long stockings, then you spent a good part of the day pulling up the socks and pulling down the elastic leg bands over them. A little history on the rite of reaching maturity for a boy concerned the end of wearing knickers at age twelve and you could now begin to wear long pants. By the nineteen forties, knickers went the way of the buggy whip and a discriminatory practice against young boys was ended. After getting dressed you made up your cot, tucking the sheet tight and folding the blanket as required and then to sit on your stool waiting until the time to line up for the march to the mess hall for breakfast, trying to ignore the growls in the tummy.

On Sundays we got up a bit later and marched to the church in the main building for mass and prayers. Then after church we went downstairs to the mess hall for breakfast. We always had a hot cereal, like oatmeal or cornmeal mush, with lots of bread and butter, and a glass of fresh milk. Second servings were not available except for the bread and butter. Sugar was always mixed into the cereal for economy's sake, although I sometimes had trouble detecting the amount of sugar. In the mess hall we sat at the same assigned table, in the same assigned seat for all of our meals. With the reasoning that an empty seat meant a missing kid, sick or off the premises, so it was easy to check attendance. We sat with our own division and age group, and a lot of fights over the grabbing of the best seat, were naturally avoided. On school days, after breakfast, we then marched back to our dormitories where we would sit on our stool, never on the bed, studying our lessons for school. St. Paul's had a fine elementary school, it was a two story building, with all twelve grades, and the teachers were all sisters of mercy nuns. The school was close to our dormitory building and being late was inexcusable, however, I did manage to be late on a number of occasions.

You had 15 minutes to get to your class, or else. This was administered by the principal, or the prefect for the habitual offenders. One personal visit to the principal's office which I can recall, was because of an escapade, my buddy, Joe Fitz and I got into one bright spring day. Although it was still a bit chilly, one of the windows was wide open. Our escapade started when the sister was out of the classroom, we were in the third or fourth grade at the time. Joe and I decided to climb out the window onto the window ledge, which was quite wide, moving up and down from window to window enjoying the admiration of the girls, and the boys as well. To our dismay, some of our more sadistic class mates did us in by latching the window, with no way for Joe and I to get back in, the ledge was much too high to jump to the ground, so there we were trapped on that outside ledge you can imagine the reaction when sister came back from the office. We could see her holding back the laughter as she escorted us down the hall to the office, to learn the error of our ways. Not one single thought about how rough we were having it as poor orphan children, or that it wasn't our fault, and that we really needed to discover our self-esteem. No, it was to be a whack by the prefect while bent over the four legged stool on the next punishment day. I really had deep thoughts about how important it really was, for a sensible person like me to try to be different.

At lunch time we went as a group to the dining hall. Lunch was usually a slice of baloney or cheese with bread and butter for a sandwich, and a cool glass of milk. A common practice with some boys was to barter their meat for trading purposes in the winter months or saving the baloney for themselves later as a snack or to trade off with someone else. They would roast the meat on the hot steam pipes near the ceiling in the washroom that carried hot water for heating the dorms. It was great as a night time snack and the smell of frying meat was hard to take for the ones who had traded theirs away. Meat was laid over the huge pipes by standing on the marble tops above the toilets along the back wall in the washroom. Amazingly, nobody ever caught any food poisoning and nobody put a stop to the practice. My feelings in the matter was to always eat the baloney while you had it, if I waited to fry it, with my luck, I would never see it again. The older boys in A & B division were the main ones who did the frying. I will admit it really did smell good on those cold winter nights. On school days, after lunch, it was back to school again until three pm, and then we had free time until six pm.

Every evening, at six they rang the Angelus bells. When you heard the Angelus bell everyone would stop whatever they were doing, whether at work or at play, to bow their head and offer up a prayer for the gifts we had received that day. It was also a reminder to return to our dorms for muster, followed by supper afterwards. The main meal would usually be stew, a soup, corn fritters, or something that could be made in bulk or dished out with a dipper. Meat was a rare treat, except for Christmas or Thanksgiving when we would get a bit of turkey or ham, due to a courtesy by some kind benefactor. When everyone was done eating we returned our metal trays to their designated spot next to the garbage pail. Very little food could be found in the garbage pail since we readily ate anything we were served. And if we didn't eat it ourselves there was always some kid who would beg for it. Our trays were so clean they didn't need much washing. By eight pm we were back in our dormitories getting ready for bed. Then at nine pm it was lights out and no more talking or noise permitted. The Sister assigned to our dorm usually stayed up until everything was quiet and then the teen age monitor from "A" division would be in charge.

Saturdays started a little differently, they were work days for all of us. After breakfast we were divided into division work groups. One group would have the job of cleaning the recreation room, working there was my favorite job, mainly because it required much less strenuous effort than the dorms and wash rooms. First, you would take a cloth soaked in kerosene, or coal oil and wipe down all the chairs, tables and window sills with it. Another group followed with dry rags to shine the same items to a mirror like finish, then everything would again be stacked to one side and the open floor area mopped, getting it ready for the wax and shine team. Old brooms were saved and cut back to the binding, then dry rags were placed under them to use as a dry mop for shining the wax, pushing the old broom made the job easier. The same was true in the dormitory where other kid's pushed the beds to one side and did the floors, others shined the stools and lockers, and in no time at all, with the work of many hands to help, everything was back in place and spotless.

Other groups were assigned to work on the washroom rooms, halls, and stairways. One thing sure, if someone shirked or skipped out we had ways of handling it on our own, no snitching about it. In addition, the floor monitor also had a major part in seeing to it that everyone had a job to do, and had completed it to his satisfaction. Once the dorms were done and lunch was over, we worked out of doors, forming up to clean up the parade grounds, walking in a line with one yard of ground between you, picking up anything that wasn't part of the natural landscape. During my days in the navy the policy was, "If it moves salute it, if it doesn't move, pick it up or paint it". Older boys had the responsibility of working the farm itself, pruning, hoeing, or using a hand scythe, hoe or shovel. They did anything which involved tools for safety reasons, because little guys weren't allowed to handle sharp tools. Weeds of course, were not so sharp and we had to pull lots of those. All in all we lived in a neat, clean environment of our own making. Any Littering or vandalizing was not acceptable, especially, since we had to do everything ourselves. Outdoor cleanup was usually a monthly or as needed, type of chore, so Saturday afternoon was normally free time. We had a several baseball teams and football teams. With the number of boys available to choose from, our teams were hard to beat. Other school teams came to expect St. Paul's to win and we didn't disappoint them.

There were times when a young visiting priest would get us together for a day of fun and football. One of those few times when we used the radio in the recreation room which, according to the name plate, was a super-heterodyne receiver radio. We would gather around the large horn to sing the fight songs and cheer for our favorite team, Notre Dame, a famous Catholic university with a great football team. Many of the seminarians and young priests who served at St. Paul's had graduated from Notre Dame, so whenever their game was played on the radio, a high spirit of favoritism was present. One occasion before a radio game had begun; our young priest decided we should go into church and pray for a Notre Dame victory in the upcoming battle.

We had about ten boys in the group and once we had said our quiet prayers, father told us to stand up on the pew seats and follow along with him in singing the Notre Dame Fight song, for God's enjoyment. We were a bit reluctant to follow his direction knowing silence was the norm in church, but once he had assured us it was o.k. We happily obeyed his instructions and soon we could be heard singing, cheer, cheer, cheer, for old Notre Dame loud and clear. Now this would be totally against all church rules and regulations, we knew our joyful noise must have been loud because, before long running feet were heard in the hall and the voices of indignant sisters were heard ordering our noise to cease.

Our mentor explained to them that when you sing you are praying twice, according to St. Paul, our patron saint at the orphanage. Our singing was a way of praying for a victory by Notre Dame. Those ruffled feelings of the sisters soon gave way to laughter, at the impossible picture of ten boys with that standing on the pew seats singing their hearts out. In those days even a whisper sounded like a shout in the ever quiet atmosphere of the church and was considered very irreverent to make noise. There were times I played football in rough and tumble scrub games, but on one occasion I did become sort of famous and it had nothing to do with football. There was a big spelling contest planned by the faculty when I was in fourth grade and for some reason Sister entered me in the competition. It may have been due to my winning personality and excellent reading ability, but Sister really wanted me to be her champion by winning that spelling bee for some reason. To be truthful, I really wasn't too thrilled being in the running, because she loaded me down with homework, making me spend many long hours in preparation for the big event which was to be attended by all orphanage officials and assembled student body. My main point about this incident was, that somehow, I really did wind up standing there alone at the finish of that spelling competition and I was pronounced the champ. I was given a neat baseball cap from the pastor and a homemade button to wear, stating I was the champion speller and for about a week or two I was famous. To this day I have this terrible ability to spell in an excellent manner to go along with my regular humility. The baseball cap became a more important part of my attire than even my knickers. I wore that cap during all my waking hours except for formal dress up periods, like going to church or school. Even then, I stuffed my cap inside my pants under my belt ready for wear. As for the button, I hid it in my locker as soon as I could; my peers were not impressed with a champion speller.

St. Paul's Orphanage - The Early Years
August 1928 to November 1942

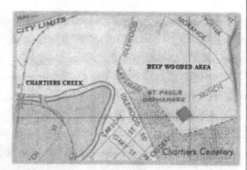

The Raft builders. Top left is Joe, at top right is me, on The bottom is Fitz. They saved my life.

A map of the route to Chartiers Creek, where our raft was being built, and where I had that close call, due to a severe cut on my ankle.

****

A photo similar to Chartiers creek, where we were building our raft to float down the Ohio river to the Mississippi. Just like Tom Sawyer.

The Orphanage Years 1928-1936

Another highlight in my elementary education period was due to an essay I had written about the Unknown Soldier. My Dad had served in World War I, and he had told me about the monument in Washington, at the Arlington National Cemetery in which the Unknown Soldier was buried. The entire school had participated in an essay contest, mainly about patriotic themes. Each class would have its winner; the judges were Fr. Quinn, our pastor, the school principal, plus other dignitaries. They would go room to room and listen to the top effort for that class and then announce the overall winner later on. My story was all about who the Unknown might have been and what were his heroic deeds in the army. A week after we turned in our writing efforts the judges came to our room and Sister handed them the winning essay she had selected for our classroom. When my name was announced as the winner I turned beet red and almost choked. Then I had to take my essay, go to the front of the class, and read it aloud. Suffering more misery than I can describe, I tried to read it in record time. The judges applauded, Sister made all the class applaud, and everyone congratulated me for being the 4th grade winner. Later, after their final judging was made, top honors went elsewhere to cause someone else all the pain and suffering of being a winner. It wasn't that I couldn't have been the winner, I just couldn't handle being famous, there was just too much responsibility involved. I realize, any ability I may have as a writer is a gift from God, to be used for his greater glory, and I have tried to use my gift as best I can in that way. We are all given gifts in this life and I believe we are obligated to use them.

One leisure activity on a Saturday was "stickball" which we played with a tennis ball, a broomstick, and at least five players. The game was played next to a wall as a backstop. There were only two bases, first and home and the batter tried to hit the ball as far as he could, running for first base and then for home before a fielder could bounce the ball off his body. If he made it home without being hit with the ball he could then take one additional turn at bat. If you were hit, it was considered an out and you had to move to center field at the end of the order. Then the pitcher stepped up to bat, allowing everyone else moved up in sequence. Some kids called the game "Rounder's" where they came from. Also we had the early version of the skateboard; they were homemade with the front and back sections of a broken roller skate left over from Christmas. The skate edges were flattened and nailed to a large piece of orange crate slat. Surprisingly, they worked quite well and we had lots of sidewalks to ride them on. We also fashioned our old skates into scooters, similar to our skate board with a high front handle and a wider base to pedal up and down the sidewalks. Except for Christmas toys, the only other skates we received would be from a parent on visiting day, but since we were there at St. Paul's because of the depressions economic reasons, that would be rare.

On a cold winter day, some of the walkways with a downhill slope were doused with water making a smooth ice surface to slide on once it froze. After a running start our leather soled shoes made great skates and we could slide for a long way on the icy surface. When our shoes showed too much wear, there was a cobbler department which resoled them with smooth leather. We didn't have sleds or skis, but we did have lots of ways to enjoy the cold and snow when it fell. Other than throwing snowballs at the girls, that is! None of us had a sled, but a side trip to the trash bin at the base of the landmark smokestack to get a square of cardboard, gave us the means for a ride down the steep hill from the school to the parade field. The hill was only a thirty foot slope, but was a hundred feet wide, which gave lots of riders a chance to slide down the hill taking turns on the sheets of cardboard or broken boxes.

Our baseball field was large enough to have two baseball games going at one time during the summer months. But there was a still lot of room for us non-sport types to enjoy ourselves. There were large shelter sheds far from the ball field for rainy days and we adapted those shelters to be our own playground. We climbed up into the open two foot by four foot raft¬ers and then through holes cut into the roof, going from one opening up onto the roof then back down into the rafters through one of the other holes, playing tag like a bunch of monkeys. We would take off our leather soled shoes to climb better, the smooth leather soles could cause your feet to slip and slide on the wood and create a definite hazard. We were high up in the rafters one Saturday during the fall when I had my first experience with the bad habit of smoking. A pack of "Wings" cigarettes, a well-known brand was only five cents for a pack at that time. We didn't have the nickel to buy any, but our one cigarette was actually just a long butt retrieved from an ashtray in the front parlor after visiting hours by one of the gang. We made the mistake of climbing high up in the rafters to find out what this smoking business was all about, since a lot of people seemed to be doing it. There were just three of the gang involved in the test and after lighting up we passed the butt around, each one taking a puff and passing it on. It didn't take long our for our heads to begin to spin and all of us were hanging onto the rafters for dear life, getting dizzy and sick to the stomach and turning a sickly green as well. Due to our self-induced condition we were unable to climb down with our heads spinning like a top. All we could do was to get a death grip on the closest rafter and hang on. We couldn't even help one another down, so there we sat as partners in misery, until our heads and nausea cleared enough to climb to the ground. That was the end of the great smoke out, we had proved what we wanted to know, that smoking was not meant for us or anybody else for that matter. Anyway, who among us could afford five cents for a pack of cigarettes?

Climbing around the shed rafters wasn't a very safe pastime either. Twice I had wound up in the hospital with broken bones and I wasn't the only one. The first time was when I broke my left arm as I missed my footing on one of the rafters and fell about twelve feet to the ground. Then the next year I fell off the roof breaking my other arm in two places. That accident happened one day when the gang was right in the middle of a game of "Rafter tag". As the game went, you were not allowed to get down on the ground or you were out, as I was running over the roof of the shelter shed from one opening to another one of my friends reached up through a hole and grabbed my leg. Off the roof I went, landing on a dirt pile nearby. When I tried to stand up everyone noticed my twisted arm. I didn't need anyone to tell me that something was very wrong; the sharp pain in my twisted arm was self-explanatory. No paramedics or 911 services to call then, I just had to grin and bear it as I walked the long distance of several city blocks down to the orphanage hospital for treatment.

Following along with me to the hospital was a parade of curious kids wanting to see my twisted arm. I had to hold my injured arm tight against my chest and those two broken sections of my arm were sharply visible. All the while I tried to keep smiling. After all, I was a supposed to be a tough guy wasn't I? At the hospital, the doctor was able to straighten the bones quickly, all the while talking about how he was going to hold my arm tight then stretch it allowing the severed ends to come back together. By the time he stopped explaining what he was going do it was already done with. During the process I only felt a short, sharp pain period as the bones came together. Then he put on a splint and neck sling to keep my arm immobilized. From then on I became a resident at the St. Paul's Orphanage hospital. I remained there among the walking wounded until my arm was strong enough to return to my dorm. Even there in the hospital, with only one arm to use, you still had to do your share for the good of the many. The nurse in charge would give us mobile patients a quart jar containing buttermilk. We had to carry it around and were instructed to shake the jar of sour milk vigorously in order to allow lumps of fresh butter to form in the jar. Thus we helped provide butter for our meals at the hospital. After the butter was removed we were allowed to drink the buttermilk. I developed quite a taste for buttermilk which I enjoy to this day.

On another occasion I was hospitalized for a few days after a sadistic dorm monitor used me for a punching bag. I was beaten pretty bad with mostly bruises and contusions, but very obvious. The guy who did it was the one assigned to our dorm as monitor to assist in keeping order and other kids had also been beaten up as I was. When my Dad came to visit the following Sunday he insisted on knowing what had caused my injuries. At first I told him the story that my injuries were caused by a fight between my friend Jimmy and me as my abuser had warned us to do. Dad and Jimmy's father knew that it couldn't be possible for two seven year olds to cause such damage and demanded the truth. When I told him the facts he said "Let's go and find him". Although parents were not permitted into the living quarters except for special occasions we went up to my dorm where we found this teenage bully all relaxed on his cot. When he saw my Dad and me, he knew he was in trouble and jumped up running to the washroom in a vain attempt to get away. There was nowhere for him to run and when Dad caught up with him he lifted him up off the floor by his shirt, pinning him against the wall. I thought sure Dad was going to begin pounding on him, but instead he controlled his anger, then nose to nose, he warned the boy what would happen if he ever hurt any of the kids in his care again, then he let him drop to the floor. Dad was a big man, over 250 lb. and very strong from carrying the heavy stepladders he used in painting houses. His message must have really got through to our tormentor, because he ran away from the orphanage that very night and never came back.

St. Paul's Orphanage - The Early Years
August 1928 to November 1942

The Annual "Auto Ride" to Kennywood Park
Every year good people gave of their time to take the orphans on a day of fun at one of Pittsburgh's amusement parks. The photo above of my sister Jeannie, my brother Jerry on the right, and myself ready to ride the tumble bug during the special Auto Ride

****

Good people in cars, like this one, acted as our parents for the day, driving us to the park, and providing a picnic lunch and a watchful eye on us as we rode the rides to our hearts content.

We were the heroes of the dorm for some time afterwards when the story got around about the episode. Abuse did happen at times, there are little Hitler's to be found in all situations, and the home was no exception. I never felt that the orphanage was to blame for what happened, some fault could actually lay with the victims, like me and Jimmy, who didn't take advantage of the available protection because of fear of retribution. We often found ways to even the score on some occasions though. One fine example I can recall was when we personally got rid of another troublemaking monitor. Feeling something had to be done about this guy, Joe and I acquired a length of clothesline, and waited until everyone was asleep then tied the rope across the foot of our tormentor's bed and then to his special table where he had all of his special goodies. For good measure we tied it to his stool and several other stools just ankle high for him to trip over. When all was in readiness a fellow conspirator at the far end of the dormitory began to make a loud racket which was against to all dormitory regulations, it just was not done. The noise woke our little Hitler, who began to run full tilt to catch that noisy culprit. We heard a crash and his loud yell as down he went on the hard tile floor, spilling his table with him. The loud noise and commotion woke up the Sister and she came out of her quarters just in time to catch him ranting and raving, while making nasty threats and in general not acting in a very caring manner toward us young innocent children. She sent him back to the "A" division dorm and after that event, at Sisters own request, the prefect replaced him with a new monitor, one who acted a little more human. Justice sometimes needs a little help to function properly.

Some other games we would play in our free time included baseball with a pocket knife, keeping score just like in regular baseball. The knife was opened up, with the small blade open¬ed fully, the larger blade opened halfway. Numerous old telephone poles, cut into ten foot sections, had been put around the area in landscaping and planting areas. They were just the ticket for our "Mumbly Peg" baseball games. We would straddle the pole with the players facing each other. Then we would each take a turn sticking the wide blade into the wood in such a way which would allow the knife to flip in the air landing in the wood. If it landed With the small end straight up it was a home run. If it landed with both blades touching the wood was a triple and with the wide blade only it was a double. If it fell over or didn't stick it was an out. We spent many hours playing "Mumbly Peg", having playoffs and even a world series of sorts. It kept us quite busy throughout the summer months.

Also popular was the game of marbles, and much trading went on for colorful aggies, plain shooters, metal steelies and some special

The Orphanage Years 1928-1936

shooters to help with winning. Western Penna. has brown clay in its soil and we would make smooth hard rings in the clay which were works of art and ideal for the sport. Another use of marbles, which was actually gambling of a sort, took place on the floor in the dormitory. At the start, all participants would gently roll a marble attempting to get the closest to the wall without hitting it. The winner got to sit in an open space on the terrazzo floor with his legs widespread he would place a marble on his own special spot in the terrazzo tile. The other participants would kneel behind a foul line, taking turns at trying to hit the target marble which was usually the smallest one in his bag. The first marksman who succeeded in hitting the target marble then sat down to take his place. The longer it took to make a hit on your target marble the more marbles you collected. It was a quick way to increase your marble holdings, as well as a quick way to lose a few. After Easter visits by parents we had lots of jelly beams among the candy, then we played the game using jelly beans. They did pick up a little dirt in the process, which may have added to the taste when you actually ate them.

Another activity on hot summer days was putting together a bug zoo. The clay earth was hard and after holes were dug the clay sides were smoothed off with water, then the opening was covered with broken pieces of glass from the dump, also smoothed in place with clay. With a glass cover in place customers could view the wild life imprisoned there. While zoo construction was underway, hunters scattered to search the rocks and brush for snakes, bugs, bees, butterflies, and just about any living thing that moved. Next to each hole was an entrance opening covered with a rock to put the inhabitant into the cage and to provide some air. The holes were so spaced that zoo customers could crawl along and observe the denizens of the zoo. The cages and ground pits were used over and over again keeping us busy on lazy summer days as long as the animals (bugs) were still alive.

There was one major summertime story which could easily have been a tragic one for me, if it were not for my best friend Joe, (Fitz), and another member of our orphan gang also named Joe, who turned out to be the human angel who kept my life from being a short one. Fitz and I would leave the grounds on a Saturday to travel through the thick woods bordering the orphanage to reach the banks of Chartiers Creek. Leaving the grounds was against all the rules and it carried the threat of physical punishment by the prefect if there was a surprise muster of the divisions while we were gone. We had sneaked out of the orphanage to visit our own private Mississippi river quite a number of times to gatherer any driftwood or other materials in order to fashion a floating raft. Then just like Huckleberry Finn and tom sawyer, we planned to raft downstream through the small town of Carnegie to the Ohio River and beyond. The creek was often used as a handy trash disposal by people living along the banks resulting in much debris being carried down the small creek.

 Fitz and I worked alone on our project, but Joe, who was one of our gang, kept after us to let him go along on our trips to the creek. We told him we only needed two and he couldn't come with us, but fortunately, on that fateful day, after our arrival at the creek Joe came out of the woods. He had followed us anyway and now we had to let him join in. As it turned out I thank god he decided to follow us, because he was the angel who saved my life that day. Getting to work on the raft, as was our custom, we removed our shoes and socks to wade out into the cold water. The creek was narrow, but fairly deep and we would try to keep our clothes dry. We had to be ready at all times to be able to get away fast in case somebody would come nosing around and discover us. Local people were always on the lookout for stray orphan kids and they knew we were not to go outside the limits of the orphanage grounds and felt duty bound to report us. On this occasion we didn't have a chance to get anything but just our feet wet, because I had no sooner stepped into the water in my bare feet when I felt a sharp pain in my foot and the water was turning bright red with my blood.

 My foot had a suffered a deep cut from a broken bottle, half buried in the mud of the creek. Right away Joe wrapped my foot as tight as he could with his undershirt and then helped me up onto Fitz's back. It was necessary to keep tight pressure on the cut, which was fairly deep, so Joe walked alongside Fitz to keep pressure on my wound. It was impossible for me to walk and at the same time keep up the pressure on my cut, so my two friends traded off between carrying me and keeping pressure on my foot. It was awkward moving around trees that were just a part of the natural scenery earlier and were now among the many obstacles in our path. Looking back in time, I can well remember the accident and the struggle through the woods with my pals. Also the doctor's table with the nurse standing by, that is also clear, but my arrival at the hospital wasn't. Later Joe told me they had to yell at me to keep me awake as they neared the hospital as I kept dozing off due to blood loss and became a dead weight, making me difficult to carry.

My Dad was called and they let me talk to him on the phone to let him know I was fine. That phone call in itself was a big event for me; I had never even held a phone before, much less talked on one. The story of our great adventure was all over the place, getting even better in the telling. The pastor commended Fitz and Joe for their levelheaded actions, which saved my life. After a short time in the hospital, on crutches, regaining my lost corpuscles, I was back in the dormitory with my friends in (E) division. Every time someone asked me to tell the story of my accident I was glad to relate how Fitz and Joe had saved my life, then to watch the two of them glow with pride. Knowing what I know now about first aid, stopping the flow of blood was key to my survival. When asked by the doctor why he had used his shirt to put strong pressure on the wound, Joe said he wanted to be a doctor and read somewhere that if you lose all your blood you will die. Thank God, Fitz and Joe were there for me when I needed them. Allowing me to live the eventful life I have had. Later on we did have an afterthought, as the three of us kept waiting to see if we were on the demerit list for sneaking out that day. Fortunately, no one ever did make any mention of it and we never did get that raft built either or even cared to.

Playing king of the hill was another great game during the hot summer, one that resulted in some pretty dirty kids. The orphanage farm would receive donations of fresh top soil at times, separate from the compost from the horse stables which contained manure. Not the thing for playing "King of the Hill". The top soil was usually dumped just north of where our shelter shed was located. At those times many truck loads were dumped, one pile on top of the other, creating a tremendous challenge for all of us hardy individuals. First we would tramp on and stomp down the loose dirt, to make it firm enough for us to climb on. Once that was done, with many feet making short work of firming up the pile, we all gathered around the base and on the count of ten, we tried to scramble to the top. It was fair game to try and pull down anyone beside you or ahead of you; it was no holds barred in climbing to the top. Those who reached the top first declared themselves to be King of the hill, but keeping the crown was another matter, because every new king had just one thought in mind, to send you rolling down the hill to the bottom. Competition gradually leveled off to those few hardy ones who were determined to be the only ones left standing at the top, but that never happened, because while you were wearing yourself out other contenders were resting themselves for their next assault on the top of the hill. When we finally tired of it all, we washed ourselves and our clothes at the edge of the farm under its big jack handled water pump. Then we would ring out our clothes and put them on to dry on our warm bodies, keeping cool in the process.

We seemed to have a knack for finding some use for almost everything that showed up on the premises. Another example was When a load of four by fours were piled up to make new bleachers on the baseball diamond. It gave birth to the idea of building a fort to play Cowboys and Indians. After we Chose up sides, we spent several hours preparing for the battle. Up near the dirt hills we made the timbers into a log cabin type of barricade for the defending settlers and cowboys. Once our fort was built we got ready for the attack. For ammunition we filled sections of newspaper with dirt, tying them into small bundles to throw at our enemies. The nearby woods had ample brush to make bows and arrows and spears. Indians far outnumbered the defending cowboys and settlers and a battle royal would begin. Under cover of the dust bombs and flying arrows the Indians would attack and always seemed to win. Other ammunition was made with a bucket of water and clay dirt. With it the defenders made piles of mud balls to hurl at the attackers, along with their dust bombs. Nobody ever got really hurt in the games except for welts and lacerations or maybe dirt in the eye, but nothing serious. As before it ended at the jack handled water pump next to the farm where we could clean off the layers of dirt, because going into the dorm all dirty was not allowed.

On occasion, older kids were assigned to work in the home kitchens and dining halls. My brother Jerry was assigned to the adult kitchen for a time, giving him a great opportunity to enjoy special treats. I remember one Sunday morning when he had let me in the side door to enjoy one of those treats. We were not allowed in an area unless we worked there, but my dear brother gave me a big breakfast roll, all soaked in butter after heating it in a heated crock jar. Using fingers only, I ate the first Danish of my young life and right then I knew the real reason God gives us brothers. Fitz and I were also fortunate to have our girlfriends working in the Sisters dining hall. Marie was his girl and Bertha was mine who I came to know through all the pangs of puppy love. Actually, I think they really became our girlfriends after we found out they worked in the kitchen. In the evenings Fitz and I would hang around the back door to the dining hall hoping for a treat. When possible, the girls would slip us a piece of crushed left over cake or a scrambled piece of pie or some other goodies. That was about that time I began to really notice girls, I found Bertha to be a very cute kid even when she was no longer in the kitchen. We would meet at school and sometimes on the girl's playground. There were not many opportunities to spend time together with girls unless they had visitors on Sunday when you did.

St. Paul's Orphanage - The Early Years
August 1928 to November 1942

Rear view of St. Paul's school
The back of the school where the great escape had begun, after I shed my inside pair of knickers and we headed for the hedges that border of the home.

Boy's Knickers
Worn until Age 12

Knickers, worn by boys to age 12. It was a rite of passage to becoming a teenager. Wearing two pair, was a bit difficult during our great escape.

Famous people like Babe Ruth, the home run slugger, on the right, came to the orphanage to visit and entertain the orphans.

Having a special girl friend at the home wasn't easy being strictly separated by gender. Except for church or school visits as I explained. In our case Joe and I did have girlfriends who we could see almost every evening while we enjoyed our goodies. We could also see each other on school days in between classes, and at church, but seldom for any long period of time. There were those times when we blew it, and the girls would ignore us and refuse to even talk to us. That was during the winter when the boys would throw snowballs at all the girls. We had to be impartial and we would throw some at Marie and Bertha as well. It was strictly political, if we threw a snowball at other guy's girlfriends, we were obliged to throw snowballs at our own. The girls just didn't understand our obligation to the code of the male. Anyway we didn't throw as hard at them and When summer came and snow season was over, all was forgiven.

St. Paul's had a large auditorium used for all activities and we were shown movies on occasion. They were the silent kind back then and in a way they helped us learn to read as we watch the show dialogue spelled out on the screen. One movie I still can remember was "The Mask of Fu Manchu", it scared me to death. One scary part had these Kung Fu types, called Tongs who were going to put a cage of hungry rats on a man's chest. Then they were going to open the bottom of the cage to make him tell the secrets of the Mummy's tomb. This was a time when all of us believed that movies were real. Sometimes the movie would be stopped because the Principal thought it was much too racy for our young minds. One example was this movie by the name of "Collegiate" it was all about playing football, with pretty cheerleaders doing their thing and there was a wacky comedian by the name of Joe Penner. He always had a white live duck under his arm everywhere he went. His standard saying was "Wanna buy a duck?" Anyway, as the pretty cheerleaders, wearing their wide ankle length skirts, began to jump around doing their cheers and kicks, Sister stood in front of the camera blocking our view of the screen during those censored parts where too much leg or ankle was in view, in keeping with the morality of the times.

Most of the films we saw were "The Keystone Cops" and "Our Dang" variety, but not much in the way of drama or mystery type of movies. One big movie event, for the fifth through the eighth grade classes, was a gift from the Shriner's organization. We were taken by bus to the Shriner's Temple in the Oakland section of Pittsburgh, where we saw a movie called "Midsummer Night's Dream", one of Shakespeare's works. It was all about pixies and little people, or fairies, filled with all sorts of weird goings on. Later on, in class discussion, it became obvious the whole thing was far above our young heads. We all knew who Mickey Rooney was from the "Our Gang" movies, but in this movie he played "Puck", a pixie who was half a human and half goat, a character who played on a flute all through the picture. Even though we recognized him we didn't understand any of what was going on, much to the dismay of our English teacher. In a way silent movies did help improve our reading skills and reading became another of my favorite pastimes. I would read magazines and everything I could get my hands on. Dad brought the comics every Sunday and we passed them around until they fell apart.

The home had a school library for me to enjoyed reading adventures like "Tom Swift", Zane Gray westerns, "Tom Sawyer" and others. There was a comic series of the "Big/Little" books, an early type comic book. These were 4 inches square and several inches thick with cartoon picture stories such as "Mickey and the Giant Spider, which had a magnetic web attached to a giant airship used by arch-villain, Peg-Leg Pete, used to capture mail planes before Mickey put a stop to it. Then there was "Bucky Bug" and "Caterpillar Princess" and others. They must have been quite interesting for me to recall them now at this time of my life. Reading was always a way to travel to an imaginary world, far away, where I could escape to a happier life of enjoyment and excitement and adventure, not as regimented as was life in the orphanage.

At times famous visitors like Babe Ruth the Yankee slugger and Honas Wagner of Pittsburgh Pirates baseball club who would come to visit the orphanage along with well-known actors or comedians, who gave of their time and talent to put on a show for us. At times it was turnabout when on some holidays we orphans put on skits for the visitors and parents. In one such skit I made my debut as the young St. Patrick taken away in chains into slavery. As the young St. Patrick I was a slave boy tending sheep in Ireland praying to God to let me preach his gospel to the pagans around me. Before the show, a kindly Nun told me how to escape stage fright, I was told to pick out one friendly face way in the back row and say my lines directly to them ignoring all the other faces in the audience. It worked very well, I didn't miss a word and was not a bit nervous A star was born. That advice came in handy at other times during my lifetime. Another thing many of us enjoyed was the opportunity of being in the "Honer Harmonica band" we learned how to play the harmonica and often sat as a group right down front during a shows, so we could play a few songs during recess or afterward. That way we always had a good seat, plus learning how to play the harmonica. I can still play a few songs like "Oh Susannah".

At Christmas time, the Shriner's and Knights of Columbus organizations sponsored Santa's visit to the orphanage providing a single gift for each child. In November, after Thanksgiving, we would receive a list of toys to choose our selection from. One toy was to be given at Christmas by a Santa. There were very few of us kids who believed, or even knew the popular story of Santa Clause, because the facts of life were very apparent to us. Although, we knew very well the true story of St. Nicholas who started the custom of Christmas gift giving we didn't know the connection to the mythical Santa. The list Christmas toys contained some really nice gifts, such as roller skates, a baseball, a bat, glove, or games for the boys. And there were all kinds of toys for girls as well. You wrote your name on the top of the form and picked your gift and waited until Christmas, knowing what would be under the tree for you ahead of time. After breakfast on Christmas morning we lined up alphabetically and received our gift from a dressed up Santa or one of his many helpers. Later, during the afternoon Dad would arrive for his visit bringing games and other small gifts as well as fruit and candy for the three of us. Dad never had much money, but he was always able to make our Christmas as happy as possible.

Easter was always more spiritual and during Mass the great hymns of the Resurrection resounded as they were sung by the children's choir. I sang in the choir until one day during choir practice Sister went up and down listening to each singer in turn. When she came to me she told me to keep singing, then after listening to my changing voice she asked me to go in the back and hum. There is a time when the vocal chords of a boy change from alto to base and I was at that point, ending my singing career in the choir. After lunch on Easter, we received a paper cup with some cookies and a few small candies. We never got many sweets, bad for the teeth you know, but as always Dad made up for it with a chocolate bunny and jelly beans. A big treat was the traditional fruit and nut egg Dad brought to share during our visitor's day. Regularly, on Sundays, holidays or a birthday, parents, relatives and guardians could come to the visitors lounge for a visit. It was a day of anticipation for many of us, but a day of disappointment for many of the kids. The names of those with visitors would be called out at one p.m., even if they had come before that. At the reception desk older kids would be given the name of a lucky ones and it would be yelled out to the waiting throng of kids standing out in the courtyard waiting and hoping to hear their name called. After an hour had gone by experience told them today was not their day, and the crowd would gradually leave the courtyard and by one thirty, very few names were being called and it was happiness or disappointment from then on. A large percentage of the orphans never even bothered, because they knew full well they were out of sight and out of mind in the their world.

One of the things those of us who expected visitors would do on a Sunday was to go out of bounds and wait along the path from the trolley stop, at the old "Bell's school house" leading up to the home, checking to see if their visitors had arrived. It was all hush, hush as they spied from the high bushy side of the path to see if they recognized someone's folks. Those who saw their visitors would run back to the courtyard to wait and carry word of any others that had been recognized. It was kind of like a happy early warning system. It may be difficult to understand that the three of us seldom played together or had any close contact other than those visits with Dad on Sundays. Jerry was in another division and had other interests, playing with his own circle of friends. There were some occasions when we would meet like the time when he worked in the kitchen, but I can't recall ever being involved in any of our games or even play activities with him. There were my early experiences in the same division with Jerry because of Dad's wishes, even then we had our own pals and didn't spend much spare time together. We did have that ill-fated runaway episode, which was one of his ideas. Jeannie was even more of a stranger due to the gender segregation, So our paths seldom crossed except after school or in church. It was as if we not only lost our mother at an early age, but we also lost a family relationship as well. Instead of all being together we hardly knew each other. Even though Dad was faithful in coming to see us every Sunday he was able to. We had lost him too as a guiding influence in our young lives. It is a fact of Christian belief that, with God's help we will never be given a burden greater than that which we can bear. For my part, I believe I was not only given enough strength to cope with what had happened and the personality to deal with it, but even blest to find the good in it. At a time of great stress in the world with homeless-ness and hunger rampant, at least we had been well cared for and blessed with a father who loved us and never failed to openly show it. As a father myself, due to that great love of my father, I was determined that my children would see me as the loving father he was.

One thing I do remember well about my brother Jerry was his exceptional art talent which he probably inherited from dad, who could draw anything. Jerry was well ahead of his time, he drew a great picture of a futuristic flying wing aircraft. On the next Sunday visit he showed it to Dad and I can remember him carrying that drawing all around the visitor's room as he proudly showed it off to other parents. This was a time when modern planes were the old Ford Tri-motor planes which carried mail and passengers between large cities. The planes flew so low you could see the pilot. Jerry worked as an architectural artist in later years. One unhappy episode I can recall about Jerry happened during one of Dad's Sunday visits. Jerry was standing up in a four wheeled wagon for some strange reason when another kid pulled on the handle. Poor Jerry fell forward, hitting his mouth on a bench and breaking off part of his top front teeth, leaving them badly chipped. He didn't bleed or even cry very much in pain, but his teeth were that way even after we left the home. Dad never had the money to have Jerry's teeth fixed and it was not until he enlisted in the Navy that he was able to have a naval dentist work on his teeth and give him his smile back.

The all-time biggest annual event of the year, which was put on at St. Paul's, was the called "Exhibition Day" show. All activities were put on by the resident kids as a token of thanks for our friends, families and benefactors. It was an event that lasted all day, including an open house of the entire complex later on. The event was usually written up in local newspapers and church bulletins of the many Pittsburgh churches. A main purpose of "The Exhibition" exercises was to assist in the local annual fund raising campaign in support of the work done by the orphanage. The day Served as a format to let the people see for themselves just how their support and funding of the orphanage was worth their effort. For weeks we practiced our assigned routines for the big pageant. Each class had a special theme to portray and in our fifth grade class we were sailors. We were dressed up with paper hats, collars and cuffs to perform the sailor's hornpipe dance when it was our turn to go out on the field. My sister Jeannie and her class performed as little Irish lassies, Jerry was also one of the sailor's, like me.

Every class did something as a group and it was done with precision. We were made to practice until we were able to do it in our sleep. Meanwhile bleachers were being built across the hill above the field and decorations were in place all around the parade grounds. On the morning of the big day, we were all out picking up loose paper or trash to have all in readiness for the crowd expected to come. Then we had to wait patiently in our classrooms for our turn to get out and do our stuff. We watched with interest through the school windows as the higher grades did their thing out on the field. One main thing we had prayed for time and time again was for fair weather, any rain would be a disaster. The decorations and all of the costumes contained lots of colored paper and rain would ruin everything. In some class somewhere in the school or in the church at any given time there were orphans on their knees praying, "Please God" no rain today! God must have been tuned in, because he really heard us. I don't recall an exhibition day ever being rained out during the eight years we lived there at the orphanage.

The Knights of Columbus, a prominent Catholic men's group, and the Shriners Fraternal organization had a special project for all of us orphans each year and we called it, "The Auto Ride". The automobile was not as commonplace then and for the orphans a ride in an auto itself was a special experience. The good people who participated in the event donated, not only use of their auto's, but gave their entire day to make it a memorable occasion for all of us. On that special day of the auto ride there was a feeling of great anticipation, watching and waiting for the cars to arrive. By ten in the morning they were beginning to fill up the open field near the ball park. The older boys were directing traffic for the parking of the cars as we began to line up at the main driveway entrance to the home. As each car pulled up we were assigned three or four children to a car and we were soon on our way. The long caravan of cars had little flags on each one to identify them as members of the orphan's day at Kennywood Park looking as we looked forward to a fun filled day at the amusement park.

Riding in a car was a special event in itself, but a first stop along the route we had a special treat as the cars stopped at "North Pole Real Ice Cream Co.", the Factory for a chocolate covered Klondike ice cream bar. There was one concern our foster parents seemed to have, worrying about chocolate and ice cream spots on their car seats. We were well trained however, and devoured those bars so quickly there wasn't time for them to drip. All of the people had badges and we were given badges with the same number as the car, so if anyone did get lost during the day it was only temporary. On the way, driving through the towns and over the bridges was a treat indeed, but one treat was very special. Sitting in the front seat right next to the driver gave me the great opportunity to watch him and learn how to drive, shifting gears mentally, as the driver took us up and down Pittsburgh's many hills. We had to cross a number of bridges traveling to the park; Pittsburgh is located at the junction of three rivers, Allegheny, Monongahela & Ohio and there are many bridges in the city. Several times the driver let me hold onto the wheel on the straight stretches of highway giving a real thrill to a seven year old boy.

After what seemed like an eternity, we arrived at Kennywood Park the largest of the amusement parks in Pittsburgh. The park was reserved for the entire day, filled with orphans from many different orphanages. We thoroughly enjoyed ourselves as only children can do, building memories to last a lifetime. There were wild roller coasters, a giant Ferris wheel, and dozens of other rides. The thrill of riding the wooden hills on the Dips, screaming our lungs out, then the feeling of being weightless on the Loop-o-Plane" was never to be forgotten thrills. For the entire day we rode on everything free. Our parents for the day, had brought along a wonderful picnic basket for lunch, filled with goodies and snacks. Many were new and wonderful to us when compared to our regular fare at the home. Those great people looked after us all day watching us as we enjoyed ourselves on the rides just like real parents would do. Finally, the great dream ended as we rode tired and happy back to the orphanage, with a promise to see us again the next year. I think they looked forward to that auto ride as much as we did.

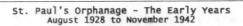

St. Paul's Orphanage - The Early Years
August 1928 to November 1942

St. Paul's Orphanage grade school
The school had grades one through twelve. It was the scene of the spring walk along the wide window ledge by my friend Fitz and I, much to the enjoyment of all. The windows, far to the right of the entrance, is where our classroom, and its wide window ledge was located.

We each had one by our Bed, also used by the Prefect on occasion.

"The tomb of the Unknown"
My essay on the story my Dad told me was my first.

In the 1920's and 1930's government control and funding was not provided for institutions such as St. Paul's orphanage. Our care was made possible due to the kind hearted people who gave of their time and treasure in order to make life a little more bearable for people in need, as we were. Even today when I meet a member of The Knights of Columbus, or the Shriner's, I enjoy retelling my story of the auto ride and what great people the Knights were in their support of the orphans in those days. The Shriner's" too, were wonderful to the orphans, providing food and funding for things like Santa visits on Christmas and the auto ride. Today those organizations are still at work providing for those in need. Thank God for people like them. Some things still remain the same over the years due to the God given good nature of people in general.

One of the most vivid recollections from my earliest days at the home was the time when my big brother Jerry and I, along with two other boys, planned to run away from the orphanage.my brother Jerry was the mastermind who made the decision to run away. I think He only included me in his plan so I wouldn't tell Dad, This great escape was made during the time when Dad had wanted me to be in the same division with Jerry so he could look out for little brother. That was when I was nicknamed "peanut" since I was the smallest kid in "D" division and boys my age were in "E" division for the youngest boys. The plan was to run away and live in the woods so we saved everything we could beg or borrow that would be a help in living off the land. I think Jerry read Robinson Crusoe around that time! Jerry's plan was to live in the dense woods down around Carnegie, the nearest town we could walk to and the master plan was to build a large tree house and live off the fruit trees and whatever else we could find on the nearby farms. We planned for several weeks during the summer, filling four paper shopping bags with extra clothes, towels, nails, cord, a small hammer, and anything else we could appropriate for our adventure. Jerry was pretty good at drawing and he had the tree house plans made and a map of locations where wild fruit trees and farms nearby and We could search for more trees in the vicinity of our new home in the treetops.

At noon on the big day I put on my two pairs of knickers, thinking it was a good idea to save room in the heavy shopping bags. Since I only had one belt I put it on the outside pair and I was all set to go. When lunch time came all the other kids marched out for the dining hall while we escapees hid under our beds until we were alone. Then Jerry got our shopping bags from their hiding place in the broom closet. We each had to carry two shopping bags as we headed for the escape route past the back of the school and across the ball field. Then we had to would crawl through the thick hedges separating the orphanage grounds from the Chartiers cemetery. Once in the cemetery it was a short trip into the miles of wooded area where we would be difficult to find. At least, that was the way Jerry had planned it to be. As we passed the school a problem developed for little peanut, my inside pair of trousers had begun to fall down making it very difficult to walk. This caused me to stop and remove the outside pair of pants and put the belt on the remaining pair.

Jerry was getting upset over the loss of time, but once again we were off like the wind for the border. Being only a little bit taller than my shopping bags I had to drag them along rather than carry them scraping the bottoms along the ground. This resulted in some holes forming on the bottom of the thin paper bags as I hurried along. The supplies were soon falling out on the ground at intervals leaving a trail of assorted socks and other lost treasures along the way. Meanwhile, up ahead without any luggage were other two escapees urging us to hurry up. Jerry was tall enough to lift his own bags up off the ground and didn't have my problem. By now I'm sure he was wishing that he had not brought his little brother along. For my part I thought that the whole idea was a bit much. Besides the idea of sleeping on the ground or living up in tree eating apples for supper was not any way to live. At least that was my thinking and I was already wishing we had stayed for lunch first. I only went along with the idea because of the great adventure story Jerry had sold me on.

Finally, we made it into the cemetery, but by then I was totally exhausted so Jerry let me flop down by a big gravestone to rest while the other two boys just kept on going. They had a different idea about how to run away, no organization required. After a bit Jerry and I set out again on our journey, but before we could reach the woods we heard the yells of a search party on the way. The prefect had organized some of the big boys from 'A" division to search for us runaways. They only had to follow that trail I had thoughtfully left behind for them. As I said earlier we had a regular seat at the mess table and when we didn't show up for lunch our absence was noticed right away. Someone must have squealed about our plans. So within minutes a search party had been organized and was on the way. They found our exit point easily by following my trail of stuff. The other two boys were long gone, but we were then marched triumphantly back to the prefects office to await the dean of boys, who was an assistant pastor. They also notified Dad so he wouldn't be worried and as it turned out Jerry was the only one who got blamed without any help from me either, but he was the only one who was punished, after all it really was his big idea. Besides, at seven years of age, I was too young to know what I was doing also; I had taken enough punishment just trying to run away, carrying those bags and all. Not to mention that somebody took the pants I left at the school. Later on Jerry did run away successfully and somehow he made it to my Dad's rooms on Pittsburgh's North Side, but for some reason he never asked me to go along that time.

As the years went by orphans would leave the orphanage by adoption, or a parent would be able to make a home for them. If they were old enough they could go to a trade school and learn a trade with help in obtaining a job to earn their own way upon graduation. It was the dream of every orphan to one day leave the regimentation of the home for the outside world to live like other kids, fulfilling the dream of living a house with your own room and parents to look after you. For we Mahoney kids, it all began when Dad came for his visit one Sunday in 1936, with him was a lady by the name of Charlotte. She treated us very nice, giving us fruit and candy and in general making an effort to know each of us. We didn't know it right away, but Dad married Charlotte and in the process he would be able to make a home for us on the outside. They had rented a house in Brookline a suburb of Pittsburgh not far from the orphanage to be our new home.

The Pre-War Years - 1936 to 1942

In 1936 we left St. Paul's Orphanage to live in Brookline Borough in Pittsburgh Penna.

Our last days at St. Paul's Orphanage - in Aug. 1936 Francis, Jeannie & Jerry with their Dad & Aunt Sr. Mary Paula.

The new home of the Mahoney family in Brookline Pgh. Pa. (Photo taken in later years.) High on the hill above West Liberty Ave. the main road into downtown Pittsburgh

Resurrection Church and School in Brookline where I attended 7th and 8th grades.

The Prewar Years
1938-1942

The big day came for our departure from St. Paul's orphanage in August 1936. We were called to the parlor, the formal sitting room in the main building and our doorway to the outside world. Dad and Charlotte were there to tell us about their marriage and the home in Brookline and we were to get ready to leave with them as soon as possible. I returned to the dormitory, dealing with the thought of leaving my friends, but pleased inside to be finally leaving for a new life, one I had never really known. The envy of my friends was apparent and as a parting gesture I gave away all my baseball cards, marbles, my rusty pocket knife, and those few possessions I had, giving them as gifts to my closest friends. After getting dressed in my Sunday set of clothes and without any further fanfare, I went back to the parlor, anxious to leave, Jerry and Jeannie waited for a while until the Pastor and several Nuns came by to wish us well as the final preparations were made. Going out the main entrance we were introduced to our new uncle, Charlotte's Brother Carroll who was there with his car waiting to take us home, to a real home at last. At that time I was fourteen, Jeannie was twelve and Jerry was almost sixteen. We had been there for eight years, the major part of our life growing up as children. We had been cared for in a loving environment, learning discipline and self-reliance and above all, a love of God, his Commandments and his Holy Scriptures.

It was August first 1936 when we left the life of the orphanage to live the rest of our lives as a normal family in a home of our own with only my brother, sister, Dad and Charlotte living there. Memories of riding in Uncle Carroll's car to the borough of Brookline in the South Hills were special ones. At one point on a high rise we could see the tall smokestack of the orphanage in the distance, etching a new memory of the end of our childhood. The smokestack was a landmark in the area since it was about 300 feet tall, standing high above other orphanage structures. The growing feeling of being family again, but still unsure of how it would be, filled my mind. Dad wanted us to call Charlotte mother, which we did when we talked to her, but it was Charlotte when referring to her. Our new home was in the same general area of Brookline as the old Mahoney family farm where I was born and where our family had lived. Our new grandmother, Johanna's farm was just a short distance from the house my Dad had rented on Plainview Ave. My new grandma was a very nice elderly lady who seemed very happy to have a few new grandkids. Surrounding that big old farmhouse were pear, plum, apple and cherry trees that I dreamed about climbing to enjoy the fruit as it ripened. There was a big overgrown garden which had not been cultivated in some time. One vivid memory I have of that first day away from St. Paul's was upon our arrival at the farm and seeing the tall pear tree at the side of the front door. There were dozens of delicious pears lying around on the ground with only swarms of bees enjoying them. At the first opportunity after meeting Grandma I was outside getting ready to fight the bees for one good enough to eat. Before I could pick one up off the ground grandma came to the screen door and told me it was better to pick ripe ones off the tree. She then gave me a big bag to fill up and take with me. I just knew I was going to love my new grandma, she knew how to treat a hungry boy.

At the time we were there, the farm was reduced to only a few acres. Over the years the original farm land was sold off and all that was left was the farmhouse and the few remaining acres. The house itself was a very old frame house built on a fieldstone foundation with a deep basement section for cold storage. In more recent times it

The Prewar Years 1938-1942

was a laundry area containing a large washing machine with a huge drum dryer, which seemed out of place with other stored equipment. There were lots of shelves along the walls that must have once been filled with canned fruit and vegetables from the farm. Much of the floor sloped with age where the house foundation had settled over the years. As in the song, "This old house", grandma's farm must have seen much better times. Now it was home for grandma, her son Carroll, and daughter Gladys. In August 1936, when we first came on the scene, I wondered how they were able to even farm that land at all, it was so hilly. Perhaps it was mostly in fruit orchards growing on the hills. You could only drive up the street from the highway below using low gear in a car it was so steep. Aunt Gladys told me how they would come home over Plainview Ave., the street along the hill above the farmhouse and leave by going down the steep street called Bell Isle Ave. No horse drawn wagon would ever make it up the steep grade. The South Hills, as the area was called, sure lived up to its name.

Another memory of Grandma Duffy was playing "Euchre" with her. She loved the card game and never missed an opportunity to get one or two of us to sit and play the game. She would bribe us with lots of cookies and milk or fruit in order to keep us there learning all about a left and right bower and how to take winning tricks. I only learned the basics of the game, but I was easy to bribe and I remember sitting by the hour just watching grandma win. She was widowed with six children; her husband had been a postman who had died years earlier. In addition to our Stepmother Charlotte, our new aunts and uncles were Aunt Gladys, a favorite aunt who always seemed to brighten up the place when she dropped in for a visit. Aunt Gladys was a clerk at a corner grocery store on Plainview Ave. owned by a Jewish family named Miller. Naturally, they called it the Miller's grocery store, located on the corner of the street and they lived upstairs in the three story building.

Before the advent of supermarkets and even in those large grocery stores of the time, like the "A & P", or "Kroger's". You went to the store with your grocery list and waited your turn to order. You called each item on your list the clerk who would pluck it from the high shelves using a long pole with tongs on the end and when you finished they would write up the bill with the item and the amount due. Most grocery shopping was only done for daily needs, buying a can of this a bottle of that, things needed for that day. A trip to the store for a single item or two was often a break in the day for many of the women who had few personal outlets. It was an opportunity to visit and keep up with daily neighborhood news. Purchases were made in cash, only a few fortunate customers had credit, which meant having your own book on file, but the bill had to be paid off monthly. Later on Aunt Gladys married a man by the name of Butch. He was a meat cutter or butcher by trade which gave him the nickname of Butch. With lots of grocery store experience between them, Gladys and Butch opened their own store on Pioneer Ave. The next street up on the hill above Plainview Ave. where we lived, it was only a short climb up the steep narrow path to reach the street where the store was located when we needed something.

The next of our new relatives was Aunt Bessie, Charlotte's oldest sister. Her husband a fine Irishman from county Donegal Ireland named John. Uncle John and his brother Jim had their own thriving ice and coal business. It was also a moving business in the spring when leases ran out and lots of people had to move. They had their big dump truck, with Helferty Brothers–363 La Marido Street – Brookline, painted on the side. The lettering for the truck was done by my Dad which was his lifelong trade, painting and lettering. That dump truck was used for everything. In summer months they delivered ice along a regular route all over the South Hills. Everyone had an icebox to preserve food at that time and some were pretty fancy, solid oak boxes with brass toggle handles on the doors where food was stored. The top of an icebox opened up for easy access to the ice compartment which was lined with rust proof galvanized steel and well insulated to preserve the ice and food. As the ice melted the water flowed down a drain pipe into a deep drain pan underneath to catch the overflow.

One of my own chores at home was to keep that drain pan emptied. If you ever forgot your job you really had quite a mess to clean up when it overflowed. Moving an overflowing pan of ice water can be very difficult chore in itself. Taking a bit of Yankee ingenuity to get it ready to empty by removing water a cup at a time into another pan saving a even worse flood from happening. When Uncle Jim, who was "The Ice Man", drove along his route he checked the card placed in each customers window, which was turned up the correct

The Prewar Years 1938-1942

side to indicate the amount of ice desired. The card had a big / 25 / 50 / 75 or 100/ number designation on each of its four sides. The "Ice Man" would drag a big block of ice from under the heavy tarpaulin with several expert jabs of his ice pick the ice would crack just right along lines formed in the block. He had heavy metal ice tongs used to grip it as he swung the ice block up onto his burlap shoulder pad to climb up the steps or down depending on which side of the street the customer was on. It was hard work to make a delivery like that at five cents a pound and a hard way to make a living, believe me.

As a privileged nephew, I sometimes rode on the truck to help slide the big ice blocks to the tailgate for Uncle Jim. The broken slivers of ice from his ice pick were reward enough and as good as any ice cream cone on a hot summer day. I became quite popular along the streets by handing out a few slivers of ice to grateful children as Uncle Jim chipped away with his trusty ice pick. Delivering ice was a summertime business since people had window boxes in winter to keep food cold. Those ice boxes were placed outside a window on the shady side of the house to keep things cool during the cold months. Also you could freeze your own ice to use in the ice box. The ice business was not worth the effort for Uncle Jim in the wintertime since most people could go to the ice company to get a block of ice. In cold weather the less food left over from the meals the better. If the temperature rose the food would spoil in a window box. At our house, Charlotte called me the human garbage can, because if there were any leftovers in the bowls at mealtime she scraped onto my plate to dispose of.

When fall came, and the approach of cold weather was imminent, the ice truck became the coal truck. Every house had its coal bin in the basement with a coal chute window at ground level that opened into the coal bin. The bin had a door in the basement near the furnace with removable boards to hold back the coal. Once the coal bin was filled the home owner could open the door to shovel out the coal as needed from the opening in the bottom. As the pile grew smaller those heavy boards in the door frame were removed and set aside to reach the remaining coal. In the event that you didn't replace the boards before a new order of coal arrived you can imagine the problem when you tried to open the coal bin door. Delivering coal was a hard, cold and very dirty job. The weight of a standard coal shovel with its deep sides filled with lumps of coal weighed over twenty pounds. One lump of coal could weigh that much by itself and there were many shovelfuls to a ton of coal. The coal was shoveled off the truck onto a metal chute placed between the truck and the coal bin window. As a delivery was made the delivery method could raise a cloud of black dust and make a lot of noise going down the chute. Making a delivery would be an assault on the ear drums as well making a black mess. Many times to save money the customers had the coal dumped near the coal bin in front of the house to be shoveled in by family members. That was a sickening sight to be seen by a boy coming home from school.

The third phase of the Helferty Brothers business was in moving and hauling. The first of May was the annual moving day, most leases would expire in May and unfortunately, everyone wanted moved right away. Aunt Bessie handled moving schedules to keep the truck moving to the right homes and to keep the crews working. She also took care of her part time job as mother of their twelve children, ranging in age from six to twenty and a fine bunch of new cousins for us. Sometimes my Dad would work on a moving when the work load got too heavy. Two of their boys, Johnny and Eddie and Charlotte's brother Carroll helped as well. It was a family affair and on a few occasions I too earned a few dollars helping to carry small stuff, like lamps and loose cartons. Moving household furniture in Pittsburgh was quite difficult since Pittsburgh is built upon nine steep hills. In the South Hills where we lived, almost every house had to be reached climbing up long steps on the high side of the street or downhill on the lower side. Either way, there were many steps to climb when moving a family in or out. Houses were mainly frame construction having two or more floors, attics and finished basements containing years of accumulation of stuff. For Uncle John's business it was fine, but as for me working in the moving business, forget it, the money wasn't worth the aggravation. The only time I would work on a moving was if Uncle John was really in need of extra help. Uncle John and his family were special to us.

Our house on Plainview Ave. was typical of Pittsburgh houses. It had the first floor on the front at street level and we had a basement kitchen opening onto a porch at the back which was twelve feet above the back yard which sloped downhill toward the next street below us. The second floor was up above street level making it two stories high plus attic at the front, and three stories plus the attic at the back. From the rear window in our kitchen you could look down and see the top of the trolley cars in the distance when they stopped at the bottom of the steps on Ray Ave. There were (294) of those wooden steps which I counted personally many times, often carrying a twenty five pound sack of flour or groceries up those steps. There were another hundred plus steps from our street to the very top to Pioneer Ave. where they ended on the top of the ridge. The steps were mapped out as a street named Ray Ave. It was so steep that it was impossible to pave so the city just put in steps for pedestrian traffic.

On moving day, when most leases would run out, people would vacate residences leaving them empty. So moving day was a good day for us kids to go exploring. We would find an empty house and use our own home master key to go in to check for anything left behind that could be useful or sell. We had a club house at the back of our property which was once a chicken coop. It had been built on the same order as the house itself and was easily converted for our own use. We also furnished it with moving day discards and we didn't have to break into a home to look around. Most homes had a standard master key for their deadbolt locks which any of the master keys could open. It may seem strange but if you lost your house key you could go to the five and ten cent store and buy another one. Few homes were closed up or locked up very often because someone was always home and break-ins were not very common. In our moving day searches we were careful not to do any physical damage and there never was any complaint about it. In one way we were helping clean out the clutter left behind by the tenants.

There were times when we would find a place where the phone was still working and we had some fun time making silly phone calls like calling a random number pretending we were the bell phone co. and ask the party to whistle for us so we could check their lines or by asking them if they had running water at their house? If a yes answer we instructed them to contact an Indian reservation. Another one was to ask if they had Prince Albert in the can then tell them to let him out. Prince Albert was a pipe tobacco then sold in a tin container. It was all in great fun especially, since kids seldom had use of a telephone. Those with a phone normally had the most common phone service providing for a set amount of calls each month. In most cases we wouldn't have caused additional charges on the phone bill because excess calls would be blocked. One thing we always looked for in the empty homes were records and steel phonograph needles. On an earlier day we had found a hand cranked Victorola record player after moving day exploring and carted it home to our clubhouse. We built up quite a large collection of the brittle, plastic 78 rpm records to play on it over the years. More about our clubhouse and the fun we had in it, later on.

The Pre-War Years - 1936 to 1942

The Liberty Tunnels under Mt. Washington. The only traffic access into downtown Pittsburgh. In the past the only way to reach the city was Through the Trolley Tunnel or the Incline.

The main industry of Pittsburgh was making steel and the mills along the river poured out the "Smog", a mixture of smoke and fog, which gave the city its Nick-name of "The Smoky City". On occasion, I rode my bike through the tubes from the sunny south

The Prewar Years 1938-1942

The Helferty family coal business was profitable until the smoke control ordinances in Pittsburgh were passed by the city commissioners, those drastic ordinances permitted the burning of only gas, coke, or hard anthracite coal for heating in Allegheny county furnaces. The ordinances limited the use of the less costly bituminous soft coal which had helped to cause the heavy smoke and air pollution which gave Pittsburgh its negative nickname of "The Smoky City", a name which was well deserved at that time. The coal business was reduced a great deal by those ordinances just as the advent of the refrigerator had its effect on their ice delivery business. Concerning Pittsburgh's name of the "The Smoky City", I can recall times when I rode my bike through the Liberty tunnels under Mount Washington from our home in the South Hills into the downtown area. There was a walkway through the tunnels with a metal pipe railing along it making it possible to ride a bike from one end to the other. Arriving at the city end of the tunnel the scene was so unreal. You couldn't see across the bridge over the river or the skyline above the city. The noon sun looked like a great orange ball shining through the smog, as the mixture of smoke and fog was called. Much of the air pollution was caused by the many steel mills built along both sides of the Monongahela River, belching the fire and smoke from their tall smoke stacks. These are the mills where my grandfather, great grandfather, and other members of the family worked for pennies a day in the early days when Pittsburgh's South Side was known as Birmingham City before being annexed by the city.

The bituminous soft coal smoke created one another great nuisance, the ever present black soot when thousands of chimneys poured black smoke into the air during the winter months. The inside of most chimney walls had become coated with a black carbon coat of soot over time. The soot coated everything and everyone when it floated softly through the cold air in winter and gave everyone black nostrils as they breathed in the dirty air. On those occasions when nature provided a beautiful white snowfall it wasn't long before a black overcoat of soot would start to build up on top of that sparkling snow. When it was cold every house poured out its share of smog pollution. The ladies had an awful time keeping their makeup clear of the black measles. The soot ruined many a white shirt and kept the dry cleaners in business all winter long. In later years many homes had switched to gas or coke and the smoke control ordinance had taken its effect on the mills as they began using methods to recapture and treat the smoke from their furnaces also new methods of making steel helped a great deal. Once again the sun could be seen shining all day in downtown Pittsburgh and the coal delivery business was drastically reduced or became non-existent just as the electric refrigerator had reduce the need for an icebox. The public need for the ice and coal man was going the way of the horse and buggy. As for the Helferty Brothers they were able to change their business to meet the changing times and moving household possessions became their primary business. Hard coal was still available for those hold-outs from the gas and electric companies. At our home dad also switched over to gas heating during the war.

One other door to door service in those days was a "The Milk Man," who delivered milk and dairy products directly to your door. Each house had its wooden milk box by the front door. You would leave your empty milk bottle with a note requesting your needs and about sunup there was fresh milk right by the door. In the winter if the temperature went below freezing the cream would push up out of the bottle lifting the cap as it froze. When that happened we all wanted some of that delicious frozen cream that had formed on the top. In the thirties some milk companies still had horse drawn wagons and horses even knew the route as they moved from house to house for the milkman. Later the move was to milk trucks except perhaps in rural areas. Most stores began to sell milk too, but home deliveries were by far the most popular way to get fresh milk. The milk man also had other dairy products available for sale, such as cheese and butter. The clatter of the milk bottles outside your door was the alarm clock and the signal for many families to begin their day.

Getting back to the Helferty brother's truck, the best use of all was in summer when the Duffy, Helferty and Mahoney families would go on a Sunday outing at South Park. The county park area had two huge swimming pools with a lot of picnic tables and shelters scattered in wooded shady locations. All of the picnic areas were equipped with a stone fireplaces and log cabin type shelter. These were built during the depression era by W.P.A., works

The Prewar Years 1938-1942

progress administration, a government funded program started by President Roosevelt to put the unemployed back to work during the depression of the late twenties and thirties. Dad worked on the W.P.A. as a painter, painting the many bridges over the three rivers of Pittsburgh. The favorite family picnic area was one called "Stone Manse". It was close to the pools for older kids and there was a small running stream with a waterfall for the tikes with a covered pavilion to serve about 25 people which was just about the number in our family group. Our picnic would actually begin on Saturday evening as the older boys worked to scrub out the truck install the canvas top and some homemade wooden benches were placed on each side to accommodate the older passengers while the children sat on mats. It was necessary for several uncles and the older boys to drive out very early on a Sunday morning to reserve the space at our "Stone Manse" pavilion. Possession being nine tenths of the law they had a tough time keeping other early birds from taking over. After attending early Mass on Sunday morning we all met at the their home and piled into the truck now converted from its moving and hauling business into a pleasure vehicle for the day.

It was probably uncomfortable for the adults sitting on those hard benches, but we kids had a ball as we sang all the well-known songs as we rode along, much to the amusement of other Sunday drivers. We harassed the cars on the road behind us, and those going the other way all in good fun, of course. State Road 88 was our direct route to the park and like most of the roads back then Rt. 88 was a two lane black top road. There were very few three lane state and national roads existing at that time and today's four lane interstate roads were far into the future. It was President Dwight Eisenhower who began the nationwide interstate system after WWII. On those hot summer days, the "dog days" as they were called, everyone came up with the same idea, to head out to the parks to cool off. It wasn't very cool though sitting in the back of the truck under a hot canvas top in heavy stop and go traffic, but in due time we arrived at our spot and the holding party was happy to give up the endless battle to hold onto our pavilion. After we unloaded all perishables to be set in burlap covered buckets in the wading pool with had a large ice block for cooling donated by the family ice co. That ice block was also a great asset for cooling Aunt Bessie's ice cold lemonade. There were no canned drinks then and most drinks were homemade except for bottled soft drinks like coke or ginger ale.

    Before being permitted to take off to the pool or elsewhere the older kid's had to listen to all of the rules: return for lunch at one p.m., no horseplay in the pool, stay off the high board, look out for the younger kids and in the final analysis the older teens were to be responsible for everything except the food, otherwise to have fun. So with our twenty cents admission in hand we were off to get sunburned and enjoy the cool water in the big pool. We had to get into our bathing suits in the public dressing rooms which had lockers for your clothes and personal items. Once at the pool area we settled the younger kids at the wading section and went to the big pool taking turns keeping an eye on our smaller cousins before going off to the nearby deep pool to swim watch the high divers. Some of the group took turns on the low diving board. Nobody had to tell me to stay off that high board! I remember an experience I had at the Moore Field pool after I learned to swim. At the time I had decided to make a try at diving from the high board. My effort landed me square on my back as I had attempted a somersault during a fancy dive. That dive cured me from diving boards any higher than six feet high for all time.

    Even at age 13, I wasn't sure if I could swim, although we had the old "Ice Box" swimming hole in the orphanage, you really could not swim there for a long distance so I never learned how. I just jumped in close to the pool wall and pulling myself along in order to just keep cool while cousins much younger than me were swimming up and down in the pool's deep end without any problem at all. I did find out quite suddenly during an earlier time at South Park pool that I really could swim I just didn't have the necessary confidence to strike out on my own. It all happened one day at the big pool when someone grabbed me from behind and threw me bodily in the deep water. As I went in I yelled that I couldn't swim and I felt myself sinking like a rock. With my eyes shut tight I imagined I was going down, down, down. And I began to panic thrashing my arms as I tried to get back up to the surface, I opened my eyes to find myself already on top of the water with my cousin

Bob Patterson in the water beside me. He was the culprit who threw me in thinking I could swim. After seeing my panic drowning act he felt bad and jumped in to the rescue. Right after that, with a new found confidence, I swam the length of the pool including the deep end. So I can credit Bob with an assist in my learning how to swim. He just happened to be there at the pool that day and spotted me before I saw him. He did succeed in surprising me I must say, but all for the best in the end.

After we had our fill of the chlorinated pool water which was made stronger then in order to sanitize the water, but after being in the pool for a while your eyeballs became red and burning and your hair was like a thick matted mop and your skin was like a wrinkled prune. Was it fun in the pool? Certainly it was, in spite of the chlorine. we rounded up our water logged cousins to head back to the pavilion and the food. First we flopped around with the little ones in the ice cold freshwater stream to lessen the effects of the chlorine. Actually it was more refreshing than the day at the big pool. When lunch was ready and we all dashed for a place at the table. There were plenty of pre-made sandwiches and lots of the peanut butter and jelly ones, Aunt Gladys could get cold cuts of meat wholesale at her store for the occasion. There was homemade coleslaw, potato salad and all the other homemade dishes that the mothers had prepared. One nice cold drink favorite of mine, which I believe I mentioned before, was buttermilk. I could drink a quart of it all by myself. Before that first big bite was taken Uncle John said the blessing giving thanks to God for all he has provided for us and Looking back at those post orphanage years we had been truly blest with new loving family.

We enjoyed the little things, the food we had, the happy times we shared, and the loving people who surrounded us. After lunch and the tables were cleared and everything packed in the truck the older kids were set to go out to explore the park. With the younger bunch back under the parental supervision and in recognition of our pre-adult position we were now permitted a bit of freedom. At South Park on most summer weekends there was not much to see except for baseball games, playing horse shoes or renting horses. Later on in the fall they had the annual county fair with horse racing, food exhibits and animal judging contests presenting all sorts of interesting activities for us city kids to marvel at. Other times through the summer there was a dance area with a juke box and a few food and drink stands to visit or we could just roam around to occupy our time. After a full day at the park the clan climbed into the truck heading for home all tired, happy and sun burned. Being one of the older ones was not always an advantage since the truck had to be made ready for ice deliveries the next day. The top had to come off and the tarp folded up with the benches and put away until it was needed for the next outing, usually once or twice a month on good weekends during the season.

Aunt Bessie and Uncle John's home was always a very special place to us and the family had become much a part of our lives during those pre-war years from 1936 to 1942. After Jerry and I had left for the Navy they were even more of a family for my sister Jeannie after she left home during the war years. At that time she went to live with the Helferty family on a permanent basis. Uncle John and Aunt Bessie had twelve children of their own and a big house to match their hearts. The kitchen was much too small for such a large family, but Aunt Bessie made it work somehow. She had the ready help of her older girls in cooking for their own large family plus the many visitors who came to share a meal as we often did. There was a fair sized dining room next to the small kitchen with one large expandable table and a smaller one off to the side. There was seating for at least fifteen people in that dining room and if extra people came the children took their meal into the living room which was a room of average size next to the dining room on the first floor. At the front of the house was a large open porch covered with a green and white canvas awning to keep it dry and shady and there was a glider to swing on in addition to the wicker chairs. Their home had two floors and a large finished attic above the second floor, all containing sleeping quarters. Somehow it accommodated all the members of the family. I am grateful that my memories of their happy home are as vivid in my mind; they are a large part of the feeling of family that I had missed living at St. Paul's Orphanage all those

The Prewar Years 1938-1942

years and they always treated us as family. That was the Helferty home in Brookline, Pittsburgh. Pa.

Their home was near the top of a very steep hill which was paved to the top of the ridge a short distance above their home and it was a downhill all the way into the woods in the other direction. That downhill path was a favorite sled ride location in the wintertime, but a long walk back up the hill after a wild ride of 10 min. or so on a sled. When parking a car on the steep street you had to be careful that the handbrake of the car was on tightly and the wheels were turned into the curb, otherwise your car could wind up in someone's yard or at the bottom of hill. Parking this way was a common practice in Pittsburgh where steep hills were common. Fortunately, their backyard was level, with parking area for the family coal an ice truck. As On most streets, behind the houses there was an alleyway wide enough for the garbage truck to pick up the garbage cans placed there by the homeowners. It could also be used as a one way driveway for automobile access in some cases, like Uncle John's truck. It was so steep behind our house on Plainview there was no alley and we had to put our garbage cans out in front of the house for trash pickup.

My Uncle John was a fine Irishman and was a very special person, who I admired very much. I marveled at his patience as a father. There were times when a quarrel would arise among his children and Aunt Bessie would send them to their father to resolve the dispute. When they came before him for his decision he was most often found sitting in his rocker puffing at his pipe while reading the daily paper. Putting his paper aside he would ask the first party to state his or her case and the other one couldn't interrupt until it was time to state their side. Uncle John would puff on his pipe as he pondered the situation and once he made his decision that ended it. His decisions were made fairly and in a loving manner and were accepted as final, if not always to the total satisfaction of both parties. I am sure Aunt Bessie must have given her own private input later on when they were alone, but not in any way to lessen his paternal authority. Their parental guidance system worked and with such a large family there had to be that wisdom given by God to fulfill the vocation of raising a family with God always at the center of their lives.

The Pre-War Years – 1936 to 1942

We enjoyed the fun of family Sundays at South Park riding in the Helferty's truck to the Stone Manse Pavilion, with its stone fire place. There was the annual Fair to enjoy at the Park as well.

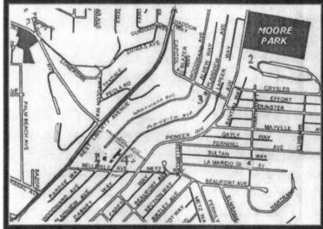

A Map of the home area, where we lived until I joined the the Navy. The Duffy farmhouse is #1 on Bell Isle Ave. The location of our new home near the Ray Ave. steps is #4. Millers grocery store #3, is where my Aunt Gladys worked, and where Moore Park pool and football field were located.

Uncle John died not long after we moved to Florida in 1959. I never had the opportunity to spend much time with the Helferty family on our subsequent visits to Pittsburgh over the years, but looking back I firmly believe Uncle John helped to influence my own attitude in raising my family. He and Aunt Bessie was a couple who knew what was expected of them as loving parents in raising 12 children. I am sure theirs was a loving relationship, although they didn't seem to make a big outward show of it when in public view. I always saw them as an ideal example of how it was to be successful parents. Aunt Bessie died in 1989 at 94 years of age and I remember when We saw her last in 1987 and her memory was amazing. She could name all of her grandchildren and great grandchildren, including their birth dates. Her family has an annual reunion on her birthday and they come from all over the map to keep their memory of her and Uncle John fresh in their memory. In the process they keep their own family circle alive. The reunion is a wonderful show of love for fine lady who was not a blood relative of mine, but she was a wonderful Aunt to us at a time when we needed her.

Their children always us like family. They may have looked upon us as poor orphans to be adopted into their relationship, but that grew in time to a much closer, brother and sister type of relationship. There were three boys in the family, Eddie was the oldest and worked with his Dad helping in the coal and ice business. Johnny was about my age and although we had a lot in common, he had his own circle of friends as I did. Except for the times we spent together on family events we were not very close. The youngest boy was Jimmy, the baby boy at the end of their pecking order along with the youngest daughter whose name was Marcella, known as "Babe" to all. The oldest daughter was Johanna Helferty who worked at Spears Department Store in down town Pittsburgh. When we arrived on the scene Johanna had met a fine man named Bert Kearns who she eventually married. Ellen was next oldest and then came the others, Mary, Bessie, Bernadette, Gladys Anne, Regina, and Charlotte, in that order. So we now had a new family which had adopted us in 1936 after our departure from St. Paul's Orphanage.

Concerning the rest our stepmother, Charlotte's family, she had a brother named Carroll, who lived with Grandma Duffy and Aunt Gladys, at the old farmhouse on Bell Isle Ave. He worked with the Helferty brothers and at other part time jobs, but did not have a specific trade that I can recall. Another sister of Charlottes was Aunt Peg Loebig, who lived in Chicago. She was the oldest of the sisters and she had a daughter named Marcella. We only met Aunt Peg a few times when she came to Pittsburgh for a family visit. Another younger sister of Charlotte's was Aunt Marcella; she was a nun in the Catholic Sisters of Mercy order where she was called Sister Mary Rosaria. It was the Sisters of Mercy who taught us at St. Paul's Orphanage, a very dedicated group of nuns. Life in our new home with our new step-mother was not without some difficulty. When you consider the fact that not only had dad been separated from us for eight years, but Jerry, Jeannie and I had also been separated from each other during that time. Then too, Charlotte had never been married before nor ever had three teenagers to deal with on a daily basis. So that was the situation as we started out on our new life together in a real learning process for us all. Fortunately, we were not a discipline problem for Charlotte due to our orphanage training we had been taught respect for our elders and not to talk back, that was a big plus for all concerned.

Dad wanted us to refer to Charlotte as mother and out of respect for Dad, and her as well. Jerry was the only one who had the clearest memories of our real mother, Regina, so he had a greater difficulty adjusting to Dad's wishes. Jeannie and I didn't have as many vivid memories of mother, but the idea was difficult for us as well. When you look at it from Charlotte's side she was taking on the task of being a mother to three teenagers she hardly knew and that was quite an under-taking in itself. As for why she was doing it the reason was simple, she loved Dad very much and was quite willing to take on that major responsibility for him. Charlotte had made a great big hit with me immediately because of her cooking. She was really a great cook, able to make great meals on a very low budget. There were never many leftovers in our icebox, I personally took care of that problem and she took great pleasure in referring to me as the "Human garbage can". A title my son Michael had inherited in later years. If there was a little bit of anything left in the serving bowls she would just scrape it onto my plate for its final disposition. I always seem to have room in my neck for another tidbit.

When Charlotte met dad, she was working as a cook and house keeper for an elderly gentleman who owned a cigar box company manufacturing the wood boxes to hold cigars. Cigars were more popular than were cigarettes at that time and his small cigar box business was quite profitable. We only knew him as Mr. Smith and there is no doubt he was sorry to see Charlotte get married, because like us, he must have enjoyed her home cooking. On our first Christmas at home in 1936, as a gift to Charlotte we kids received the very best Christmas gifts in our young lives. He gave us brand new sleds for Jerry and me and there was a huge doll for Jeannie. We really felt rich that Christmas thanks to Mr. Smith's generosity. That same sled was still in use when our children, Mike and Eileen were little.

In the thirties many movie theaters had a "Bank Nite" on Wednesday's with a cash jackpot door prize for the holder of the lucky ticket number. Dad and Charlotte went regularly to have some time together and were always hoping to win the jackpot. We were left alone to look out for each other on those occasions and since it was on a school night we had our instruction list; clean up the kitchen, do our homework, turn off the radio at nine p.m. and get to bed. Once in a while our brother Jerry, who had a flair for cooking, would make us some fudge by using just enough ingredients so Charlotte would not notice just a little bit of cocoa, chocolate, and sugar was missing from her pantry. We would enjoy a fudge treat while listening to the radio before going to bed, but somehow Charlotte always seemed to know what we had done and Dad would give us a talking to afterwards. The economic depression was still going on and work was still scarce for Dad. Charlotte must have been able to account for everything she had in the way of food and our fudge might have been the special ingredients for a birthday cake or some treat she had planned. Maybe that would account for her negative reaction to our pilfering, but there was no way to put back the wonderful taste of forbidden fudge. How did she possibly know? It could have been the delicious odor of chocolate still remaining in the air even after we cried crocodile tears cutting up a small onion to disguise the smell in the kitchen. Mothers and step-mothers seem to have that special instinct of knowing, maybe it's because they did it themselves in childhood.

Dad and Charlotte went out on other occasions, usually to the local pub for a cold Iron City beer and an evening of dancing. There was not a lot of extra money for anything fancy. There was one favorite place called Rudt's Tavern on Brookline Boulevard which had a small dance floor. Another favorite place was the American Legion Veterans Hall where Dad was a member. Dad and Charlotte loved to dance and they could dance up quite a storm. To this day I can recall the fast music of "The Tiger Rag" and visualize my 250 pound dad and extra thin Charlotte moving around the floor like dancing stars Fred Astaire and Ginger Rodgers, a well-known song and dance team of the time. Everyone in the place would stop and watch them as they whirled around the floor they were that good. For other dancers there was always the possibility of getting run over by Dad as they whirled around the dance floor area. There was no doubt that Dad did love Charlotte or that she loved him. She seemed to be quite jealous as well. Deep down I know Dad never got over the death of our real mother and I'm sure Jeannie was a constant reminder of our mother for Dad. As she grew older Jeannie became a closer image of mother so that Jeannie could have been a competition for dad's love as Charlotte saw it.

Being a boy of 15 I was certainly no psychologist, but I saw animosity growing between Jeannie, Jerry and Charlotte. There were times when Dad would come home after a disappointing day and a few too many nickel beers. Feeling very low, he would confide in me as he talked about our mother and his love for her. My heart went out to him during those days when he carried such a load on his shoulders. You would never know that he was anything but a happy painter who seemed to know everyone in and around Pittsburgh. Considering my own lifetime and how fortunate I have been, I often wonder if I Would have been able to raise a family under those conditions. Work was very scarce then and to come up with the carfare for a daily ride on the trolley into town to the union hall, was a major problem. At the union hall he waited with other desperate men for a painting job to become available. Somehow, in spite of being always short of funds, he always managed to have a coin or two left to buy us a treat when he could. We didn't own the home we lived in, Dad just rented it with an annual lease. Very few people were able to own their homes during the depression, unable to earn enough income to handle the kind of credit required to purchase a home. There were occasions when the owner would try to sell our house and potential customers would come by to look over the property.

The Prewar Years 1938-1942

The Pre-War Years - 1936 to 1942

This side view of our new house shows the steep hill the house was built on and the deep valley beyond.

The ice box was the only way to keep everything cold and it had to have a block of ice to keep it that way.

The three windows visible on the left were: top, my bedroom, middle was the kitchen and bottom was the basement kitchen.

My father served in France, with the 28th Division in WW-I. his fear now was for his sons going to fight in another war.

A six tube super-het radio our entertainment center. and our link to the news of a world in turmoil.

Naturally, we didn't want to move so on those occasions it was my duty to answer the door and with my well-rehearsed white lie. Dad could not stand telling a lie. but In this case it had come under the heading of self-preservation so, I would smile my million dollar smile and tell them I was alone in the house and couldn't let anyone in. They would then look around the outside and that was it. Anytime we saw strangers at the door we just did our bit to keep them out just in case they were potential buyers. Dad and Charlotte finally were able to buy the house in 1946 after I came home from the war. They had won $1,000 on a raffle at church and I was able to loan them $500 which I had saved while in the Navy. They put it all together and paid off the mortgage. The house was 50 years old at that time and thanks to dad's hard work and handyman ability it was in very good condition. Actually, it was the hard work of each one of the family working together under Dad's direction to make it possible. When he painted the house I helped him as his gopher, you know, go for this and go for that. To give an idea about the area where home was, our black top street had two very narrow lanes and must have been the original farm wagon road, considering the way it wound along the side of the hill, running parallel to us Hwy.#19 down in the valley below. Pittsburgh is located at the foothills of the Allegheny Mountains and its streets and houses seem to cling to the sides of the hills. Our local hill started in the valley where U.S. Hwy. #19, called West Liberty Ave. In our section, ran fairly straight and level down to the Liberty tunnels which ran under Mt. Washington. Along this road, trolleys and buses traveled on their way into the city of Pittsburgh.

To get up the hill to our house on Plainview Ave. from the trolley stop on West Liberty Ave., you had to go up Ray Avenue. Now I don't mean drive up, because Ray Ave. wasn't a paved street, as it was indicated on the city map, it was too steep to be useful as a street. Ray Ave. was a set of wooden steps with landings at intervals, 295 of them in all and to reach Plainview Ave. you had quite a climb ahead of you to arrive at our home. The steps were sturdy, kept in good repair, and built through some heavy wooded sections, which had a few pear and crab apple trees that I visited in season. If you lived higher up on Pioneer Ave. you had many more wooden steps ahead of you to reach the very top of the hill. The alternative was to take the Brookline bus, which went along Pioneer Ave. from the tunnels to the Boulevard, then walk down the steps to Plainview. Dad would use the trolley and the steps to get home. Try that after an eight to ten hour day or carrying a 25 pound sack of flour, along with the groceries from the Streamline market on West Liberty Ave., as Jerry and I did quite often. We didn't need pep step machines or tread mills to keep thin, nature provided a dandy one without cost. In my case, I was so skinny, that when we played a game of hide and seek I could hide behind a big tree, or a telephone pole, without being seen. Is that skinny, or what?

At our end of Plainview we were in a row of frame houses, placed close together, all much alike, built at the same time, and perhaps by the same builder. Our house was the third one in from those steep Ray Ave. steps. On one side of our home, there was fifteen feet of space for the steps leading to the back yard between houses, with a zero lot line on the other side. On the steep hill across the street was a small section of woods, which covered the area between our street and Pioneer Ave. at the top of the ridge. There were apple, cherry, oak, and other trees growing wild, although some of the cherry trees were from the original Duffy Farm orchard land, further down the street. We spent many a happy hour roaming those woods, and enjoying the fruit, but more about that later. When new houses were built back then, the lumber was usually fresh from a mill, and green as can be. They didn't have drying kilns as they do now to provide dry lumber for building construction, so the basic framing was completed first, and then left bare to cure in the weather. After several weeks of curing the siding was put in place and the construction would go forward with the interior. In hilly Pittsburgh most houses were built to fit on the geographical level of the property, and many of them were built into the side of the hills. If an advertisement of property was listed in the newspaper as being on a large level lot, it was definitely not in Pittsburgh. The only level areas were along the river banks in the downtown area around the Point, where the many steel mills were located. They say Pittsburgh was built on a total of nine hills, and any postman can attest to that, considering the many steps they had to climb when delivering the mail.

All of the houses in our row had a wide porch across the front, with four tall wooden circular pillars supporting the heavy roof, and keeping the porch dry and shady. On the lower level at the back of the house, was a smaller porch off the basement kitchen. On some of those sweltering summer nights my brother and I would sleep out there. We would borrow a padded moving blanket from Uncle

John to make the hard floor more comfortable, and enjoy the cool breeze outside instead of trying to sleep in our hot bedroom. The frame houses of the era had no insulation in the walls, making them hot in summer and cold in winter. The basement kitchen was only used as a laundry and a canning area in season. It was equipped with kitchen cabinets and a gas stove, and could have been a studio type rental if desired. Coming in the front door, which was actually on the second floor of the house, you entered into the hallway leading to the large country style kitchen. It was equipped with its wooden ice box, large gas stove and vintage Hi-Boy tableware cabinet, which once belonged to Grandma Duffy. There were no wall cabinets at first, until Dad built several wood cabinets above and below the heavy iron sink for our everyday dishes and food storage. The type of dishes were limited, with one good set and one ordinary set, so not much cabinet space was required. The under sink cabinets held Charlotte's own selection of pots and pans, the tools of an expert cook. They were mostly cast iron skillets and heavy enamel pots and pans of many sizes. We were duly warned that care had to be exercised when washing them because; the thick enamel could easily chip. The kitchen table seated six normally, or we could crowd in eight for meals. It was always kept against the open wall, so the three of us could do our homework in the evening.

The kitchen was the real family room of the house. It was the only heated room during cold winter months using the gas cooking stove and its burners and oven to heat the room. The rest of the house was not heated unless extremely cold weather came along. The house had a hot water radiator system heated by our coal furnace. Coal was a greater expense than using gas, so the furnace was used sparingly during the hard times. On the left side as you came in the front door, there was an archway to the living room. In it was a piano, which no one could play, on the right side. That was the favorite spot for me to curl up in, and I usually fell asleep under the overhanging keyboard as we listened to the radio. There was a couch and Dad's favorite stuffed chair on the left. Our entertainment center, a small cathedral style six tube radio, was in a corner on the end table. In the middle of the fireplace, on the back wall, was a gas fired heating grill, with ceramic bars over the gas jets. These bars became white hot with

The Prewar Years 1938-1942

the gas flame, and generated lots of warmth on cold evenings. They were only used during the coldest winter months after supper, when we listened to the radio, and it was usually turned off the rest of time for economy reasons. Above the fireplace was an ornate mantle holding my grandmother's hand painted vases, her wedding gift in 1879. Some family photos were also on the mantle below the large oval mirror, which Dad always painted with a water color Christmas scene each year for the holidays.

The radio in the living room was our evening entertainment for listening to the news and special radio shows. Dad had a great interest in the news, having served in the First World War, "The War to end all Wars", in 1918. Serving on the Siegfried line of trenches in France, He was becoming disturbed by the news of the growing threat of Germany arming for war. The British tried negotiations, believing Hitler only wanted prosperity for his country, but events were proving he only wanted revenge for their defeat in World War I. The German "Bunds", groups of immigrant German youth, were even forming in America in support of his goals. Dad's greatest fear was that Jerry and I would be going into harm's way if America became involved. He felt the British and French, wanting their "Pound of Flesh" from Germany after the war, had forced them into the terrible depression, which gave rise to a dictator like Hitler. When we talked about the coming danger, Dad told us more about his service in the trenches on the German Siegfried line. In later years I was able to get a copy of the day to day operations of his company in the war. Reading about his hardships in trench warfare, and about his personal stories, I was convinced he had lived up to the true statement that "War is Really Hell", not something glorious as some might think. In the late 1930's the news was of great concern for young men and teenagers, like Jerry and I.

Down the entrance hallway to the left of the kitchen door, were the stairs leading to the second floor bedrooms. There was a master bedroom to the left at the front of the house, looking out on the street, for Dad and Charlotte. Off of the upstairs landing were two smaller rooms for the three of us. Jeannie had the smaller one, which had a great view across the valley at the back of the house. Jerry and I shared the other larger bedroom, with a great view of the peeling paint on the neighbor's house next door. We were also close to the favorite nesting spot of some pigeon's that made a nesting spot just outside our window, providing us with a continuous serenade during the summer. Our bed and other furniture were made of beautiful grained oak, which had come from Grandma Duffy's house. The bed had a very high headboard and a lower footboard, and also had a much softer mattress than the thin cotton one I had on my bunk in the orphanage. It was big and wide enough for both of us boys to share, without kicking one another except occasionally. Located on the landing at the top of the stairs next to the window, was Charlotte's, foot operated, treadle type, Singer sewing machine. Jeannie learned to use it very well when she studied economics at vocational school, and became quite a seamstress, just like our own mother had been. When I left the Navy she recycled my uniform into a suit for her son Skippy.

There was only one small bathroom in the house, located on the main floor just off the kitchen, and next to the stairway to the basement kitchen. Needless to say, any time spent in the one bathroom had to be short, in consideration of the other family members. It had porcelain, free standing, iron bathtub with the traditional lion clawed feet each holding a ball. The space under the tub made it easy to clean the entire linoleum floor, which was one of my chores on a Saturday. Taking a bath was a new thing for me, which required filling the tub halfway, adding hot water from the stove, then getting into the lukewarm water to bathe. It was a big improvement over those Saturday baths, by Aunt Agnes in a portable tub at the Mahoney Farm, when we were small. Built in showers, were not a common bathroom standard in older homes like ours. We were used to rationed showers in the orphanage, but now water was in great supply. Drawn and treated by the city from the three great rivers. Saturday was bath day; extra baths were only taken when it was deemed necessary. A daily bath was not the normal thing; taking sponge baths was the more common method. That meant filling the sink with hot water, also heated on the stove, and using a washcloth all over to do the job. Sponging was more sensible than a tub of lukewarm or mostly cold water to bathe in.

Baths in the Navy when at sea, were not the best either, we each got a bucket of cold water to do the job when water was in short supply, and we would take advantage of a rain squall to shower down. Deodorants for use by men were not even considered then, and not just from a male point of view. There was a soap called Lifebuoy, used to eliminate what they called, B.O., body odor. Today, men use all kinds of smelly stuff to impress the ladies. We always thought it was not only okay to sweat, but a real necessity for good health, body oils help fight disease, from a medical point of view. I heard trivia somewhere that the reason for weddings being scheduled for June in earlier times, was that now, in warmer weather, people would have had their spring bath by then. Honest, I read it somewhere!

Down the stairs in the basement kitchen, which I mentioned earlier, was a very large room equal to half the area of the first floor of the house. There were laundry tubs, which could be used for a kitchen sink hookup. Nearby, was a wringer washing machine for doing the laundry. Many of the other houses used it as their main family kitchen. Our main use for the kitchen area was for canning fruits and vegetables when in season, and for making jelly from fruit on Grandmother Duffy's many trees or from the wild ones we could find. The actual basement, partly underground, was under the living room at the front of the house, with the entrance door at the foot of the stairs to the kitchen. It had the coal fired furnace, Dads workbench, and under the front porch, was a small room used as a fruit cellar. The walls were lined with shelves for the canned fruits, jellies and vegetables, put up by Charlotte and Jeannie, with our help in doing the picking. Also stored there, were bulk potatoes, onions and bulk canned goods. Next to the furnace, underneath the porch, was the big coal bin with a metal window chute to the outside for coal deliveries, as I explained earlier about Uncle John and Jim, the coal & ice men. One thing was certain, that basement represented a lot of hard work for us young teenagers.

All summer long, Jerry and I would pick all the fruits and berries we could find for home canning. Vegetables were bought from the farmers market in town, or grown in our own garden. That was another major chore of mine, caring for the garden. Many weekly hunting trips were also made to get elderberries, blackberries, cherries, apples, or whatever else could be found. Getting the stuff picked and carried home was one thing, but then came the actual canning stage. Charlotte and Jeannie bore the brunt of the cooking preparation, and we helped fill the mason jars. There was lots of competition in the woods to find the wild fruit, because so many people were out of work. Many of them were also out looking for the same fruit trees and berry patches as we were. As kids we spent a lot of time in the woods, and we were always on the lookout for any new locations, traveling over a wide area of woods in the process. When the fruit ripened we were out with our sacks & baskets getting what we could. One good example was the picking of elderberries, they grew on six to ten foot high bushes in great clumps, and the tiny berries grew in clusters at the end of the stalks. We would fill our bushel basket with just the berries, stripped from the ends, and then we had to carry the heavy basket home on our shoulders using an old rake handle through the handles of the basket. Looking like a couple of Chinese coolies, Jerry and I had to keep in step to prevent the heavy basket from swaying side to side. It took a while before my shoulders were back to normal after a trip carrying those heavy baskets.

 Another tough basement chore required filling that coal bin with a ton of coal, which first had to be shoveled from the Helferty Co, truck and into the coal chute. Then all winter long it had to be shoveled into the hot furnace a little at a time, mainly during the very coldest spells. Otherwise the kitchen was the only warm spot in the house. Since the burning of coal made ashes, which fell through the iron grate into the bottom of the furnace, they had to be removed. So on a Saturday, ashes were removed from the furnace, and then scattered all over the garden area. Was that the end? Oh no! The ashes had to be turned over into the soil mixed with the clay to loosen it, to get the garden ready for spring and another vegetable crop. Across the back end of the garden area was a well-built former chicken coop, which Jerry and I converted into a fine clubhouse. More about the clubhouse later on! The furnace was the hot water circulating type with water passing through the fire chamber, there it was heated and circulated through pipes to metal radiators. We had two radiators; one was positioned below the window in the kitchen, and the other near the front door. The rising heat warmed up the air coming in around the drafty window and door. Insulating between the inside and outside walls was not a building construction standard when these houses were built, making them more difficult to heat. On winter mornings, with the furnace cold, Charlotte would get up early, and preheat the kitchen before we got up, which meant we had to dress in record time to head for its warmth and eat breakfast, before venturing outside into the cold for the long hike to school.

The Pre-War Years - 1936 to 1942

 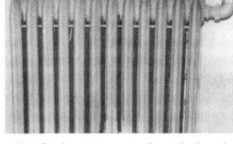

The basement kitchen was also the laundry and the canning area in the fall.

Circulating water was the main heating system with only two of these radiators for the entire house, both located on the first floor. No heat in the bedrooms.

****

During the season we roamed the woods looking for fruit to can. Everything from cherries to elderberries to help stretch the food budget. We all had our part in the operation, Jerry and I picked, Jeannie helped Charlotte with the canning and Dad built shelves.

Sunday evening had a lot of great radio shows, such as Amos and Andy, Fibber Magee and Molly, George and Gracie Allen, Bob Hope, Red Skelton, and many other great entertainers. Listening to the radio required an imagination to enjoy the stories, which painted a mental picture along with the story line. Orson Wells, a realistic actor, scared the country with his Halloween story of "The War of the Worlds", which had the Martians landing in New Jersey in their destroyer spaceships. People were arming themselves, and taking their families into the countryside to hide from the invaders. I listened to the broadcast, but didn't believe it, because they announced in the beginning it was a fictional story, thousands who tuned in later, only heard the story part. Charlotte and Dad were the ones who controlled the radio, for economical, as well as parental control reasons. Anyway, we enjoyed what they liked too. There were no PG or R rated radio shows as far as I know. Perhaps, I understand their reasoning more now than I did then, because vacuum tubes were expensive, and had a limited operating life before burning out. Marking the tube sockets, then taking the tube to a repair shop was necessary at times. I can recall when we were without our radio entertainment, because the budget could not handle the expense of a new vacuum tube. Dad and Charlotte picked the shows we all listened to, usually prime time comedy and variety shows on Sunday nights, but in the afternoon after school there were the kid shows we were allowed to listen to, after homework was done. There were shows like "Jack Armstrong, the all-American boy", "The Lone Ranger and his Indian companion Tonto", and others.

Our home was built before electrical wiring became the standard for home construction. Each room had a gas jet outlet for a gas mantle, which would glow brightly when the gas flame burned inside to heat the element, which created the light. They were very fragile, falling apart very easily if mishandled in any way. Fortunately, the owner of the property had an electrical service line brought into the house, so we never had to use the gas jets for lighting, except in a few power emergencies early on, like when we couldn't pay the bill. Two separate wires for the 110 volt service came to glass insulators mounted on the side of the house from the power pole. They entered into the house through the basement foundation wall, terminating in a steel fuse box in the furnace room. It had the glass, screw in, type of fuses, one for each room of the house. Electrical outlets were located in the floor the living and master bedroom, and the outlet serving the room required extension cords for lamps or appliances. All we had was a floor lamp and a radio to worry about; our clocks were windup table types, and in the kitchen we had a toaster and a waffle iron, with one single overhead light, which hung on a long electric cord from the ceiling. All other rooms had only the ceiling outlet for lighting, obviously we were not yet into the full electrical age. Another aspect of the power service, was the two separated heavy copper wires going from floor to floor, inside the walls up to the bedrooms. The separate wires to the first floor outlets were in full view passing through the basement floor support beams.

In later years, Dad removed all of the metal pipes serving the gas lights, except for the gas supply to the gas fireplaces in the living room and main bedroom. He also extended the power to additional outlets in the house. Those electrical outlets in the floor turned out to be a potential hazard for crawling babies. After the war, when my sister Jean and her husband Fran came to visit, their little son "Skippy" would crawl around in the living room, on this occasion we heard him scream, and found him crying his heart out next to the outlet in the floor. Close to the outlet was a fairly large puddle, which had flooded through his cloth diaper, creating a wet contact for the electrical current, giving him quite a shock. Cloth diapers didn't hold much water, and plastic pants were usually worn on babies. Unfortunately, Skippy didn't have any on to protect him from the electric shock.

Concerning winter and the steep hills of Pittsburgh, and our brand-new sleds, let me tell you about Pittsburgh style sled riding and its hazards. Actually, riding a sled down most of the city streets was a threat to our life and limb, but that didn't stop us from risking our necks or our sleds. The most hazardous street around was Capitol Ave., which crossed Plainview Ave. not far from home. Nobody would dare to try it from Pioneer Ave. up at the top, but halfway down at Woodward Ave., below our street, it was possible to make the sharp ninety degree turn halfway down, then have a straight run down to the main highway at the bottom. The curve was bordered by thick woods and the many trees, which prevented a sheer drop onto the roof of the auto dealership on U.S.#19 below. We spread coal ashes on the hard packed snow on and above the curve permitting us to slow down enough to make the sharp turn. You tried to hit the curve as close to the inside as possible, with feet dragging then, if you did not slide into the curb, or into the trees, or flatten your runners. You had a full ten minute adrenaline filled ride down the remainder of Capitol Ave. At the bottom, if you wanted to, you could ride down West Liberty Ave. on the sidewalk for as far as you could go. I might add that Capitol Ave. was not available for traffic when we did our sled riding; it was just too steep of a hill for any car or truck to climb, when it snowed or iced up. We would travel the slight downhill grade on W, Liberty Ave. Hwy.#19, and all the way to the Liberty tubes. That is, unless someone had cleared off their sidewalk, stopping you dead in your tracks. Walking back and taking the climb up steep Capitol Ave. you were ready for another try, if you had the energy to do it again, that is. In Brookline they would usually block off traffic on a number of good sled riding streets. Those streets, which were not too steep, and had an upgrade after reaching bottom, would bring your sled to a safe stop as you went uphill for a short distance. On any Saturday, when it snowed, I was usually gone all day until dinner time, challenging the hills.

 Cars were not a big problem then, not that many people had a one, even at less than a thousand dollars to buy a new car. We didn't have a car in our family, except for Charlotte's brother Carroll, so walking was the main method of local travel for us. Rain, snow, or shine, we walked to school, to church, and the store. There was trolley and bus service available at the bottom of Ray Ave. steps for longer trips into town, but no help in getting to church or school. One story regarding riding the trolley was often told by Uncle John, on himself. On this occasion, he and Aunt Bessie and their large family of twelve, were on their way to downtown Pittsburgh by trolley. Uncle John was the last of the family to get on, and as he stood at the front, after paying the fee, Uncle John looked around and there didn't seem to be any seats left. The conductor looked over the car in his big rearview mirror, and commented to Uncle John, "Mr. It looks like you did yourself out of a place to sit down". In good humor Uncle John said, "No problem, it's a good thing I have one little enough to sit on my lap". Nobody got a bigger kick out of telling the story than Uncle John.

Our church and school was Resurrection Catholic Church in Brookline. Based on our own family history the Mahoney family had grown with that church. Begun in 1903, the Resurrection Church congregation had come together for the first time in a vacant store warehouse on Brookline Blvd. In 1913, when the main church and school were built, the Mahoney family farm was purchased by my grandparents, Jeremiah and Margaret Mahoney. They and their children were among the early members of the new parish. In 1936, when we returned to Brookline, Resurrection Church was about two miles from our home on Plainview Ave. So with five days to and from school, and to church on Sundays we walked a lot of miles in a week, or a month. Of course, we never had a reason to complain about the walking, there was no other option. We did what came naturally in those days, we put one foot in front of the other, and in no time at all you were there. Very few cars traveled along Plainview Ave., but when they did we had to move to the side of the road as we walked along, since there were no sidewalks. It wasn't until after we came to Brookline Blvd., the main street in Brookline, that the auto traffic increased. For pedestrians, the sidewalks were smooth, wide, and thankfully, totally level. In the middle of the Blvd. were two sets of trolley tracks, with cobblestones in between them. There was a single lane on both sides of the tracks in each direction for auto traffic, and parking spaces all along the curbs. As the center of the Brookline community activity the Boulevard was a very attractive looking thoroughfare. Along the business section, which ended at the World War I Memorial Park, there was every type of store to provide for needs of the public. The stores and restaurant-bars were on the level side of the street, with homes high above the Boulevard on the higher side. On special holidays, parades were organized by the BBMA, the Brookline Business Men's Association. The parade went from Pioneer Ave. to the Memorial Park at the other end. The Boulevard was the center point of all community activity and a walk down "the Boulevard" was a walk down memory lane for anyone who grew up in the community.

The Life & Times of "Himself" ... The War Years

Starting at the American Legion hall, where I had cast my first vote as a young sailor. Dad was a devout Democrat, and he went with me when I first registered to vote. The clerk asked me what party? And when Dad said Democrat, the clerk warned him that he couldn't influence my decision, but he was very pleased when I did register as a Democrat without his help. Next to the American Legion hall was the bakery, the owner hired Dad to paint the Saturday specials posters, which he put on the store windows. The owner always tried to get Dad to take his pay in baked goods, but Charlotte told Dad we needed cash only. Fresh baked bread and pie sounded fine to me, though. Next there was Joe's tavern, where Dad would decorate the mirrors behind the bar at Christmas time. Dad made extra income using his fine artistic talent, carrying his painting suitcase as holidays came along. In my grade school years I went with him on occasion, enjoying the coke and pretzels I received from the owners of the establishment, while Dad did his artistic painting. When I attended South Hills High School I met the owner's daughter, Betty. Most of my popular records came from Joe's tavern jukebox. When the music records were changed out by the Jukebox Co. Betty would give me some of the used one's. Betty and I dated from time to time, and after a movie we would go to the tavern, and dance to the records in the family living room above the bar. Her dad would provide us with snacks and cokes, making the evening even more enjoyable. I think he approved of me, since any father would like to have their daughter meet an (almost) perfect gentleman.

Next on the Boulevard tour, was the Brookline News agency, which sold newspapers from all over, and also magazines, soft drinks, model airplane kits, and boat kits. When my brother Jerry began his model airplane club he bargained with the agency owner for a club discount. He also bargained with the school principal for the use of the school drafting room at Brookline Elementary, quite an achievement for a teenager. Next, on the corner of a side street was our old time Brookline Firehouse, where you could see the firemen playing cards, or washing down the shiny red fire trucks. When Dad got his job with the WPA and the city of Pittsburgh later on, it included painting all Pittsburgh county buildings, firehouses and police stations. During his many years with the city Dad got to know

The Prewar Years 1938-1942

most of the police and firemen personally. Another connection with the Brookline fire station when I was growing up was, Charlotte's Uncle Elmer Mills, who was a retired fire chief from the Brookline Fire Dept. The tall hose storage tower at the fire house was used to hang the hoses to dry out after use. Down the street from the fire house were a variety shoe and clothing stores, and the Brookline Movie Theater, where Saturday was always kid's matinee showing a main family feature, then a regular weekly serial.

The Pre-War Years - 1936 to 1942

The Brookline fire station of the times, where my step-Uncle Elmer had been a fire Chief. Dad painted city fire and police stations on WPA.

Mom and Pop grocery stores, similar to this one, were the main food shopping source of the times.

The World War I Cannon Park at the end of Brookline Blvd., where we often ate our lunch on school days before exploring the Blvd.

A record player like the one we used at Joe's tavern to play old jukebox records.

These serials were the ones which ended with "to be continued"; they were all great adventure stories ending in death defying cliff hangers. They were short films designed to bring you back next week to see what happened to your hero. They starred "Flash Gordon on the Planet Mongo" or "Buck Rodgers in the 25th Century A.D.", and none of us wanted to miss the next installment. For the next week we searched at job sites, around garbage cans, or empty houses to search for soda pop deposit bottles. We could cash them in for our .25 cent price of admission. The quart size bottles were worth a nickel, the small ones were two cents. I earned my admission other times by working for Millers Grocery Store, passing out special sales circulars in the neighborhood. I earned fifty cents, delivering hundreds of them climbing up and down many steps in the process.

There were delicatessens such as Bards and Isaly's where you could get cokes or ice cream cones for five cents, banana splits for fifteen cents, and many flavors of ice cream sodas. At Isaly's you could get those delicious Klondike ice cream bars. They were hard frozen ice cream squares all covered with chocolate, like the ones we received on the "auto ride" in the orphanage. At Isaly's you could get the best chipped chopped ham around, and in later years when we came to Florida, Mom would send our son Michael to the local grocery for some chopped ham, chipped wafer thin, the way Isaly's did in Pittsburgh Pa. When the butcher saw Mike coming he would remark, "Here comes chip chop". Another popular place for sodas and banana splits was the Edgewood Pharmacy on the corner, where Edgewood St. met with Brookline Boulevard. The street dropped off at a steep angle to the next street below. During my high school years I had worked for a time at Edgewood Pharmacy dishing up sodas for the teen crowd, enjoying a few of my own making as well.

Perhaps I shouldn't be telling this, but one stunt my friend Jack McCahan and I would pull was quite spectacular, at least we thought so. When hanging around at the drug store on our bikes, we would douse one hand with lighter fluid, light it and wave our flaming hand at the passing cars, much to the amazement of the drivers and passengers in the cars going by on the Boulevard. The flames didn't actually hurt, as long as we kept our hands moving back and forth quickly. No harm except for a bit of singed arm hair. It was very spectacular, but perhaps just a little bit on the dumb side, as well. All I can say about my friend Jack is that some people will do anything to attract attention, he thought up the idea. Also on Brookline Blvd. was an assortment of grocery stores, like Donahue's, Butlers, Atlantic and Pacific Tea Co. and the A&P, plus several small individual grocery stores. In each case you had your prepared list of food items then waited your turn in line, then your order was filled when your turn came up. At the counter the clerk would select your items from the many packed shelves on an individual basis. The only supermarket, as it is known today, was the Streamline Market, which was down Ray Ave., and about half a mile on West Liberty Ave. It was the closest store to home as the crow flies, and always had greater bulk food sales, especially on the larger sacks of sugar and flour Charlotte needed for bread baking and canning. Carrying a 25 lb. sack of flour up the 295, that's two hundred ninety five, wooden steps of Ray Ave. was no picnic.

The Streamline Market was the very first supermarket which compares to the ones in use in the fifties. It was the first self-service store in our area, and because it was self-service they had to hire an extra assistant manager in charge of watching for all light fingered customers, who had a different view of what self-service really meant. I worked there as Asst. Manager during my senior year at South Hills. My Aunt Gladys worked at one of the small boulevard grocery stores for a time, and got me a job sweeping up, emptying trash cans, etc. on Saturdays. Besides a small wage I had a fringe benefit of making my own lunch from the meat display, the fruit counter, and beverage section. The pay wasn't much, but I made up for it with my creative meat sandwiches. Meat was definitely a luxury item for me, normally a Sunday treat like meat loaf, chicken or pork. During the week it was peanut butter or jelly for our school lunches, with soup, stew, or pasta for dinner. When Charlotte sent us to the store to buy our Sunday meat we always had to ask for a piece of suet, when buying beef for a stew. Suet was the fat cut off by the butcher when trimming a side of beef, and at home Charlotte would cook it in the skillet as she rendered it down for soup stock or gravy base. We also would ask for a beef bone, which she used for making soup. Charlotte really did know the ways to stretch her food dollar.

The high value of that scarce dollar in our household was really brought home to me on one memorable occasion. Charlotte had sent me to buy a broom, which was on sale at the Donahue's Grocery down at the far end of the Blvd. When I arrived at Donahue's I reached into my shirt pocket for the dollar to buy the broom, but in spite of a frantic search it had disappeared. The last time I remembered having it was up near the firehouse. While I was walking along I had rolled it around my finger for a while, and then placed it in my shirt pocket still rolled up. In desperation I retraced my steps a number of times before giving up to go home without the broom or the money. I listened to Dad and Charlotte as they read me the riot act about being careful with money, being responsible, etc. The next morning, on the way to church, everyone searched along the sidewalks and in the gutter as we walked along looking, without much hope, for that lost dollar bill. Praying all the while, I might add. Then, within sight of the Donahue's Store I spotted my lost dollar. There was a billboard in an open space between two stores, with wooden planks instead of a sidewalk in front of the billboard, and there, wedged down in a crack between a set of the boards, was my coiled up one dollar bill. Dad retrieved it by putting a pencil into the coil, and we all felt thankful for its safe return. The coiling helped to hide as well as save it, but it would have taken just a bit more vibration on those wooden planks, and my dollar would have joined the pile of other trash beneath the platform. During mass I gave thanks that my many prayers had been answered. It was only a missing dollar bill you may say, but it was much more than that, it was needed to provide for our very basic needs, and not just our wants. An average wage then was only $20 a week.

When Charlotte gave us lists to be filled at stores on the Blvd. we would pick up different items at those stores, which had a sale going on or, where the price was a few cents cheaper. Even if it meant walking quite a bit further between stores to get the savings. As the saying was, if you watch the coppers they will soon turn to green. Getting back to our Brookline Boulevard tour, at the end of the main business section was the World War I Memorial Park, with its big WW I artillery cannon and flagpole. There were nice shade trees, and benches for people to relax on. I don't believe there was a boy in Brookline who didn't shinny out to the end of that high cannon barrel at some point in his boyhood. Following the Boulevard beyond the park was Creedmoor Ave., a steep street,

The Prewar Years 1938-1942

where the Resurrection Church and school were located. It was a two story square building, which didn't look much like a church at that time. It had the school on one level and the church on the upper level. Because of the steep grade of the hill they both had entrances off Creedmoor Ave. Later on, when the main church was built at the top of the grade, the school was on both levels of the original building. Charlotte's family, the Duffy's, had been members of the parish for a long time, well before Charlotte and Dad had met.

Father Quinn was the pastor, known as a very determined man; he and Grandma Duffy had a big misunderstanding, to put it mildly, during Mass at church one Sunday morning. At the altar rail waiting to receive Communion, Father Quinn passed by Grandma Duffy as she waited to receive the Eucharist. She then remained in her place and he passed her by a second time. After that Grandma Duffy got up then went to her seat to wait until Mass was over. Then, as the closing hymn was being sung, she got up and walked into the sacristy, the place behind the altar where vestments were put on. When Father Quinn came in she demanded to know why he refused her communion. He had a policy of not giving communion to any woman wearing a low neckline dress. Due to his poor eyesight, he couldn't see that grandma's dress was a light pink around the neck and really was not cut low. He apologized for his mistake, and offered to give her communion right there in the sacristy. Grandma Duffy told him in no uncertain terms, you embarrassed me in front of the church congregation, so you can give me communion in front of the congregation. She immediately went out to kneel down at the communion rail to await Fr. Quinn. Soon he came out with the chalice, and with lots of interested parishioners looking on he gave her the sacred host. Grandma was as strong willed as Fr. Quinn was. She stood her ground, and we admired her for it. We were sitting near her and saw the entire episode up close.

In 1936 after we had left the orphanage we began attending the Resurrection Parochial School, completing 6th to 8th grades there. Those were memorable times and one day was exceptionally so. It was a day when I became the center of attention, as well as being a subject of great curiosity by the faculty. Maybe I should not tell this on myself either, but I will, one warm day in early spring, after lunch was over the windows were opened, and I just couldn't seem to work up any interest in the lesson at hand. I was putting my hand under my desk to check on the location of my bubble gum on the underside, when I found a knot-hole in the wooden bottom. A book covered the opening, and I felt the challenge to try and balance the book with the middle digit of my right hand. As I was raising the book up past the knuckle of my finger the book fell off, when I tried to remove my finger it wouldn't budge. The skin on my finger had bunched up around my knuckle and it wouldn't come out. Raising the desk lid a bit, I tried hard to push it back out with my free hand, without any result. As panic began to set in, I started raising the lid higher, twisting and pushing my now swollen finger. For some time I just sat there trying to be calm, also asking God to lend a hand, but I am sure he had other more important prayers to be answered at the time.

    My panicked actions grew, and the teacher, Sister Clarissa, took notice of my strange activity and after a short statement concerning my lack of attention she invited me to stand, and read a few historical passages from the lesson at hand. Of course, I had to decline the invitation to stand up due to obvious conditions. I tried my very best to explain my problem to her, and even made a futile attempt to stand up as far as my imprisoned hand would allow. It was then she came to see what I was up to. As I raised the desk lid everyone came to see my problem. By now the entire class was gathered around my desk enjoying the break, and also seeming to enjoy my discomfort. There it was, my poor finger, just sticking out like a post, or like a worm poking out of a red apple. Sister Clarissa vainly tried her luck with a few tugs and pushes, and then sent one of the boys out to get some soap, that would do it for sure. With all the members of my class gathered around other tourists were dropping in, laughing and shaking their heads as they came and went. I quit trying to tell people how I did it, that really sounded dumb. I could say it was the desk that attacked me as I was searching around for my bubble gum. Al, my former good friend, asked me if it hurt, then he tugged on my finger to see if he could fix it, I kicked him in the shins, and he yelped down the aisle feeling a little pain himself. The soap was tried unsuccessfully leaving my finger still impaled in my desk,

The Prewar Years 1938-1942

Now it was time for more drastic measures. Sister sent someone for Charlie, the janitor. He was the handyman and janitor, but anything needing to be done had to be taken care of early in the day, because by late afternoon Charlie was hard to find, usually asleep someplace. Fortunately for me it was still early in the day, when Charlie came in to inspect my personal emergency. He gave me a strange look, then after inspecting the bottom of the desk imprisoning my digit he left to get his tools shaking his head, and mumbling something about damaging school property. I tried hard to believe Charlie would be able to set me free without any personal harm. When Charlie returned he had a hammer in his right hand and a wood chisel in his left. When he positioned that sharp chisel near my finger I closed my eyes and prayed. He made one whack of the hammer then a second whack, and a twist of the wood chisel giving me a sharp pain due to the pressure, but my finger was freed from its wooden prison. More importantly my finger was unharmed except for the swelling, and Charlie had done a good job. The desk was made of solid oak, and the knot hole was on the line, where two boards were joined together. The chunk of wood Charlie chiseled out had split around the knot hole, and what a relief, I was not wearing the desk any longer. Charlie handed me the piece of wood as a souvenir, and I wrote on the side of the section of wood; "This is the hole my finger got stuck in on May 10th 1937", then I passed it around the room for everyone to see. Sister called the class back to order, but I had the feeling that whenever she looked my way she was finding it very difficult to keep from laughing about the incident. Somehow, I never thought it was all that humorous, at least not until much later, when the damage to my ego was all healed. I can imagine it was a general topic of conversation around the convent supper table a while.

Another memory of my grade school days at Resurrection concerned our lunch time activities. During the lunch hour we often left the school grounds to eat our peanut butter and jelly sandwiches at the Boulevard Memorial Park. On one such day, four of us were taking a walk up the Blvd., and during our stroll we came upon a parked car, left there at the curb, with the engine still running, near Joe's Tavern. One of our not so clever pals suggested we all take a joy ride back to school. He reasoned we would not be stealing it, but just taking a little joy ride. It was nothing too serious, and we could park it where the owner could find it eventually. The boy came from a well to do family, which had cars, so he knew how to drive, and he convinced the others go with him. As for me I declined for personal reasons, and they were soon off down the boulevard tooting the horn, having great fun. Upon my arrival back at school the news was out, they had all been caught by an alert motorcycle policeman. The policeman would have thought it really unusual for a fourteen year old to be out driving, with only other teens in the car. They were taken to the local police station and their parents were being notified. Needless to say, I was glad I had refused to join in their escapade. I had the best of reasons for keeping out of trouble, because after we left the orphanage my father told me that he would never do anything to make me ashamed to say that he was my father and he hoped I would never do anything to make him ashamed to say I was his son. To this day that statement by my father, who loved me as I loved him, has been a guideline in my life, and I have passed Dad's message on to my own family with those same positive results. When I was invited to go along on that joyride that day, Dad's message came through loud and clear in my mind. Another rule of his was, if you want to stay out of trouble, stop and think of the consequences before following the crowd. From a spiritual standpoint; what we do in this life will determine whether we enjoy an eternity of joy, or an eternity of regret in the next life.

During my first year at Resurrection school I became re-acquainted with our Brookline, Mahoney relatives. Especially, my first cousin Jim, who was in my brother Jerry's class. His younger brother David was in Jeannie's class. One day after school Jim had invited me, Jerry, and Jeannie to go home with him to visit his family, Dad's brother Jim and Aunt Estelle. I knew of my Dad's Mahoney relatives, but my memories of them from my childhood were dim. Anyway, we had a nice visit getting reacquainted, and I was glad to know I had family so near to us. Our visit was short, but as a result we got back home a little later than usual, and Charlotte was really upset about it. Dad asked us not to go there again, apparently because of some past family disagreement between them. When young Jim asked me to visit at another time, I didn't lie to him, I just told him we weren't

The Prewar Years 1938-1942

allowed. So we only saw our new first cousins at school. It wasn't until years later in Florida, that we became close to Uncle Jim and Aunt Estelle, known then as "Nana" to the family and to her many friends. My cousin Jim, his wife Bernadine, nicknamed Bunny, and other Mahoney cousins lived in the Melbourne and Eau Gallie Florida area as well. The only close relatives, which we had seen in the early years, were the Patterson's, Uncle John and Aunt Margaret, who was Dad's older Sister. They lived across the valley, high up on another ridge, in the suburb of Beechview. Their three sons, Will, John, and Robert were friends as well as cousins in later years. We also visited often with Mary, Dad's oldest sister, who taught at St. Catherine's church school in Beechview. She was a nun in the order of St. Joseph convent, and known by her religious name as Sister Mary Paula. Dad would decorate her classroom blackboards on special holidays, as had done for the Sisters at the orphanage. On occasion, Aunt Sister Paula would come to our home to share Sunday dinner when she could get a ride from some kind car owner. Another younger sister of Dad's was Agnes, who also came to visit occasionally.

During our visits away from the home there had been some contact with our mother Regina's family, the Picard's. Mother had two sisters and one brother, Aunt Genevieve Vogel, Aunt Agnes Fitzpatrick and Uncle Julius Piccard. Aunt Genevieve and Uncle Joe Vogel had ten children. Aunt Agnes and her husband Uncle Al Fitzpatrick had no children, and Julius never married. During World War II Jeannie was able to visit the Vogel family on a number of occasions at their home on Camp Horne Rd. in Ohio Township, northwest of Pittsburgh. In the 1990's I was in touch with my cousin Betty (Vogel) Reese, in Ohio Township. Another Cousin, Bob Vogel, lived in the nearby town of Deltona, Florida, with his wife Louise. Their son Robert Vogel Jr. was the sheriff of Volusia County on the east coast of Florida, near Daytona, at one time. Sheriff Bob Jr. had gained national recognition with his anti-drug war along I-95 on the east coast. While we were in St. Paul's, around 1930, we visited with Aunt Genny and Uncle Joe Vogel, where they lived high above the Monongahela River, on Bonifay St. overlooking Pittsburgh's South Side. I can remember the path going down toward the steep drop-off behind their home. They had a garden in all the usable space, but I never went to see how far it went to the edge of the tree covered hill, but the Vogel kids didn't seem to give it a thought. Uncle Joe and Aunt Genny were very kind to us on those visits. It was Aunt Genny who wanted to take Jeannie into their family even though they had a large brood as it was. Dad always wanted us to be together, but the way it turned out we were completely separated from each other right from the start in St. Paul's Orphanage. Even though Dad thought he was doing the right thing.

A big part of growing up in the 1920's and 1930's was the opportunity go exploring in the woods. St. Paul's Orphanage was in a country area of small farms and wood-lands. There were many types of fruit trees, such as cherry, apple, pear, and many berry patches were scattered all through the woods. Even though we were not allowed to leave the orphanage grounds, on pain of punishment, we managed to spend many summer hours in the woods. We would work on our tree house and roaming far and wide, to find trees to visit when fruit to ripen. The same thing was true after we left the orphanage, and lived on Plainview Ave. in Brookline; there were lots of woods to roam in, one was a wooded area right across the street from our house, running along the high side of Plainview Ave. There were cherry and apple trees growing wild among the oaks and other trees on the old Duffy farmland. One large apple tree on my list was so high that from its very top branches I could see some of the tallest buildings, like the Gulf Building, in downtown Pittsburgh. I had one heart stopping occasion up in that tree, when I made an attempt to go higher than I ever had before, trying to reach one elusive group of apples near the top when, a rotted limb splintered, then broke under my weight. Fortunately, the tree had lots of big secondary branches below me, which did the great job of slowing my fall. I found myself riding that broken limb down to the ground, just like riding a bucking bronco. In the final analysis, I only some minor scrapes and bruises to show for my wild ride. The apples were still way up there ready to fall when ripe, and as for me, I was ready to wait them out.

Another time, while enjoying the woods and climbing trees for fun, I was not so fortunate. It was on a summer Saturday after doing my chores, that I headed on out to see what the day had in store for an adventuresome fourteen year old. Not far from home I came across a coil of steel cable left there by the power Co., when they

The Prewar Years 1938-1942

installed a new power pole nearby. It appeared to be long enough to make a great ride for life cable ride. It could begin at a big tree up close to the street then run to a higher tree further down the hill in the woods. It had all the makings of a great fun project for a quiet Saturday. I went back home to search through Dad's junk box to find a pulley wheel, the kind used on painting scaffolds. I found the pulley, and enough rope to attach a seat on our cable ride. With the help of my brother Jerry and my good friend Skippy we got busy constructing our cable ride. Running the cable through the pulley wheel first, we fastened the wire at each end, struggling and pulling it as tight as possible to make it a smooth ride. With the rope seat attached to the pulley, and after hours of hard work, it was ready for the test run. Brother Jerry volunteered to be first, but it was my cable and my idea, so there was no question in my mind who should be the test pilot. It really would have been better to learn just a little more about the downward angle of the grade, and the height of the trees before making a live person test, but even though I had no engineering skills, I thought it looked fine.

Impatient to try it out, I climbed up on the platform then onto the rope seat, and once I let go of the holding rope I was off, flying like the wind and I do mean flying. As I saw the end tree looming larger in front of me I was a bit sorry that I had greased the pulley. Sorry also, for giving a push at the start, and most of all, sorry I didn't let my brother Jerry go first. The ride was downhill all the way and predictably, when reaching the very end of the ride I was wrapped all around that big tree. Jerry, seeing me hanging there half unconscious, ran home to get Dad. A short time later Dad had me untangled, and helped me down out of the tree. That was the end of our "ride for life" cable ride, because Dad had called the power company to come and get their cable out of the trees. In my opinion, with just a few minor modifications, like a stop on the cable before hitting the tree, it would have been a terrific ride. I might have been able to sell tickets and make a young fortune. I must have done something right though, I heard Dad telling the story on a number of occasions, and he sounded quite impressed with my ingenuity and my lack of engineering skill.

Grandma Duffy, still had a few acres left of the original farm, down the street from us on the corner of Plainview and Bell Isle

Ave. Their original farmhouse was still being used by Grandma Duffy, Uncle Carol, and Aunt Gladys Duffy. There were pear, apple and three of my all-time favorites, those delicious big, black, Bing cherry trees. When the Bing cherries began to ripen, my brother Jerry and I, along with the Helferty boys, would take on the job of guarding against predators, especially the two legged variety. Mainly we scared off the birds, which must have come from everywhere to feast on our cherries. We tied tin cans with twine, and placed them high up in the trees, so we could just pull the string and frighten them away by remote control. The birds wouldn't just eat one cherry; they took one bite out of every cherry in view, causing them to turn bad. When the fruit was finally ready to pick all the families gathered for the joint picking effort. The older kids climbed into the trees with baskets attached with ropes to pick the delicious crop. Before our picking began in earnest Grandma Duffy allowed the pickers five minutes to pick and eat, after that it was whistle and pick.

The Pre-War Years - 1936 to 1942

OUR CHICKEN COOP CLUB HOUSE - 1937
Our converted club house was a great place to build our model planes, and enjoy the old records on our crank up Victorola. We even had a pot bellied wood stove for heating in the winter.

****

The Brownie camera was the first one for general use, and very simple to use.

Our pot belly stove, rescued from an empty House one day.

The "Victorola" record player. No batteries, no AC. only arm power.

Then we would fill our basket and lower it to be emptied, presenting another opportunity to sample a few more cherries as we waited. After the picking, the pitting and canning operation, there were lots left over for refrigerating and eating later on. For weeks afterward we were back in the trees looking for any we may have missed, those Bing cherries were great eating. Another great pastime we had were the high swings. The woods were made for swings, not that little; push me, type of swing, but the twenty five foot, out over the side of the hill, heart in the throat, type of swings. One such swing was on a great oak tree high above West Liberty Ave. near the Brookline junction. You had to pull the swing back to the take-off platform on a nearby tree, then putting your foot in the loop while holding onto the large knots for a good grip, off you went in an high arc, which carried you out over the edge of the drop, and you could look down on the tops of the cars, trolleys and local businesses along the avenue. To an adult it probably looked only 100 ft. up, but to us it was a mile high. One thing was sure, the adrenaline flowed wide open until the swing slowed enough to get off. Every ride on that swing was a totally new experience. For safety sake, a clothes line was fastened to the seat of the swing to bring it back from the cliff edge to help getting on and off. There was enough slack in the rope to prevent interference with the ride itself. It gave us a safety feature in case we had trouble getting someone on the swing back to the platform. Any high tree with a sturdy lower limb was a good candidate for a tire type swing, or rope one with a seat. There were lots of those, but exciting ones with a challenge were meant for adventurous types my age.

    When a boy reached thirteen years of age, it was the common practice to make the attire change from knickers; these were the knee length trousers of the times. Getting his first pair of long trousers was sort of a rite of passage from childhood to teenager, and a milestone of growing up in those days. Wearing knickers was the style for young boys, they had elastic cuffs just below the knee, and the knee length socks were held up by garters, which would sometimes cut off the blood circulation. The use of Knickers was practical for young boys, considering the padding at the knee to protect against the scrapes and scratches, common with rough and tumble boy stuff. They were not very practical for walking through brambles and bushes with legs protected only by thin stockings. Along with those long trousers came another growing up item, a watch pocket, which was located at the right front side of the long trousers near to the belt line. Having a watch pocket made for a very popular thirteenth birthday gift, getting the dollar railroad watch with a belt or a chain to pull it out and to keep from losing it as well. That two inch Ingersoll dollar watch was like a railroad conductor's watch. It had a diameter of two inches with a spring winder at the top plus a ring to fasten a chain or a watch fob, the same kind used by adults, who weren't supposed to lose their watches. A watch fob was a decorative piece of leather, used instead of a chain. It was attached to the top of the watch, making it easier to remove from the new watch pocket, or vest pocket, as desired. Vests were also a normal article of young men's attire.

Another regular part of any boy's attire was the cap, which was similar to golf caps in use today. You wore it wherever you went, especially church and school, and it was always a nuisance keeping track of it indoors. There was also a colored celluloid sun visor hat with a cloth edging, and stretch head band, great for shading the sun in summer. Celluloid was the early plastic material used as movie film and other uses, even men's fake collars were made of the stuff. Girls always had their heads covered, with bonnets or hats as a matter of custom, in church women were expected to have their heads covered. Wearing a hat did have one advantage; it covered up our home style haircuts. At St. Paul's everyone had close cut hair for practical reasons, and to prevent spread of head lice, ringworm, or other such juvenile scourges of the scalp. For boys, the barber simply used a bowl to trim in around the head, and the neck was shaved clean making haircuts short and sweet. When we lived at home, Dad was the barber, and I always had the impression that he hated that job of cutting hair as much as his customers did, make that victims! His hair clipper was the mechanical, hand operated, type, there were no electric clippers, then except in barber shops. There were times during a haircut, when clumps of hair and scalp were removed suddenly, if Dad's fingers got too tired, or the clippers jammed. A five ouch, haircut was considered a good one. Those clippers are

The Prewar Years 1938-1942

still in my possession, but only as a souvenir or a keepsake of mine. My two sons, Michael and Billy, never had to endure the pain and anguish of a haircut the way their Dad and their Uncle Jerry had to, fortunately for them electric hand clippers were invented for home use, and the best place for Dad's hand operated torture device was in the memento box.

Without air conditioners windows and doors were always kept open wide during hot weather, and flies were plentiful. They would lay in wait by the doorway for the screen door to open up for them, and then in they would fly in, in droves. There were no useful bug sprays like aerosol available, so the method to control the fly invasion was one continuous effort all during the summer months. There were some basic items used in the battle against the common house fly. Every kitchen had its roll of sticky fly-paper hanging down to attract the pests, which then became stuck to the tacky surface. Those fly-paper rolls were effective, but being tall was a real disadvantage. If you bumped into one of those messy, sticky rolls, they stuck to your head, with or without flies attached. For use on window sills and food tables was a flat fly paper sheet, which worked the same as the flypaper roll. When it became fully covered with dead flies it was not a very appetizing decoration at mealtime. The hand-held fly swatter was the most effective weapon, usually assigned to the older children, especially us boys, to hunt down and swat every fly anywhere near the premises. The swatter was made with a sturdy wire frame and a four inch square section of window screen material, which we swung with deadly accuracy. First we had to chase the fly away from the food onto another safe surface before swatting, for very obvious reasons. There was a hand operated pump type sprayer used for garden pests, but not suitable for indoor use. The oily, smelly spray did not lend itself to enjoying the delicious aroma of the food. A bit of trivia from the thirties about the multitude of flies indicated that if the automobile had not replaced the horse, our larger cities would have become so deep in horse manure the fly population would be almost impossible to control, allowing disease to run rampant. As it was, even with the automobile, the fly has been responsible for the spread of many diseases and illnesses over the years.

In case one of us really did get sick, the doctor always came to the house, checking your eyes, heart and tongue. From that inspection he decided on aspirin or some other pill he had in his bag. Many doctors learned their trade from medical schools or correspondence schools, and were not as fully educated in the practice, as they are today. The last time I remember the doctor coming to our home on Plainview, was when Dad bought some industrial life insurance on each one of us, and we needed to have a really good physical to qualify. When the doctor came he was examining Jerry first, and as the doctor did his thing, Jerry must have had a different idea why the doctor was there because, he complained about a pain in his chest, giving Dad a fit. Dad was hoping to get us qualified for the insurance and Jerry was about to mess it up. As it turned out the doctor had a laugh over the episode, and assured Dad that everything was fine. One despised home remedy was the use of Epsom salts for keeping the digestive tract in shape. A full tablespoon of dry Epsom salts followed by a glass of water required you to stay near the bathroom all day. When we were in the orphanage we would get in line to get a big square of baker's yeast, to prevent zits on our faces, I guess. That was followed by a tablespoon of Epsom salts, making your mouth dry as a desert. Then you had to wait for your turn at the water fountain to wash it down. Yuck, and super yuck! Can you imagine the dozens of kids waiting in the bathroom lines?

Cars held a great deal of interest for us as teenagers. We could name every make and model of the cars that passed below us, as we perched on the grassy hill high above West Liberty Ave., at the Brookline junction, on lazy summer days just passing the time. Few people owned cars then, and all of the paved roads were mainly two lane black top. Some main streets, like West Liberty Ave. and Brookline Blvd. did have cobblestones down in the middle along the trolley tracks. Most streets weren't bothered with traffic, and our street especially, had little auto traffic to interfere with our street games of tag, hide and seek, and run sheep run. In 1922 there were ten million Model-T Fords, known as Tin Lizzies. From 1906 to 1926 they were rolling off the very first automobile assembly lines in the world, and you could get one in any color you

The Prewar Years 1938-1942

wanted, as long as you wanted black, according to Mr. Henry Ford himself. The most well-known cars in 1936 were from the Ford Motor Company, and other top companies, such as, Lincoln, Nash, Pontiac, Oldsmobile, Packard, Chrysler, Pierce-Arrow, Hudson, Studebaker and Plymouth. In 1939, the Ford Mercury came on the scene, and my friend Jack's father bought one. The rumble seat was a standard in some coupe models of the 1930's. Instead of a trunk in the car, the trunk lid located on the top could open up as an upholstered, extra open air seat. It was great in the summer, if you didn't mind the heat of the sun, or the wind and rain, but those rumble seats were only used by the more hardy individuals in the cold winter months. They were the forerunner of the convertible to a degree. There is a little poem I remember about the rumble seat, which goes like this: My auntie liked to ride with me to enjoy the fresh clean breeze, so I had to put her in the rumble seat, then I watched my auntie–freeze!

There is very little photo record of my childhood years; some of those I do have are shown in this book. Few people had cameras in those days, and the luxury of buying a camera didn't fit in the family budget. Those who did have a camera usually owned one of those Brownie pinhole cameras made by Kodak. Nothing fancy, no frills, just frame the picture in the viewer, push down the mechanical switch and that was it. Before the Brownie camera came on the scene, if you wanted to have a picture taken, there were photo studios, and traveling photographers who visited the local neighborhoods, usually with a pony or a donkey, taking a picture of all the tots. Every family album seemed to have that photo of kids on a saddled pony; Jerry is pictured on a donkey in our own family record. Once the Brownie camera came along everyone became an expert, it was a very simple box shaped device. After opening the back of the camera, which used 120 film, the starting tab on the film was wound around the top spool and the remainder slipped in the bottom slots. When film was installed and the case was closed, film numbers showed through a red cellophane window as the film was used. The single up and down lever, and the one position lens, were all that was needed to take the photo. No flash, no focus, or light settings to deal with. The pictures I have in my record look as good now as they did when they were first snapped, looking better than some of those taken in more recent times. There was only black and white film then, colored photo film did not become common until after World War II.

The economy of the times didn't permit a money allowance for kids, so if we wanted to buy something we had to find ways to earn the money. One way to earn a few coins was to search for scrap copper, iron, brass, rags or even bones to sell to the junk man. Finding anything to sell wasn't easy, since most parents saved their rags and metal for the same reason, extra money for their families. Our best opportunity came after May 1st, the traditional moving day in Pittsburgh. Yearly leases expired soon after the cold and snow had passed, and when a local house had become vacant we would sneak in to explore and look for anything of value left behind by the former tenants. Soft drink returnable bottles were worth .02¢ or .05¢ each, copper was always a great find, so was brass. The "Junk Man" came around in an old truck piled high with scrap metal, bags of old clothing and rags. He drove his old truck slowly up every street, calling out, "metal and rags to buy", as he rang a big bell. On the back of the truck he had a giant scale to weigh each purchased item. There wasn't much competition; he always controlled the value of the scrap, unless you were able to take it to the junk yard yourself. Whatever we were given was 100% profit, so we didn't complain as we counted our coins, and planned what to buy. As for me, model airplanes were my favorite toy choice, and I always seemed to be saving for some special item. After we left the orphanage Jerry and I became closer as brothers. Besides sharing the same bedroom, bed, dresser, chest and closet. Together we worked to make over our back yard chicken coop into a great club house, furnished with leftover furnishings from vacant houses. We built bunks, for sleeping out in the summer and made work tables for our model airplane club to use.

Jerry had started the club with only a few members, and it soon grew in size. He even arranged for the club to use the Brookline Elementary school drafting class-room for our meetings and model building, which had large tables for our use. Jerry seemed to have a knack for organization, he also arranged for wholesale prices when we bought our model kits at the Brookline News Agency on the Boulevard. His club grew to about twenty members at its peak, quite an accomplishment for a young teenager. We used the clubhouse to build our own models, and as a place to spend our spare time. We had acquired a wind-up Victorola with a collection of old time records from our visits to empty houses, which we played over and over. I learned many of the very, moldy, oldie tunes from those old, turn of the 19th century records. Even learning by heart, some of those really heart wrenching songs. Tunes like, "That Letter Edged in Black", "A tender loving Lassie used to live a happy life, until Father turned her picture toward the wall", all designed to bring a tear to the eye. They were often a hit at parties when I sang some of them, although, there seemed to be more laughing than crying, when I did, for some reason. Everyone was amazed that anyone would want learn, or even remember such songs. Later on, my grandkids could sing some of them. One song I taught them was called, "Oh we're crazy, we're simply crazy, and that's the way we pass the time away". They called them Pap-Pap's silly songs, so those old songs may continue to live on. Someday my family will thank me, maybe!

There was a few times, which maybe I should not own up to, when I went to South Hills High School and used our club house as a hideout for skipping school. We made a trapdoor in the floor, so we could enter from behind the club house from the back street. The front door had a big lock in plain view, hiding our presence to anyone up in the house. We didn't do it very of ten mind you, only on rare occasions, when my friends forced me to join them. Anyway, my grades were fine, and I had no problem with being able to be the only one of the family to graduate from high school. My brother Jerry never graduated from grade school, he only finished seventh grade, before going on to learn a trade at the Vocational school. Attending a Vocational school was a common practice at the time, a good choice, in lieu of regular schooling. Jerry's special talent was in drafting, art, and mechanical drawing, and the vocational school prepared him for his lifelong occupation, as a draftsman. Jerry always had Dad's talent for art; even as young as age eleven he was drawing planes. He drew a flying wing aircraft before the popular science magazine had a futuristic one on its cover.

The Pre-War Years - 1936 to 1942

Archival photo of a typical CCC camp, where young men, like my brother Jerry, were employed in a military lifestyle planting pine forests, building state park pavilions, and other projects. It was a government program called, The Civilian Conservation Corps. Part of the WPA, and designed to put young men to work.

✯✯✯✯✯✯✯✯✯✯✯✯✯✯✯✯✯✯✯✯✯✯✯✯✯✯✯✯✯✯✯✯✯✯✯

My graduation photo from grade school in 1938, now enrolled in South Hills High.

My skinny tire bike, which cost me $2.50. It had one tire and no brakes. It had wood tire rims with steel spokes & no fenders.

At age 18 Jerry joined the government "CCC" camp, known as the Civilian Conservation Corps program. They employed young male volunteers, who lived a military life style in camps, receiving pay and lodging. They worked mainly in reforestation, planting large areas of pine trees for future building uses, and also worked on state park construction projects. It was part of the "NRA", President Roosevelt's "National Recovery Act", to help in bringing the nation out of the depression; they called it Roosevelt's alphabet soup. After his tour with the "CCC", Jerry went down to Miami Florida, working at odd jobs, washing dishes, and working with a surveyor for a time.

The Prewar Years 1938-1942

One story Jerry told on himself about those difficult times, was how the Army would not even take him when he tried to enlist, because he was so malnourished. Not long after he arrived in Miami, with high hopes of a good job, he was close to the edge of starvation until he decided to take a job as a dish washer in a local restaurant, so he could get his meals free. After that he hired on with a surveying company, and soon became self-sufficient. Eventually, he put on enough weight to join the Navy, rather than wait for his number to come up in the draft. Jerry returned home for a time before joining the Navy in early 1942. I had helped finance his trip to Miami, so in part payment for what he owed me, he gave me several of his neat sport coats and slacks. They were nice, but I was expecting my money back!

As it turned out I joined the Navy myself in November of 1942, so I didn't get very much use out of those duds until after the war. Jeannie was still attending Resurrection Elementary School, but when she did graduate, she went on to vocational school, as Jerry had done. She studied hair dressing, home making, and sewing. After graduating she went to work for Western Union, delivering telegrams, which was the major method of quick communication at that time.

Dad was working regularly now painting the many bridges over Pittsburgh's three rivers. He was working for another of the government "Alphabet Soup" programs, the "WPA", or Works Progress Administration. The "WPA" was a nationwide government effort repairing roads, bridges, and decaying infrastructure of the cities. The "WPA" got a publicity black eye over the image of workers standing around, just leaning on shovels, watching others work. It filled the employment gap, until the war effort brought about full employment, and it did repair a lot of public streets and services in the process. Dad worked with the bridge painting crews who worked from scaffolds. There was competition among painters to get on the bridge jobs, to the extent that sabotage, by radical workers, was a danger. Dad told of how they had to check all the ropes and tackle used to support the hanging stages before they put them over the side of the bridges to do the job of painting. The ropes were stored in metal drums, and there was a time, when someone poured acid over the ropes weakening them with the obvious potential result. On windy days those swinging platforms would blow around, and during heavy gusts of wind the painters had to sit down quickly, using their feet to keep from hitting the bridge, or its framework with force. Dad was happy to have a steady, even if dangerous job. During the war, he went to work for the city of Pittsburgh painting city and county buildings, such as fire and police stations. He remained with the city until his retirement. Sadly, he wasn't retired for even one year, before dying of cancer at 65.

About my little sister Jeannie, as I said earlier, we were unable to be very close at the orphanage, but after we settled in our new home we became real family at last. Even to getting into brother, sister squabbles, which we couldn't enjoy while at St. Paul's. One memorable incident of disagreement came when Dad and Charlotte were gone, and we had our assigned chores to do. Jean had a bucket and was getting ready to wash down the stairs to the second floor, when we got into a nonsensical fuss over nothing. She had begun the aggravating action of repeating every single word I would say to her. Naturally, that upset me, plus the fact, that she refused to accept my superior logic or listen to reason, it was enough to anger a saint. Push came to shove, and then my sweet little sister swung her bucket overhand at me, and almost put my lights out. The reason I still remember this minor spat was because we never had that many fights, in spite of that secret "violent" nature on Jeannie's part. Just kidding Sis! My little sister is, was, and still is a sweetheart. Another incident involving Jean had to do with her trick knee, which would just pop out of its socket on occasion. We were walking home from church one wintry Sunday, and as we started down the snow covered, shortcut path through the woods across the street from our home Jean slipped on the snowy path, and out of the socket went her trick knee. Jerry and I made the fireman's carry with our arms, and down the path we went, slipping and sliding to the bottom of the grade. We carefully carried her across the street up onto our front porch, then as we carried our patient through the door; her knee bumped the door frame popping her trick knee back into place. Then miraculously, she stood up and hurried into the kitchen, leaving her two tired brothers to wonder if they had been taken in. But she couldn't have planned anything like that, not Jeannie; she really did have a trick knee!

The Prewar Years 1938-1942

Not to pick on my sister, but let me tell you the sad tale of my very first bike, and its destruction by that same sweet girl. Of course, it was only an un-fortunate accident; even Dad was convinced of that, but it was more like a gross negligence on her part, in my opinion. Anyway, I had found this second hand bike for sale at a local gas station. Two dollars and fifty cents was the price, but it was in need of lots of "TLC". I was happy to get it, even though it was basically, just a bike frame, fenders, wheels, without tires. The wheels were made of wood, and badly out of round, supported with heavy wire spokes to adjust the alignment of the wheels. In its day it must have been a very sturdy well-built bike. Dad supervised repainting of the frame, while I became an expert on wheel and spoke adjustments. Next, I saved my money, and bought two new tires, "skinny tires", as they were called, without inner tubes. The tire itself was like an inner tube with treads, almost rigid. Balloon tires did not become available for all bikes, until much later. Finally, it was ready to ride, except in the rain, because I was still saving up for the fenders. So, for a time I enjoyed my bike, such as it was, riding up and down Plainview Ave. The "New Departure" brand brakes were a bit tricky, and I planned to get a new set later on when I saved the money. Because of the poor brakes, stopping was a matter of expertise on the part of the rider.

This brings my tale to that eventful day, when my little sister begged and pestered me for a ride. As always, being a pushover for tearful women, I agreed to give her one short, make that very short, ride. My next mistake was to leave her all alone with my bike. I had gone in the house for a minute and when I came back out; there she was coming down the steep path across the street, to get a good start she said. Without any brakes, she crossed the street, and went over the sidewalk to drive into the solid concrete porch steps. She had splintered the wooden front wheel beyond repair, and also bent the fork. In general, no other way to describe it, she destroyed my poor bike. So, after months of work, spending a fortune in hard earned cash, I had only enjoyed that prized possession for about one month. Jeannie herself had just a few minor scrapes and scratches, I was really glad she wasn't badly hurt. However, the final irony was to listen to Dad's recriminations for allowing her to ride on a bike with bad brakes. She always did get her way, but then brothers are rewarded in heaven, of that I'm sure.

The front porch was the main center of family activity during the summer months, especially in the evenings. Everyone sat out on their porch to enjoy the coolness of the outside air. The inside of the houses after a hot day, and due to the lack of building insulation, the rooms were hot and uncomfortable. Up and down our street children played on sidewalks, and in the streets, playing games like tag, one giant step, and all those games kids loved to play. There wasn't much car traffic to interfere, since not many families had cars, even though a new one sold for less than a thousand dollars. Uncle Carroll Duffy had a car, and a single lady, who lived alone in a house that stood by itself down the street, had one. She was so short she had to sit on a cushion to look through the steering wheel as she drove along. We all ran to get out of the street, whenever we saw her coming; we knew she couldn't see anything, except for the little bit of road visible directly in front of her car, and in between the steering wheel spokes. I'm sure she never saw many of the shorter kids. That didn't stop her from driving like the wind, though. Generally, there was very little to interfere with our evening fun. Our porch had its wooden swing, a rattan chair, settee and rocker. After dark, when everything got quiet and neighbors put their little ones to bed, we sat with the radio on low next to the open living room window. Listening to those great evening radio shows, like Bob Hope, Fred Allen, Red Skelton, or Inner Sanctum. Whenever a championship boxing match between Joe Louis and Billy Conn, who was a Pittsburgher, were fighting it out for the world championship title, every house seemed to be tuned in.

Main title bouts had greater public appeal then, than they do now. It may have been, because there were no professional teams in hockey or basketball, and even professional football was still in its infancy. All sports were part of radio listening, along with other shows. Popular with a lot of the public, were our Pittsburgh Pirates baseball club, they were well supported, even though they often fought it out with the Chicago Cubs for the bottom spot in the standings of the National League every year. At St. Paul's I had been a member of the Pirates Benchwarmer club, which entitled members to free seats during Pirate home games, depending on whether transportation was

The Prewar Years 1938-1942

available to the park at Forbes field. College football, with home teams like Pitt and Duquesne, were also very popular, as well as high school regional teams. I was active in Sandlot football, which was well organized in Pittsburgh's suburbs. Professional football was in its infancy, and the Pittsburgh Steelers trained at Moore Field, where our local sandlot team played. The Steeler players were former college players who worked at their own regular jobs, and then came together on weekends to play their games, getting a share of the gate for their efforts. Our local sandlot team, the "Moore Pro's" as we called ourselves, benefited from the Steelers know-how and equipment. The Steeler players often helped to coach our team football players as well, and also made their training equipment available for us to use. Due to that asset of having the Steelers on our field, made our team quite unbeatable during the years I played with them at left tackle, only 130 pounds, soaking wet!

    If a good fight was on too late, I had my crystal set, with its one earphone, in my room for listening while in bed. The radio had a Piezo electric crystal, with a radio frequency coil, and a cat-whisker. Moving the whisker over the crystal you could locate the right spot, where radio station KDKA was the strongest. You could hear other nearby stations like KDKA, as well. Some crystals would work best with certain stations. Dad had a story about my grandfather's first crystal set, which he had made himself using a mother's oats box wrapped with copper wire for the radio frequency coil. After he tuned the cat-whisker to KDKA Pittsburgh he let my grandmother, Margaret, listen to the music on the headphones. She screamed throwing down the headphones, unbelieving that music could be coming out of the air, calling it a tool of the devil. When you consider all of the problems caused by the violent programming on radio and television in modern times, she may have been right. The evenings on the porch gave relief from the heat of our upstairs bed room. There were some nights, when Jerry and I would sleep out on the back porch, using Uncle John's moving quilts to lie on, because our room was so unbearable.

    Pittsburgh winters were generally damp and drizzly, it didn't snow often, but if it did the snow packed hard on Ray Ave. steps, and it was almost impossible to go up or down without taking a fall. Then when a thaw set in it all turned into ice at night. Usually, the kitchen was the only room heated, and using the oven on the gas range caused the windows to fog up. In the evening, before Dad came home, there was a strained atmosphere in the kitchen as Charlotte was preparing supper, and the three of us were doing homework at the kitchen table. Every so often we would take a turn wiping fog off of the window pane looking for Dad on the Ray Ave. steps coming from the trolley stop. The unnatural quiet was very upsetting to me, and I felt a compulsion to break the silence by talking about any subject, which came to my mind. I kept it up until Dad was spotted on the steps and was in the door. Just like the sunshine breaking through the clouds, he would break that strained silence. In 1938, after two years living as a family, there was now a very strained home atmosphere. Dad was doing all that he could to calm the discord, but it was growing in spite of his efforts. We were older now, and our differences were becoming more pronounced.

The Pre-war Years - 1936 to 1942

The 1936 Ford belonging to Jack's Dad, which we used for our night time cruising without permission.

My first elective in high school was typing. A wise choice for the future.

CASEY AT THE BAT

CASEY AT THE BAT
SOUTH HILLS HIGH SCHOOL
PRINTING CLASS - 1941

This booklet was printed and published as a fund raiser for the school Athletic Dept., when I chose printing as my second elective. I still have my copy of the booklet.

The Prewar Years 1938-1942

Anyone who grew up during the thirties would remember the process of coloring oleo-margarine inside the package itself. Even though butter wasn't too expensive, especially fresh tub butter, which was sold in bulk at Donahue's. Charlotte occasionally bought butter as a treat, but oleo-margarine was the choice of necessity for most families. "Oleo", as it was called, was purchased in one pound, snow white blocks, without the yellow color of butter. This was due to the dairy lobby, which forced Oleo to be sold white, so it could not be confused with real butter, and compete with real dairy products. Each pound package had a small capsule of coloring powder to be mixed into the Oleo giving it the look of butter, although it didn't affect the actual taste. When we had to buy another block of Oleo we took turns at squeezing the coloring into it, although I believe Jeannie had the chore more often. You would take a large mixing bowl, sprinkle the powder on the Oleo to add in the coloring, and then squish it by hand, until it was evenly colored. It was formed into a block shape again, and placed in the ice box to firm up. Later on, the coloring method was improved by putting both the Oleo and coloring in the same squeeze bag making the job less messy. Oleo eventually became an accepted table spread, on a par with real butter and sold, already colored yellow, in the package.

Walking to school in winter was difficult; we all had our galoshes, or overshoes, to wear. They were heavy, but did a good job of keeping your feet dry and warm as toast, unless, you jumped in a deep snow bank and filled them with snow. We had lots of shortcuts on the way to school, but with ice and snow on the ground we stayed on the well-traveled paths, where people put down coal ashes on their sidewalks. Often, we followed the alleyways that ran behind all the houses. Talking about the alleyway, reminds me of a time when my brother Jerry had the occasion to actually run up a six foot fence between a house, and the back alley. There was a delicious Bartlett pear tree in this back yard, and morning after morning, in the fall; we passed it on our way to school. We drooled over the ripe fruit, and thought about how we could acquire maybe just one. Our problem was, the old man who owned that tree sat there on the back porch, or in the yard, admiring and protecting his prized fruit from predators like us.

One morning as we came by he was nowhere in sight, and several pears were down on the ground. We both had the same idea, why not climb over and get one? Jerry volunteered to climb the fence, while I would stand by to catch the fruit when he threw it over to me. Up and over he went, but just as he reached the tree, and before he could touch a pear, the door flew open and this madman came rushing at Jerry with a broom club. In nothing flat Jerry was at the fence, and honestly, I saw him actually run up that fence without stopping. I helped catch him as he jumped down the other side, then we were off running before the old man could get his gate unlocked. I never will forget the sight of seeing Jerry go up and down that fence. We began to take another route to and from school for a while after that, rather than take a chance on meeting that wild pear man again, talk about being possessive! The winter holidays were not the long drawn out affairs then, which we have now. Christmas season started in late November, and ended after the wise men came, on the feast of the Epiphany. Sometime during the Christmas season, we would make a family trolley trip to downtown Pittsburgh to see the decorated department store windows. The great, annual, animated window displays were a high point during Christmas, and were meant to lure the customers into the stores to shop. At home, we decorated our tree using those light strings where all the lights went out, when any one light burned out. We really could have used the later ones that showed only the burned out one. Trying to find that bad one would almost wreck the tree. Dad always painted a Christmas scene on the mantle mirror, which we left there for months afterward, because we really hated to wipe it off. Christmas presents were usually, the practical things you had a need for, like underwear, socks, or a new cap. The stocking on the mantle held a little fruit and candy.

I remember getting my first fountain pen for Christmas one year. It was a Schaeffer pen, which had a rubber bladder to store ink. To fill up the reservoir, you placed the point into a bottle of ink, and pressed a metal lever on the side of the pen to deflate the bladder, then by releasing it slowly the ink was drawn into the rubber bladder until full. Those pens were also a potential hazard if they developed a leak while clipped to your shirt pocket. The ink would run out of the bladder, ruining your shirt, and your disposition as well. In school we had wooden pen holders and pen points, which fit in the end. To write a lesson in ink the method was to dip in the ink and write until the small amount of ink was gone, and then you dipped the pen in again. It was quite an art to write, without making a big ink blot on the paper, or to run out of ink in the middle of a word. Oh yes, the old story of the ink well, and the girl with the braids in front of you, don't believe it, the girls were too smart to let their hair hang down where a boy to reach it, and teachers made sure the punishment would be far too great for any boy in his right mind to even want to try it.

The Christmas holiday dinner was more of a treat, than any of the gifts, at least for me. It was turkey, with all the trimmings, apple and pumpkin pie, with a small glass of port wine to go with it, a special treat at Christmas. All the really great food we seldom saw, except on the holidays or special family days, Charlotte was a fine cook, no doubt about that. Thanksgiving was centered around the turkey, and for that big meal one year, Dad had a live turkey given to him. He really had a struggle trying to put the ax to that bird. It wasn't until Ed, the next door neighbor, brought his farmer expertise to bear, and came to Dad's assistance. That bird was a lot of trouble to prepare for the table. I had a hand in pulling out all the pin feathers in the process. Dad's one main comment about live turkeys for dinner was: "never again". For about six months in 1938, the difficult time at home due to conflict between stepmother Charlotte and her teenage age step-children. Came to a head, and Dad was in the middle of it, trying to cool things down. Animosities that had been brewing ever since we left the orphanage caused a separation between Dad and Charlotte. During that time she went to live with her mother and her sister Gladys, at the old farmhouse down the street, on Bell Isle ave.

During the separation Dad had asked his sister, our Aunt Agnes, who lived alone in Lawrenceville, if she would come to keep house and prepare meals for us. The arrangement worked out for a while, and I really loved Aunt Agnes's fresh baked bread, often checking on her big bread pans to watch the dough rise under the covering. She was a good cook too, with one exception; Charlotte could make a meal out of almost nothing, with minimum cost, while Aunt Agnes did not seem to be able to control costs very well. Dad was far from being well off, and their disagreements over such things as food, money, and other things, soon had Dad and Aunt Agnes in conflict. I can only speak for myself, but I had begun to feel that we were better off with Charlotte. Then too, Dad would get feeling really down, and often asked me if it would not be better for Charlotte to come back. When it was just the two of them, they seemed to really enjoy one another's company. Another side of the situation was Charlotte she would often intercept me, when she saw me going along the street, and would ask about Dad and us, almost pleading with me, without actually saying that she would like to come back. I was glad to pass her wishes on to Dad each time she spoke with me. Finally, Aunt Agnes took off in a huff one day over differences, and sadly, I had to carry her special bread pans down Ray ave. to the trolley for her, I was sure going to miss her wonderful fresh bread, believe me! Dad never told me why she left, but shortly after that we had a family conference, and we all agreed to make another try at working together if Charlotte was willing to do the same. All seemed to be much more peaceful within the family after that. Later on, in 1942, when I left for the navy, as Jerry had done earlier, Jeannie still had problems between her and Charlotte. As a result, to get away from the hassle, Jeannie went to live with the Helferty family. She later went to work for Western Union, and never did go back to live at home with Dad and Charlotte.

In June 1938 I left behind my early years, graduating from Resurrection grade school in Brookline. Then at age sixteen, in Sept. 1938, I began my higher education at South Hills High school, the largest high school in the South Hills of Pittsburgh. The school was located on Mount Washington, next to the ventilation shafts for the Liberty Tunnels. The traffic tubes ran for over a mile under the Mt. Washington, an elevation of over 300 ft. The name of our school football and basketball teams was "The Tunnelites". Instead of a name, like the Panthers, Bears, Lions or some name to strike fear in the hearts of our opponents. Then again, considering the team losing record, perhaps the name was appropriate. I suppose my high school years were unusual by today's standards, a World War was now in the making. Nazi Germany, under dictator, Adolph Hitler was threatening the world with destruction with his aim of world domination. He was aided by Italy's dictator, Roberto Mussolini, and Hirohito the Japanese emperor. The empire of Japan was already on the march throughout all of Asia. Together, the three dictators were known as the Axis powers. Russia was in turmoil as the Bolshevik dictator, Josef Stalin, had forced the Russian people into a communist, atheistic society. Stalin was an evil man, but as the slogan goes: the enemy of my enemy is my friend, so we had to support the Russians in their part of the struggle against the Nazi's in the east. History proved we could not have won the war without them by keeping the Nazi forces busy On the eastern front, making the D-Day invasion possible.

    Here in America, under our president, Franklin Delano Roosevelt, we were only able to support freedom by providing the tools of war, under the "lend lease act", passed by congress. The world was again on the brink of another world war as more countries became involved. Once again, the forces of good and evil, were confronting one another. When war did come, those who would do the fighting and dying were the young men now in high school and college. We didn't need to be told to keep up with current events; we were part of the events. We listened each night to the radio or read about it in the newspapers, the tragic news of how country after country fell to the military might of the Axis powers. News of the World each day gave us a bleak outlook for our future. Dad often talked of the wasted lives and treasure that was spent on that First World War, called "The War to end all Wars". We had allowed Germany to fall into chaos, ripe for dictatorship. Instead of having a reasonable peace with them in the interest of the future as America had done with the Marshall plan after WW II when we funded the rebuilding of the Europe we had help destroy. Dad was always impressed with Germany's technical ability, and he felt that America and Germany, as allies could maintain the peace of the world. He blamed the mess on the

The Life & Times of "Himself" ... The War Years

British whose ambassador had believed Hitler's big lie, leading to a policy of "Peace at any Price". Most of us high school students knew we had only a few years to go, before the war would arrive at our front door. Discussions on where we would serve when called were commonplace.

At home the life of the new high school freshman was changing; my sister Jeannie was still in grade school. Brother Jerry was in Vocational school learning drafting, and Dad was working regularly on the "WPA", painting the many bridges over Pittsburgh's three rivers. He worked on the government's alphabet soup program, called the "WPA", or the Works Progress Administration. It was part of the new national effort by President Roosevelt to repair America's roads, bridges, and the decaying infrastructure of the cities. The "WPA" got a bad image over pictures of five workers standing around leaning on shovels and watching one or two others working. "WPA" put men to work repairing public streets and buildings to help bring the country out of the depression. These programs were in force until the growing demand for the tools of war brought about full employment. For me the challenge at hand was to get a high school diploma. Completing high school was the main goal back then. Col lege was not generally planned for. Most students and the average parent had not even completed grade school. So a high school diploma was something to strive for. My dad expressed his hope that one of us would be successful, and I was the one having the best chance, if the war would let me. My first year was transitional, leaving grade school at eighth grade, no junior high or middle school then, to take on the life of a high school student. Our arrival each morning at south hills started in the school auditorium with popular songs being played by some of our music students, who took turns on the great Wurlitzer organ, playing the top popular hits of the day, while students relaxed as they waited for the warning bell to call them to classes. Courses were very basic then, dealing with all the subjects, which would be helpful in getting a job to earn a living. The only elective subjects available were, wood shop, auto shop, machine shop, drafting, typing, and home economics, all courses dealing with the workplace or homemaking. No frills just a basic education for a working lifetime.

The Prewar Years 1938-1942

The Pre-War Years - 1936 to 1942

After graduation from South Hills High school in June 1942, I got a job on the B & O Railroad at the Glenwood Yards in Pittsburgh. My job as Yard Clerk required checking the freight car numbers of the trains ready to pull out for destinations across the country.

****

Railroad switching yard where trains are assembled by switching engines to route freight to correct destinations.

Smoke belching engine of the 1940's. Cinders in the eye were common.

During my four years at South Hills we could pick electives to gain extra points for graduation. My first elective was typing, which came in handy during the war when I had to type up navy reports, and during my years at Western Electric Co., as a supervisor, when I used on a regular basis. During the retirement years with my personal writing, and working on the computer it has paid off well over the years. Another elective, was woodshop. Among my few, but extremely well done wood shop efforts, were a night stand and a four legged Kitchen Stool of solid oak. The instructor required the use of all mitered joints, without any nails, just glued wood joints only. That stool is still in my personal possession, and should last forever. My very first effort in woodshop #1 was a precisely made pine wood door stop, which earned me the first "A" in woodshop. Sadly, the doorstop was lost to posterity during the war. My last elective, taken in my sophomore year, was print shop. Our biggest project was to make a commemorative booklet to be sold as a fund raiser for the school athletic committee. The booklet featured a well-known poem called "Casey at the Bat". The poem was about this baseball hero who struck out, and caused Mudville to lose the game, when everyone was convinced they couldn't possibly lose if only their star Casey came to bat.

Contained in the booklet was the story of how the poem came to be written. That poem was always one of my favorites, and I knew it by heart. I would recite the poem anytime for un-interested groups and luke-warm friends, who didn't appreciate my rare memory ability. A still have a copy of the booklet in my historical record. The booklet was published by the 1939 senior class, with assistance by us lower classes. The seniors set the type and did the proof reading and printing. We had to do all the messy jobs, like cleaning up and resorting used type slugs, cleaning up the ink rollers, and in general doing the menial stuff. We did get some experience putting the type into the blocks to prepare them for the seniors. Printing methods were very archaic compared to the methods used today. The first thing we had to learn in print shop was to memorize the "Pi" assembly box, which was used to sort out the alphabetic slugs. These were tiny lead characters of the alphabet, periods, commas and spaces all arranged according to highest usage. We had to know all type locations in the "Pi" box for sorting as well as composing.

···

After the written article was ready we placed the appropriate alphabetic pieces into blocks according to the page being printed. The article was then assembled, clamped and ready for a sample proof to be printed. Each page was placed into a larger block with the necessary spaces in place ready for printing. The senior students would then place the assembled pages into the printing press and ink was rolled on the face of the type for a finished run to be made. As each page rolled off the presses the instructor did the final proof reading. Once all pages were printed out in the planned quantity, all of the paper pages were cropped, assembled, and made ready for delivery. That was the good part, because now the printing type cleanup began, by us lowly freshmen and juniors doing the messy job of removing all traces of ink from the blocks and type. We had to clean each metal slug individually, and return it to its own proper compartment in the "Pi" box. A final inspection of your "Pi" assembly box was made by the shop teacher, and if he found any slug with ink remaining, or placed in the wrong compartment he had a novel method of discipline. He would pick up a big handful of dirty slugs and scatter them at random over your assembly box.

Then you had to redo the whole box to find them. I had a method of my own if that happened to me; I just carefully looked for those messy ones up on top and removed those using tweezers. Then I used a soft cleaning brush with ink remover and wiped over the surface slugs then by stirring up each compartment I would successfully remove all evidence of the dirty type. I never got an "A" in printing class, but I think I should get one for using my noodle and saving myself the job of resorting everything. Another major difficulty with print shop was to get all the ink off your hands and from under your fingernails. Printing today is done without the need of the "Pi" box, so that was one high school elective, which I could never use in later life as I had with typing and woodshop, my others electives.

We had the Moore field playground, which we considered to be ours, and we considered the Olympic pool to be ours as well. Our football team was called "The Moore Pro's", because of the close association we had with the Pittsburgh Steeler's Professional football team. The Steeler's used our field for team practice, and we had the benefit of football advice and equipment to make us one of the best sandlot teams in the Pittsburgh sandlot league. We were undefeated during the years when I played on the team. Our games were played on Saturday mornings and even though I only weighed 115 pounds soaking wet I played tackle on the first team. At times when we trounced a team and the rematch would be played at their field, and we often played against the older brothers, or other ringers, rather than the team we beat. After one tough game I went home with an arm in a sling, a swollen jaw and a sprained knee, not to mention brush burns and contusions. Dad didn't have any hospital or medical plan back then, and at times like that Dad would tell me, "No more football", but come Saturday during the fall I was out there, getting pulverized. It was great fun, really! Times when I did get hurt and couldn't play my substitute, who was a big, strong lanky kid, filled in for me at tackle. One team from Sheridan played their games on a steel mill dump site, and the field had cinders mixed in the dirt. It took a week to get the tiny bits of cinders removed from our hides after those games. The Steelers were the greatest help with our quarterback and the passing game. Most of our games were won with passing plays resulting in touchdowns and with the Steelers help we had great plays to use in winning games. During those days the Steelers and other Pro players were former college players who played for a percentage of the gate on weekends going back to their businesses or jobs in between. The Professional football days, when men would play for big bucks were far into the future.

During most of the summer months the Moore Park playground and pool were the big attraction for us, but hanging out on Brookline Boulevard at the Edgewood Pharmacy soda fountain was a favorite evening spot as well. For a time during my high school years I worked behind the counter dishing up sodas, banana splits and ice cream cones to customers. Another job I had while in grade school was as a delivery boy for the Pittsburgh "Post-Gazette" newspaper. My paper route was just off Brookline Blvd. up on the hilly side of the street. The paper cost three cents, you kept one cent and gave two cents to the route man, who picked up the papers and gave you your quota to sell. I made more money by selling papers inside the local bars, where customers would usually give you a nickel, so you made three cents for yourself. A paper for only three cents may seems cheap, but an ice cream cone was only five cents, a postage stamp was three cents, and the 5&10 cent store was just that, a place where you could buy many small items for nickels and dimes, if you had dime to spend, that is! Selling newspapers wasn't bad in summer, but in the wintertime with ice and snow and slush it was no fun delivering papers up and down those high steps on Brookline's hills. Dead beats were the people, who for economic or other reasons did not pay their newspaper bill, and were a problem on any route. Charlotte often helped in that department by calling their homes every day, until they paid up, and if they didn't pay on time after that I only delivered for cash.

....

Another income source for boys my age was setting up pins at the bowling alley. Before the automatic, pin setting machines young boys worked down in the pit picking up the pins and resetting them for the next frame. Under the alley floor there was a foot operated pedal, which raised metal pins through openings in each position. The bowling pins all had a centering hole in the base to seat them on the metal pins. Once seated the foot pedal was released very gently to prevent pins from falling over then the bowling balls were put in the return chute. For safety sake you had to get out of the pit in a hurry before the next ball came whizzing down the alley. When a ball hit the pins they flew in every direction and bruised shins were an occupational hazard. In Pittsburgh at that time most bowling was done with "duck pins". These were short stubby pins with a wide ring of rubber at the middle; the bowling ball was about the size of a softball and much easier to handle than the large ten pin balls. The main reason for the popularity of the duck pins were the problem with setting the big ten pins by hand. Usually only one alley had ten pins available and none of us pinsetters wanted the job of setting up those clumsy things.

If you were pretty fast at setting up duck pins you could make good tips by setting up pins for "Pot games". These were games with cash riding on each frame, and the winners were very generous. After midnight when the bowling alley closed we usually headed for "Jimmy's Diner" on West Liberty Ave. Jimmy's was a favorite gathering spot for us, but not exactly a teen hangout. It was Just a hamburger place with pinball machines. The hamburgers were fried on a sheet metal gas fired grill, and delicious milk shakes were made on mixing machines. We enjoyed a milkshake and a delicious sizzling hamburger with lettuce, tomato and mayonnaise. Then spend a few coins to make a try at winning the secret jackpot on the pin ball machines. Gambling was illegal, although everyone in Pittsburgh knew how to play the numbers game. Every day the winning number could be found in the upper right hand corner of the Sun-Telegraph newspaper. In was always the last three digits of the day's stock market quotation. Gambling may have been illegal, but everyone knew the winning number and the name of some numbers bookie where they could place a bet.

Very few high school students had cars, but a friend of Jack's had a 1936 ford coupe with a rumble seat which was like a trunk lid that opened. It had a cushioned seat and the raised lid became a cushioned back for comfort. It could seat two or three, but you had no protection from the wind or the rain. All you could say for it was, it's better than walking, and we went out in it often on dates or just cruising around. There were no cars with anything like air conditioning, but for cold winter days we did have hot water car heaters circulating heat from the cooling system. If it was really cold the engine never would warm up enough to give off much heat. Jack's Dad had a new Ford Mercury, which had a gas vapor heater that put out lots of heat, but we had to open a window to get rid of the fumes. Jack's Dad kept his car in a garage about five minutes from home due to the lack of decent parking space in front of his house. On occasion Jack would borrow the keys, and we went for a joy ride around Brookline or over to Dormont. One eventful night Jack called me to meet him at his house, he had hi-jacked the car keys again, so we could go cruising. Walking up the street to the garage we were planning our itinerary as we walked along. Once at the garage Jack found the lock had been left open somehow, and when he opened the door there was his Dad with his arms folded and a half smile on his face. Without any comment his Dad just told us to go ahead and take our ride and he would just sit in back.

Jack didn't know what to think, perhaps his Dad wanted to see how well he drove the car, or something like that. It didn't take long for us to find out that he was really planning a parental lesson for his car key swiping son, as any father should. It was wise of Jack's Dad to nip this kind of activity in the bud. I totally agreed with his thinking, and besides doing wrong Jack was getting another innocent person involved in his escapades, me! Well, to be perfectly

The Prewar Years 1938-1942

honest, I wasn't all that innocent, I guess. Jack did turn out to be a good man later on, in spite of his early youthful misbehavior. As we drove along, to impress his dad, Jack stopped at a gas station and put in one dollar's worth of gas at the cost of 19¢ a gallon. Our usual plan was to mark where the gas gauge was then put in one gallon, and drive around until the gas gauge got back to where it was when we started out. His Dad said it was o.k. for us to ride to Dormont or to Mt. Lebanon, which was much further away. Jack drove to Dormont, a distance of about three miles from home as the crow flies. After a time he told Jack to stop and then asked us get out. We watched as he got in on the driver's side and took over the wheel. Then without a word of good-bye, good luck, or any kind of angry comment, he just drove down the road leaving us standing there. His lesson had lots of time to sunk in as we hiked on home. We did make a stop at Jimmies Diner for a delicious hamburger and to rest our feet, so it wasn't a total loss. Jack's Dad never mentioned it again, and even though the keys were still in the vase on the mantle as always he knew they were safe from those midnight riders. My Dad did not own a car, but I am sure I would never have done such a thing. Jack and I were the best of friends all through the years, just so I could keep him on the straight and narrow path.

In high school Jack and I often double dated using his Dad's car, this time only with his permission and under strict regulations. The main requirement was no smoking in the car. In the forties smoking was advertised as being good for you and not as harmful as we know it is now. Some cigarette's ad's claimed. "Not a cough in a carload!", "Take a treat instead of a treatment", and other misleading ad's to make you think the weeds were good for you. We all smoked, because it was "hip" and everybody was doing it. When I wanted to smoke on a date I held my cigarette out the window and blew the smoke out of the window to prevent giving the upholstery the smell of smoke. Jacks Dad would get very upset and we could lose the use of his car if that happened. One date night as I was hanging out the back seat window puffing away, and as I held the cigarette out the window it burned faster, which limited the duration of my nicotine fit. Then as I finished my smoke, I flipped the cigarette away, but the wind blew it back into the car and I yelled for Jack to stop. We all got out while I scrambled to find the smoldering butt. I could see it lodged between the seat and the side of the car and it was starting to burn the paint. I risked getting my fingers burned as I tried to get to it, but it only fell down deeper inside. It was no longer burning the paint or the seat, but it still glowed brightly on the floor beneath the seat. The solution would have been to remove the seat to get at it, but we had no idea on how to do that without tools. After a while we just got back in the car, deciding it would probably never be known, and continued on with our date plans. It was years later, after the war, while on a visit at Jack's home and we were talking about the times we used his green Ford Mercury, Out of the blue, Jacks Dad asked who it was that had left a cigarette burning beneath the back seat in 1941. When we told him the true story we all had a big laugh over what had happened. He had taken out the back seat sometime during the war years, and when he discovered the burn mark and what was left of the cigarette he knew full well who to blame for it. Those youthful days had ended, but we did leave our mark in some ways.

In Sept. 1938, until graduation in June 1942, the ever present threat of a World War overshadowed high school life. Most of Europe had already fallen, and country by country went on the Nazi list of the conquered. The battle of Britain was in progress, and the greatest air war in history took place on my 18th birthday, Sept. 16th 1940. The Nazis sent 300 bombers and fighters over Britain to level the city of London. They were met by 200 English Spitfire fighters, constructed of plywood on a steel framework. The battle lasted all through the daylight hours as the German air force lost two planes a minute in the battle. It was the greatest defeat of Germany's air armada in the war. Winston Churchill, the English prime minister, praised the heroic airmen with the statement, "Never have so many, owed so much, to so few! Nightly on the radio we listened to the terrible suffering of the free world as the axis powers ruthlessly destroyed everything in their path. The three most brutal dictators in the world were headed for a confrontation with the United States, and we were all waiting for the spark to ignite.

Russia, under Dictator Josef Stalin, first joined with Hitler in conquest of Poland, but sided with the Allies later to defeat Germany.

The Prewar Years 1938-1942

That put the free world in the position of working with another Dictator every bit as ruthless as Hitler, Mussolini, or Emperor Hirohito, the Axis powers. In our high school classrooms the number of juniors and seniors declined as many older boys left school for military service rather than finish out their full school terms. My Dad had made me promise to wait for my diploma and then for me to join the navy, and "only the navy", as he put it. Remembering his experiences in the trenches in World War I, he didn't want his sons to endure that kind of life. It wasn't easy being a senior with many of the young men already gone, and everyone wondering when you would be joining up. I stuck it out as Dad had wanted, and in June 1942 I achieved my goal and that of my Dad by receiving my high school diploma. It was nothing fancy; I was just an average student, but a graduate nonetheless, one of a new educated generation and the first in the family. One month earlier my brother Jerry had enlisted in the Navy and Dad wanted me to wait a little while longer before going in. With my diploma I was now able to get a job on the Baltimore and Ohio Railroad just as Rev. Father Fallon had predicted at my christening. He had told my Dad at the time that with a name like Francis J. Mahoney I would either become a priest, or go to work on the B&O. My position on the B&O Railroad was as a yard clerk. The job involved visually checking the sequence of the railroad freight cars as the trains were being assembled. I had to make up the bill of lading for the train, which required six carbon copies. There was no Xerox copier then, and getting six readable copies gave my fingers calluses so thick my fingers would not meet at the sides. Railroading was a hectic occupation, because of the heavy load of military cargo and the shortage of railroad cars; as a result, every antique engine, coach, and freight car was put into service. We worked around the clock until we were out on our feet. Cots were provided to catch forty winks when needed, anything to keep you moving military freight.

One night that I clearly remember after twelve hours of walking the tracks I felt like a walking zombie. I had been warned to never go between the open couplings, which connected the cars. That was a major "no-no" in the rail yard, but this night I really believe I was sleep-walking, when I walked through a two foot space between two of the freight cars. At that same time a freight car had been sent down the track by a yard switching engine. The couplings slammed together just seconds after I had passed through them. That scare got me awake long enough to punch the time clock and grab a cot for a few hours. A yard locomotive was a smoke and cinder belching monster, causing a pall of smoke to hang over the yards, and a cinder in the eye was a daily routine. Diesel engines were in limited use at the time, and the job of railroad firemen was to shovel in the coal and keep a watch on the steam gauge. In my off hours I could hitch a short ride to a nearby town at times and getting a ride on the engine, fulfilling a childhood dream. Normally, I rode in the Caboose, that little red sleeping car for the conductor and crew which was always the last car of the train. It was very enjoyable to pass through the railroad stops and have people waving at you. It was a pleasant memory of my short railroading career. The railroad was such a priority job that I could have had a deferment from military service. In that case I would never have had to leave home, but like most young men of my age I felt it was my patriotic duty, and I had an obligation to serve my country as best I could by enlisting in the Navy.

"The War Years", Serving aboard the USS Patrol Craft #606 From November 1942 to April 1945 - Convoying troop and supply ships in the Atlantic and Pacific war zones.

BATTLESHIP ROW - PEARL HARBOR, OAHU HAWAII - DECEMBER 7, 1941
BURNING WRECKED AMERICAN WARSHIPS AFTER JAPANESE ATTACK

"December 7th 1941" - In the words of Franklin D. Roosevelt, "On this day, which will live in infamy, the United States has been cowardly attacked by the Empire of Japan, and a state of war now exists between the Japanese and the Axis Powers".

****

"Patrol Craft Underway" - A painting by Jim Kennedy of the Patrol Craft Sailors Assn. Typical of the small ships, which served by the hundreds in WW II.

The War Years- Aboard a U.S. Navy Sub-Chaser- 1942-1945

Duration of the war plus an additional six months. That memorable morning six of us close friends piled into Jack's Ford and headed for the main enlistment offices in the old county court house in downtown Pittsburgh. Jack and the others had all decided to join the Air Force in hopes of staying in the same group, while I was on my way to the Navy enlistment office as I had promised my father. After my physical I received my orders to report to the P&LE-RR station after ten days for transportation to Great Lakes Naval training Center in the frozen northland on lake Michigan, near Chicago Illinois. My father had served in the trenches in the World War one, and stated he never wanted me to go into the army and endure what he went through living in the mud and grime of trench warfare. From my own point of view the idea of sailing the seven seas to visit strange far away countries all sounded fine to me. The first thing I learned in dealing with the Navy, was the truth of the saying, "Hurry up and wait". So, while I waited to take my physical, those Air Force recruits were down the hall having their photograph's taken by the Pittsburgh Press news photographer, showing the "V" for victory sign, as buddies went off to war. They could have waited just a little while for the lone Navy man to show up. Anyway, that newspaper picture should show six buddies going off to serve their country, but shows only five.

Now there was a two star banner in the front window of our home on Plainview Ave. It was the practice of the war years for homes with men in service to display a white banner with a blue star for each family member serving in the military, replacing blue with gold for those killed in action. It was a visible way to let friends and neighbors know about how their boys were faring in the war. My ten days of preparation to leave for the Navy went quickly, and as it had turned out I didn't have to leave for boot camp alone. Ralph, a friend of my sister Jeannie, who I had met on occasion, heard about me joining up and decided to enlist with me. He asked the recruiter to let him go with my group, which was to leave shortly before Thanksgiving. On Nov. 16th 1942, He and I assembled with other navy enlistee's at the P&LE, "Pennsylvania and Lake Erie", railroad station in downtown Pittsburgh. Typical of those war years were the sweethearts, sporting new engagement rings and there to see their loved ones off to war. The Sisters, Mothers and Dad's, were also on hand for the tearful good-byes. We knew we would be back for leave after boot camp, but still it was mentally difficult to accept the separation that would soon follow. My sister Jeannie was also there to say goodbye to her friend Ralph. Dad and Charlotte were there, but no girlfriend for me to say good-bye to. There was no close girlfriend I felt that strongly about. Actually, it made leaving a little less difficult for me, but as I think back on it, I did feel a little left out. After a last sad goodbye our names were called out and we boarded the train that would take us to the Great Lakes Naval Training Center, located on the shore of Lake Michigan, in frigid North Chicago Ill.

Jack, and the others had already left for their training center with the Air Force, having only one week to get ready to depart, but I did have the opportunity to see them off when they left. We had no way of knowing at the time, what our service would bring, but two of the six friends wouldn't be coming back, both shot down and lost over Germany after the invasion of France. It was the end of our youth as we knew it, and the end of an era for everyone. I can recall how dark it was, when we pulled out of the depot. I had a seat on the river side of the train and I watched, with some misgivings, as the familiar skyline of Pittsburgh disappeared from view. Now the feeling of being on my own again, as I had basically been at St. Paul's orphanage, began to sink into my consciousness. Having the ability to deal with my peers and look out for myself was a real asset during my Navy tour of duty, which took three years, four months and 28 days, out of my young life as it turned out. During the eight weeks of boot camp the presence of my buddy Ralph was a real asset. He was a big husky farmer type and with him around I wasn't totally on my own, and any occasional run in with a trouble maker was rare. After boot camp we were separated, but after the war we were reacquainted and I was best man at his wedding.

We arrived at the Great Lakes Naval Training Center after a long overnight trip, sleeping as best we could in our tilt back coach seats. I can remember well how cold I was from the very first day, when we went from one cold building to the next, much of the time in our shorts or just in our birthday suits, lining up for our physicals, a baldy haircut, clothing, medical shots, sea-bags, hammocks and mattresses. From then on until the very last day at NTC, when I was sent to Key West Florida for Anti-Submarine warfare training, I stayed cold. Adding to the chill was our baldy haircuts, which was the identifying feature of all new arrivals. Old Timers" had varying amounts of new growth on top. The finality of leaving our civilian life behind came at the end of the first day when we were given a box to mail our "civvies" home. From our hats down to the last item of clothing, except for personal things like our watches. Beginning our new Navy lifestyle we now had all of our necessary possessions packed in our sea-bag, plus our personal hammock and mattress. We didn't need anything else as far as the U.S. Navy was concerned, unless they issued it.

To identify our new possessions, we were given a name stencil kit to mark each item in bold letters right down to the socks with our last name. I lucked out I found that my kit was missing, so I didn't have to ruin all my possessions by putting an oversized label on them, even if it was my own name. The following day I was sent to have one made, and my new stencil was the regulation 1-quarter inch size, everyone else had been given a big three eighth inch stencil, making their name stand out like a sore thumb on everything. Some lamebrain clerk had cut the wrong size stencils, and the men had to put those oversize letters on all of their clothes. This was the very first of many incidents of good fortune to come my way in the Navy. Fortunately for me all of my clothes were standard size, some guys with odd sizes had to put up with ill-fitting clothes until they could be corrected. Fifty recruits were assigned to a company, each composed of recruits from all over the east. After formation of our group of new recruits in the main building we were marched to our new home, Company Barracks #1636. We came to a halt before a two story, dormitory building with a large sign, Company #1636, above the entrance. It looked exactly like all of the other barracks square wooden buildings we had passed on the way. There were ladders against the building, which were still in process of being painted by the construction crews. The interior was all ready for us as we were marched into the building. We were now 50 navy "Boots", officially known as Company #1636.

We were assigned to lockers and hammock spaces, there were no regular bunks to sleep in just hammock spaces. My good fortune smiled again, my buddy and I had upper and lower in the last hammock spaces, furthest from the door and well out of the limelight. The Chief Petty Officer in charge had his private room located near the door entrance far from our territory. The fact that we would be actually sleeping in a swinging hammock really didn't sink in with us until we assembled for instructions on how to sling and tie our hanging beds. At each station was a gray foot locker to contain your Navy and only Navy belongings. There were two four by four wood stanchions, or posts to civilians, for us to secure the hammock ropes. There was a long crossbar above it to assist in getting in and out of said hammock. Sleeping in a Navy hammock may sound simple enough, but the thud of falling bodies during the first night was proof that it was not a normal practice for most of the land lubbers in our company. Once you climbed in and relaxed you couldn't try to change position unless you used the overhead crossbar to move into position. Otherwise, you came spilling out onto the hard wood floor. By the end of that first rugged week we were all qualified in the use of navy hammocks and other mainly unfamiliar Navy activities. We were also very black and blue in spots.

Typically, reveille sounded at six a.m., and by six thirty we had to be dressed, standing at attention and ready for a day of full activity.

The War Years–Aboard a U.S. Navy Sub-Chaser–1942–1945

For starters it was double time to the drill field for calisthenics before breakfast. If it snowed, as it often did, push up's were a bit more difficult with your nose poking into the snow. Then we were marched to breakfast eating by the numbers, all start at the same time, all to finish at the same time. Then it was double time again, a bit like slow running, back to the barracks for the day's orders. Each day was broken up between marching drill sessions, class room instruction, weapons handling, and with hand to hand combat training as well. There were continual medical checks to monitor physical problems, with a break for meals in between. At the end of the day it was back to our barracks, always on the double, of course. Recruits ran everywhere they went, unless ordered not to by their Company C.P.O. After dinner we had free time to do laundry, write letters, or relax, until lights out at nine p.m. The folks back home didn't know it, but those regular letters we sent were required by the Navy. They didn't like getting calls about how poor Johnny was doing, and not hearing from their offspring in service for a while. So we had to turn in a letter home every week to the C.P.O. Who would put a check mark in his record, so he could see at a glance, who was and who was not writing home to let their folks know how they were having so much fun away at camp.

There were times when slumber did not come as easy for the entire barracks. Any talking after lights out brought swift action. Barracks lights were turned back on, and orders were given to assemble out on the drill field for discipline drill. Instead of being all snug in our warm beds we were in the freezing cold in the middle of the Polar Regions running laps around the frozen tundra learning all about Navy discipline. Revenge was usually subtle, but swift for those who caused our discomfort. Teaching us recruits discipline sometimes took a sadistic turn. One example that I can recall vividly, involved the new asphalt on our drill field. The recruit barracks had unfinished wooden floors, which were prone to stain badly, and for Saturday inspection we used steel wool to clean decks and ladders, "floors and steps" in civilian talk, to the satisfaction of our CPO. On this day in particular our regular drill field was closed due to final recoating of the asphalt surface. Our personal Adolph Hitler marched us out onto the field anyway, running us through our drill schedule on the not quite hard asphalt surface. Needless to say our shoes and boots were now spattered with black asphalt lumps. We were then marched back to our barracks, while still in step two by two up the ladder and into our quarters. Our fearless leader then gave instructions to all hands for the immediate cleanup of floors and uniforms. We had very little spare time that week. The Navy message to be learned was follow all orders given, without question, no matter how difficult it may be or how we looked at it from a personal viewpoint, that didn't matter. There was your way, the easy way, and other good ways, but the only one that counted was, The Navy Way.

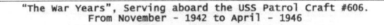
"The War Years", Serving aboard the USS Patrol Craft #606.
From November - 1942 to April - 1946

The gang of six who went to enlist in 1942. The five in the news photo are Chuck, Paul, Jack my best friend, Bob and Jeep. They were at the recruiting center joining the Air Force, and getting their photo taken by the Pittsburgh Press. While I, the lone Navy man on the right, joined the Navy and was left out of the photo.

Entrance to Great Lakes Naval Training Center in N. Chicago. where a recruit spent eight weeks learning how to do everything, not your way, not any way, but the Navy way. You are now a lowly "Boot", trained to serve for the duration of the war, plus 6 Mo.

Barracks and personnel inspections were always held on Saturday mornings. Every piece of gear we owned had to be laid out on our neatly folded hammock, according to strict regulation patterns, which are outlined in detail according to the Blue Jacket's manual, our Navy rules bible. Each item of clothing was rolled up and tied with white braided twine, and then secured with a perfect square knot, with the bitter ends tucked under. All shoes had to have a mirror like shine, the uniform of the day unblemished, the Head, "Navy for lavatory", had to have sinks and commodes sparkling. Decks and ladders were all sanded clean as all barracks life came to a standstill, while we waited for the Officers team of inspectors to arrive. Nothing could be disturbed, you had to wait even go to the bathroom until after the inspection. To dispose of the last little pile of dirt was something of a challenge, and at times we would end up taking it outside to bury in the snow. It all seemed very illogical, but I must admit that after six weeks of non-stop doing things the Navy way, we were becoming a well-disciplined group of "Boots", and had developed a great deal of pride in Company #1636. Even our formerly bald heads were now showing enough hair to rub, if not to comb, as we became Old Timers ourselves, able to harass the new recruits with their shaved skulls.

As our Boot Camp training progressed we learned about how the U.S. Fleet had given America its first major victory over Japan at the battle of Midway in mid Pacific. A total of 20 Japanese warships and 275 planes were destroyed by the remaining carriers of America's Pacific fleet. The Navy was decimated at Pearl Harbor, but our carriers had been at sea and survived. The battle of Midway prevented a Japanese invasion attempt of Midway, America's outpost in the Western Pacific. Other good news came when Gen. Jimmy Doolittle, and his group of B-25 bombers took off from the carrier, USS Hornet, to hit mainland Tokyo in force with a daylight raid, and in doing so they gave America a much needed morale boost in the war against the Japanese Empire. The planned invasion of Australia was stopped dead in its tracks by American and Australian troops at Port Moresby, New Guinea and in the naval air battle of the Coral Sea. It was the first sea battle in naval history fought entirely by aircraft, with opposing vessels not visible to one another. Our losses were great, but so were the losses to the Japanese fleet. Then in early 1943, American forces seized Guadalcanal Island in the Solomon chain, where I was would spend much of my war service, giving the Americans a valuable airstrip at Henderson Field to strike back at the enemy bases in the Asiatic/Pacific Theater of war.

During 1942 and 1943, in the American Theater of War in the Atlantic, the Nazi submarine war against allied shipping was at its peak, and hundreds of American ships were being sunk, some just after leaving safe harbor. In support of the convoys Liberty Ship gun crews were being manned by the Navy. After graduation from boot camp many of those not going on to Navy schools were almost sure to join the Liberty Ship gun crews; this was one of the navy's most hazardous duties at that time. Part of each days schedule in boot camp included an update of American forces action around the globe, so we had been kept well informed. During classroom sessions we were tested for our aptitude in such things as radio, radar, technical and mechanical ability. I must admit I tried hard to excel at everything I was tested for, since progression in the Navy hinged on taking and passing tests for every Petty Officer rating. On Dec. 11, 1942, with a final short graduation ceremony, boot camp was over and we were now second class seamen in the United States Navy. We were given thirty days home leave and our assignment orders. Once again my good fortune was apparent; my orders were to return to Great Lakes NTC for further evaluation as a radar, sonar, or radio operator. As it had turned out, my final assignment was to be trained as a Sonar operator serving in the anti-submarine warfare in the Atlantic against the Nazi U-Boats, possibly aboard a Destroyer-DD, Destroyer Escort-DE, or other anti-sub vessels, such as Patrol Craft-PC, or Wooden Sub-chaser-SC, engaged in escorting convoys along the east coast from New York to Havana and Guantanamo Bay Cuba, assigned to the Navy Eastern Sea Frontier with Guantanamo Bay as our southern base.

"The War Years", Serving aboard the USS Patrol Craft #606
From November - 1942 to April - 1946

-Great Lakes Naval Training Center. Graduating recruits pass in review.

On December 11th 1942, Company #1636 graduated from "Boot Camp" at Great Lakes Naval Training Center. After a short period of evaluation I was ordered to Key West Sound school for training in the Anti-Submarine fleet of the Eastern Sea Command.

This photo, from the Blue Jacket Manual, shows the method of laying out all of your earthly possessions, ready for inspection. On the right is seaman 2nd Class Francis Mahoney, now trained to serve in the U.S. Navy.

Every recruit, received thirty days of home leave before being required to report to their new stations, and after weeks of nothing but regimentation a trip home was welcome therapy. The fact that it included Christmas at home was a happy plus. Christmas was very special in another way as well, my brother Jerry had been listed as Missing in Action during Operation Torch, the North African invasion at Algiers, and was now home on survivors leave. He had piloted one of those assault boats, which carried the invading troops from the transport to the beaches. His ship was sunk, and then the ship that rescued him was also sunk. He made it to shore, where the beaches were in American hands. After days ashore he was unable to find his command group. With his dark beard, Jerry said they thought he was an Arab, when he went to rejoin his task force. Fortunately, Jerry hadn't been wounded or injured in any way, although that Missing in Action letter from the Navy so soon after his enlistment caused Dad quite a bit of heartache. As it happened we both arrived home at the same time, and you can bet the Christmas of 1942 was definitely one of thanksgiving as well. Our thirty days of leave went by all too swiftly, and for Dad I know it was difficult seeing both of his sons going off to war. He was truly concerned for our safety, and we had no way of knowing when it would all end.

Dad's hugs were much stronger and more often as the day of parting grew closer. Jerry and I went with him into town during our leave, and to the local Pub in Brookline, where he enjoyed being able to introduce us all around and exercise his bragging rights about his sailor boys. It was times like that when Dad told us more than he ever had about his experiences in the trenches during WW I, "The war to end all wars". That war only served to create a broken and beaten Germany ripe for a madman like Hitler to take control. Visiting the pubs with Dad at our young age we couldn't buy a beer legally, because the drinking age was 21 in those days, but service-men didn't have to pay for a drink in his hometown anyway. There was a strong spirit of patriotism in the country, and people were proud of those in the service. Charlotte was no less proud of her boys, and with her great cooking skill she made every meal a Sunday special. With all her great cooking am sure I gained back every ounce I had lost in boot camp. My sister Jeannie was now attending a vocational school and working part time for the Western Union Telegraph Co, which was quite busy delivering telegrams due to the war. Jeannie was now living with the Helferty family because of the difficulty living at home. When Jerry and I left for service her problems with

Charlotte became more frequent, so aunt Bessie Helferty invited her to come live with them for a while, and that turned out to be the best solution for all concerned. We had our share of family gatherings during our leave and there was no room for family feuding. It was through a girlfriend at Western Union that Jeannie met a special soldier named Holden and they began to correspond. In 1945 they were married and from that time on Jean started a life of her own with her husband the former soldier boy.

    Jerry left before me and with my leave over I said my farewells again at the P&LE station where I boarded an old, rickety vintage coach with its big pot belly stove at one end, vainly trying to warm the frozen occupants of the car taking me back to Great Lakes NTC for evaluation. Listening to the sound of the clickety clack of the rails, my every thought was of home, wondering just how long it would be until I returned home again. Later on, in letters from home, I learned of friends and acquaintances who would not return. Although I always thought about my own chances with the confidence of youth, never really doubting I would come through the conflict o.k. One memory I have about the war years was the strong faith people had in God, and praying wasn't just a sometime thing, it was a necessity. The churches were filled on Sundays; people needed faith to deal with the uncertainty of life and to pray for those in service, and to pray for guidance on how to deal with the potential of a loved one not returning home. Almost every home had a family member in harm's way, somewhere in the war. All gasoline, food, clothing, and basic necessities were rationed for the people at home. The entire country was involved in the war, not just those in service. We weren't sure at the time that we would even be victorious in the war. The Axis powers were at the peak of their conquest, every day brought news of allied reverses. German mines were discovered just outside New York harbor. We were not living in very comforting times then, and we seldom discussed what might happen, rather being satisfied with what we had at the time while hoping and praying that God would see us through.

    On January 11th 1943 I was back at the Naval Training center for several weeks of personal evaluation. The Navy had a priority for new candidates in anti-submarine training, and that was where I had landed. I was assigned to base personnel barracks With minimal drill or work sessions, receiving regular liberty passes. I took trips into the big city of Chicago, and into towns like Waukegan Ill., Jack Benny, the comedian's home town. My good buddy had gone on to his station, but there were other sailors from company #1636 in our liberty group to team up with on shore leave. As a group they all seemed to like bar hopping, and I joined in with them for a time. I quit bar hopping one freezing night after trying to put away all the beer in front of me, all purchased by kind, well-meaning, grateful civilians. After losing contact with the world I eventually came back to my senses, with a lot of help from a true angel in my young life. I had wound up on a bench of the elevated railway platform, and somewhere I had lost my Navy Peacoat. Without it I was well on the way to freezing to death. It could have been a short naval career for me if it hadn't been for a wonderfully persistent, elderly lady who kept shaking and talking to me, even hitting me with her purse as she tried to wake me up. I have often thought about my elderly angel, and how she had awakened me just in time to catch a train back to the base. She helped me up on my numb tingling feet and gently shoved me through the doors of the coach. She looked so pleased and happy to see me getting into the warm car, still scolding me for hanging out in bars and drinking. It took me a while to warm up and thaw out my nearly frostbitten limbs in the warmth of the train. Then as my senses came back I began to realize that if it was not for my elderly angel I might have wound up like a frozen popsicle in that Chicago elevated station.

From then on I spent my days of liberty in small towns like Waukegan, where a man in uniform had numerous opportunities to enjoy delicious dinners, attend great dances, and where he could meet lots of nice young ladies who appreciated a man of the sea. Well, I would become a man of the sea shortly. The local people worked hard to make our life away from home a little more bearable and it was well appreciated. By Mid-January 1943, after three weeks at Great Lakes, I had my final orders, and welcome orders they were. Leaving the frozen north in mid-winter for sunny Key West Florida and the Fleet Sound School. There I would be given an eight week training course in anti-sub warfare methods to stop the enemy threat of Nazi submarines on our very doorstep. Because of my good scores in Morse code, my acute hearing and mechanical aptitude, not to mention my natural good looks and matching humility, I had been selected to train as a sonar operator involved in convoy escort duty. Serving as an operator of the underwater sonar detection equipment, and being trained to locate and track the enemy subs by the use of echo ranging methods to attack and destroy the enemy U-boats.

In layman's terms, sonar sent out a pulse of sound, transmitting it under water by use of the sonar head, which extended below the ship. When the sound wave struck a large object the sound was reflected back to the receiving equipment and recorded. The Sonar operator tracked back and forth across the target until the ship passed over the sub to make its attack with depth charges. Sonar was the undersea eyes and ears of the convoy. At the Fleet Sound School they had training rooms set up for a simulated, programmed, search and destroy mission. The Submarine trainees tried to evade the attacking Sub-Chaser with both crews striving for a victory. After our hands on training with the simulation equipment, we were sent out into the Gulf of Mexico to track a vintage WW-I submarine, which in turn tried evasion tactics against our Sub-Chaser. Our ship during training was a converted yacht commandeered by the U.S. Government as an emergency measure. The Navy had purchased a number of private motorized Yachts, and installed sonar gear on them to fill the escorting gap until the regular fleet was built up. The classroom training went fast, but the shipboard training was more difficult, and also a new experience for us landlubbers. We also assisted with shipboard duties as we waited our turn at the sonar stack. On our first day out in the Gulf on our converted yacht, called a YP or Yippee boat. The swells were kicking up and it was becoming very rough on the deck of the small ship.

Until my turn would come I had been assigned as a ship's mess cook, helping the cook to make coffee and sandwiches for lunch down below decks in the galley. The cook assigned me to prepare the sandwiches, and as I worked at my chore the roll and pitch of the ship was having an effect on my equilibrium. When the cook saw me starting to turn pale he wisely sent me topside for some fresh sea air. I wasn't seasick, just feeling a bit queasy, but once I hit the sea breeze I was fine, not so for many of our class. In fact, when the instructor saw me standing there with my apron flapping in the breeze and not leaning over the rail feeding the fishes he put me to work operating the sonar stack. Since most of the others were incapacitated off and on for a good part of the day I spent a lot of time operating the sonar stack, tracking our ancient submarine and operating the equipment. Actually I have never been seasick, even in the roughest weather, during my three and a half years in the Navy. Those old submarine "R" boats from World War One, which they used for our sub training were a plumber's nightmare inside. They were tin buckets filled with a confusing array of pipes and valves. They say you needed an engineering degree in order to flush the toilet. Considering all of the antiquated equipment required to operate them, and the cramped living quarters for the crew I had great admiration for the crews that put their lives on the line taking them down each day for our anti-sub practice. One particular incident while at sea, during our training duty, brought us into contact with the war itself. We were out on patrol as usual running through training drills when our Yippee patrol boat received emergency orders to take up a search station off the dry Tortugas Islands near the Florida keys in the Gulf of Mexico, because a U-boat had been sighted in Gulf waters. Ship convoys along the Atlantic coast were attacked on a regular basis by Nazi submarines and at times in Gulf waters. Our YP, boat was equipped with depth charges and deck guns, no match for a Nazi U-boat on the surface, but effective against submerged subs. The Key West naval command gave search areas for us to patrol until dark in hopes of a contact for the PBY's to attack. While we were screening for subs in the area there was one solid contact, which carried the ship on a good four hour search including a depth charge attack in the process. Although we didn't have any confirmation of a target we had really been part in our first actual anti-sub run on a real contact, even though we were just observers. Returning to base I realized that the war was not only very real, but very close at hand.

  On a scale of one to ten, enjoying life at the Key West Center during our period of training was a two. No nights on the town, but we could attend the base movies, or visit the large ship service store where one could get a cold coke or ice cream. There were recreational areas to play cards, just sit and relax, or bat the breeze with our shipmates. There were sailors from all over the east, making for interesting conversation about our homes and families. On a Sunday after church we could go into the town of Key West to see what there was of interest to young adults far away from home. There were no surfers or swimmers around, all of the beaches were closed and closely patrolled by armed Navy guards. Our group of sonar students often had to perform those duties as well, such as patrolling the officer's compound. The photos in my pictorial history show me with my shipmates in full dress white uniforms, all according to regulations, and not really ready for a day in the surf and sand. In most cases, except for a visit to the U.S.O., the United Services Organization, which was a program started by Hollywood movie stars and other entertainers. I spent my time trying to catch up on school lessons knowing full well what would be expected of me once I went aboard a ship on convoy. I felt compelled to make sure I would have the ability and knowledge to do my job. Training classes were from 7 a.m. To 7 p.m. Six days a week with only an hour or so after dinner before we crashed, exhausted in our bunks. After a while it seemed as though we had always been there and life was one continuous classroom. If there was one thing at Key West that made our lives bearable at the school it was the chow, as food is called in the navy. The mess hall had big signs, such as "Take all you want! Eat all you take" and they meant it. A guard was stationed at the garbage cans and sometimes the cook himself would stand watch at those G.I. Cans. They would send you back to finish up your plate if anything was still edible. The cook hated having his food wasted and you soon learned not to let your eyes get bigger than your stomach. Going up for seconds was always a better idea. The meals were a high point of the day and you had to really exercise restraint to keep from overfilling your tray.

Key West was one of the hottest places in the southeast just as the Great Lakes Naval Training Center on Lake Michigan, was the coldest. The humidity in Key West was so high your bunk was almost soaked every morning, because of the dampness. We had to air out bedding on a regular basis in order to stop mildew, which turned things black and green. Another joy of living in Key West was the size of the roaches attending fleet sound school with us. You may not believe this, but we had to tie our shoes to the bed legs to prevent them from being carried off by those huge critters. In order to catch them we left out hambones for them to take, and once they had one in their sharp pinchers they wouldn't let go for anything. After that it was easy to throw a rope over them and tie them up to be taken away and shot. I wanted to keep one and raise it as a pet, but I was sure that Pennsylvania wouldn't grant me a state license to keep one. I may have embellished this tale just a bit, but believe me they were huge!!

While at the school we were considered part of the Naval Base basic crew, and were expected to stand regular guard duty. This required standing at the main gate with a loaded rifle to protect the base from potential intruders. We also had to guard the VIP complex at the officer's residences and along the shoreline. Some of us had been trained to serve as Shore Patrol in Key West. One major coincidence during my navy service is the fact that I had been a Shore Patrolman, "Navy Military Police Officer", when I began my Navy career at Key West, Fla. And I ended up serving as a Shore Patrolman in Wildwood New Jersey in 1946 after the war ended. During that time the Cold War was beginning between Russia and the world, and we patrolled along the shores of Cape May N.J. guarding against any Cold War communist infiltrators. Only petty officers could serve as Shore Patrol and it was only after I finished Sonar Operator School as a Third Class Sonarman, while I was attending Sonar Maintenance School that I qualified. Shore Patrol duty was mainly a case of checking identification cards and keeping the peace. The drinking age was 21 and was enforced by the naval authorities. It seems a man could fight and die for his country, but he couldn't handle alcoholic beverages for some reason. I wasn't yet 21 myself, but adults or having older shipmates to share a beer with you solved that problem. After completion of operators school those who had scored highest on technical aptitude tests rather than just having the highest grades, were selected for advanced technical training in maintenance and repair of radar and sonar electronic equipment.

As it turned out I was part of the group that would be remaining for training on how to care for Sonar equipment in addition to being able to operate it. We learned the operation of the huge foot high vacuum tubes, motor generators, and other electronics which was needed to transmit and receive sound waves using the Sound Stack and Sonar head to detect the enemy sub. The tubes generated a great amount of heat and cooling fans were needed to keep them cool in the high temperatures of the equipment room. Later on, aboard ship when we operated with the added excessive heat at the equator, I had to use additional fans for cooling. The school was an intense training period and not all made the grade. With successful completion of the maintenance course on April 30th 1943, we received a Petty Officer rating of Third Class Sonarman. The SOM 3/c rating had just been designed as a left arm rating depicting earphones pierced diagonally by an arrow. There were no Sonarman rating patches available for our uniform when we left Key West for our assignments, so they gave us permission to wear the Coxswain 3/C rating temporarily. We had a letter to prove why we were illegally wearing a right arm rating on our left arm. It caused no end of questions and problems with the regular Shore Patrol, until the new patch became available. The pay for a third class Petty Officer was $60 per month, a nice raise in pay since I started as apprentice seaman at $21 a month when I enlisted, and was now a Petty Officer after only six months of service, a fact which didn't sit well with Regular Navy types later on.

My new orders were to head home for leave followed by assignment to a ship at Brooklyn Navy Yard in N.Y. First there were 15 days leave to spend at home and I now had a serious girlfriend, a five foot two blonde named Lois. We had been introduced on my previous leave and in the keeping with the spirit of the times and the fear of never seeing one another again caused lots of usually sensible people to make wrong decisions, just as it turned out for Lois and me. Our letters while I was at Key West were filled with love and dreams of the future. One day I bought her an engagement ring in Key West intending to present it to her when I came home after Fleet Sound School. My previous leave had been in Dec. 1942 and it was great to be home again if only for a short time. During the war years, service men were required to wear their uniforms at all times no civvies allowed. In fact very few of my clothes still fit me. That high protein food, forced exercise, and the strict routine of Navy life had added a few muscles here and there. Each of us had pride in our country and in our branch of the service. Being home on leave was also a great opportunity for parents, relatives, friends and sweethearts, to shower us men in uniform with lots of attention in their own way. Showing appreciation for the many sacrifices they were making to protect the nation. The Axis powers were at their peak and there was a nagging fear that the war could somehow reach our own American shores.

As for those of us in the military, we had to pack in as many memories as we possibly could to carry us through until we would return. Getting home on leave was a bit of a ritual attempting to hold onto the past while trying to avoid thinking about the future. Some of the loneliest times of my life in service were those hours that I spent riding on trains returning to base after a visit back home. Now Dad and Charlotte had to share my time on leave with Lois my new sweetheart and my future bride. Lois was only seventeen and her mother had given us strong hints that she was not in favor of any quick marriages, so I gave Lois the ring and we were now secretly engaged. She wore the ring on a chain around her neck until she would be able to break the news to her mother. She did tell her older sister, but she didn't tell anybody else. The fifteen days of leave passed all too swiftly and I was soon boarding the train in Pennsylvania station, heading for the Brooklyn navy yard in New York City, to begin my new career as a seagoing sailor on a U.S. Navy fighting ship. According to my orders it was called the USS Patrol Craft"–PC 606. After the war at the time of decommissioning the ship was given the name of USS Andrews, named after a small town in Texas. To me and the crew who served on board her, she was proudly called by her number the "Six O Six".

On the train, as I traveled to New York for assignment to my ship and the anti-submarine fleet, I settled down for the scenic ride across Pennsylvania. The ride was scenic, but not very restful, because my coach was of the early 1900 vintage, with its wood burning stove and recliner seats. The seats were locked in the uncomfortable position, air leaked in all around the sash windows and fine cinder dust, as black as pencil lead, was in little piles along the window sill. At least I was wearing dark navy blues, and the soot was not obvious, as for those in light colored clothing; they had a problem keeping clean. Fortunately, it was springtime and there was no need to open any windows. The train engines burned wood and coal, resulting in smoke

The War Years–Aboard a U.S. Navy Sub-Chaser–1942–1945

and ash blowing back over the coaches and to open windows would mean a car full of smoke, until the wind shifted. The railroads were crowded with freight and passenger traffic. Little effort was spent on the comfort of the passengers riding in the coaches. A large percentage of train passengers were in the military traveling under orders to new stations, or to home on leave. The trains were crowded with them, and every piece of rolling stock owned by the rail companies had been brought out of mothballs and was put into service for the war effort. Some of the coach cars were no better than riding in a box car and an open one at that.

"The War Years", Serving aboard the USS Patrol Craft #606
From November - 1942 to April - 1946

Operation Torch called for the capture of five Vichy French-controlled ports in North Africa. All objectives were secured within four days.

Second Class Sonarman rating. My highest rating at discharge. After training at Key West I had earned a third class rating. My brother Jerry was in "Operation Torch", the invasion of North Africa, as indicated on the map. He was listed as missing in action, until he arrived home for Christmas, as I did, in 1942.

****

Another painting by Jim Kennedy of the P.C.S.A. The Association of PC and SC sailors in Bay City Michigan, who manned these small escort vessels.

My disappointment at being assigned to such a small vessel changed to one of pride in what we were able to do in the service of our country in time of war.

My journey ended in Grand Central Station in the heart of New York City. Grand Central was the largest, oldest and most famous RR Station anywhere. It was built by Railroad tycoon Vanderbilt who owned all the railroads in the early 1900's. He had it built to satisfy his achievement of total control over the Railroad industry. I had no trouble finding where to check in; a military information booth gave detailed directions to find the Brooklyn Navy Yard bus stop. In due time, I was on my way by bus through the city of towering Manhattan buildings heading for Brooklyn's huge naval base. It was a complex of boat docks, dry-docks, supply depots, and mooring berths for warships of all types. There were barracks for personnel and administration offices. Having been asked the same old question hundreds of times, the bus driver would announce the exact number of bus stops for arriving personnel to reach the base receiving office, where all personnel had to report in. At the sign in desk I presented my orders to the officer on duty. After checking my orders he assigned me to a barracks location to await the arrival of my ship, the USS PC-606, which was now on its way from Stamford Conn. where it had been built. After arrival at Brooklyn Navy Yard it would be outfitted and prepared for shakedown exercises, and to pick up its five Officers and its 60 man crew, including myself.

Those awaiting their ships in the barracks at the Navy Yard were assigned to "make work details", and given liberty in New York on an alternate basis. The barracks bunk locations were divided into port and starboard group's for work, or for liberty assignments. As luck would have it I met a fellow Sonar technician I knew in Key West Sound School, a smiling Irishman who lived in the Bronx borough in NYC. He had been waiting at the Navy Yard long enough to learn the ropes, as they say. Each day one or the other of the two groups had duty, and since large numbers of men came in and went out, no records were kept of who occupied which bunk. His plan was to switch bunks each day when outgoing crews left and before new arrivals came in. With his plan we avoided any Navy "make work projects", like washing down the decks of the barracks and doing kitchen duty. We enjoyed liberty on the town every day, avoiding any work projects as well.

His family came from Ireland, except for him and his sister, and they were as Irish as you can get. His family treated me as one of their own, trusting me to take their sixteen year old daughter Irene out on her first date into New York City, although it was a double date with him and his girl along to chaperone.

Another shipmate I met at Brooklyn Navy Yard lived in the Bronx. He also had an eligible sister, and knowing what a sterling character I was he was proud to introduce me. She enjoyed going to dances, plays, movies etc. As opposed to my Irish buddy's sister, who was more of a home type, and had much more appeal for me. The family had glass cabinets filled with awards and ribbons won in the Irish reel dance contests back in Ireland. The house was really jumping on weekends; I enjoyed the home atmosphere more than the night life and crowds of the city. Even though I enjoyed the home hospitality the most, I still found time to go with the other guy's sister on occasion. Being kind of engaged to Lois back in Pittsburgh my association with girls was basically platonic and based only on fun and companionship. However a lot of girls seemed to have different ideas wanting to have that boy in uniform to show around. It was a time of deep feelings and emotions due to the troubled times.

There were times when my buddy and I would go to the local pub to fill his Dad's one gallon beer bucket. It was a common practice in the Bronx to bring your own container, a throwback to the thirties during prohibition. The bartender would grease the bucket with lard to keep the beer from going flat. On the container lid there was a clamp with a tiny breather hole to keep it from spilling. His Dad would only drink draft beer considering bottled beer as too flat according to his taste. The people at the bar treated us like heroes. Both of us were in anti-sub warfare and the general knowledge of the sub menace off the coast was well known to all. Later on after we were on our ships they wanted to hear our eyewitness accounts of convoys and submarines on the high seas. Our money was no good even the bucket of beer was on the house. It was a time when saboteurs had been put ashore by U-Boats, and mines had been placed right in American harbors. A feeling of helplessness seemed to prevail among the people. America only had a few major victories and we weren't anywhere near winning yet, but the tide was beginning to turn. By December of 1943 those fun days in the big city had ended, my buddy's Destroyer Escort went to the European Theater of War, and I was on my way to the South Pacific aboard the PC-606. I did correspond with Irene from time to time, but I never saw the family or my shipmate again. I always did hope and pray he had survived the conflict as I did.

During the weeks on the town I learned all about life in the Bronx and the other borough's, which make up the City of New York, especially in Brooklyn with its famous Steeplechase Park. I went there on occasion while on liberty to experience one of the most exciting rides I ever rode, the three hundred foot parachute jump. The tower of the parachute ride was the highest structure in the park; its lacework metal column was topped by a huge ring holding the cables to pull the parachutes. You sat in a comfortable seat with seat belts tightly fastened and the canopy of the fixed parachute above. Slowly the parachute rose on its cables, taking you higher and higher as the view of New York and the harbor, with its prominent Statue of Liberty coming into view. Never having been in a plane before I felt this must be what it was like to flying over the area. I became so interested in the view that the shock of the click when the parachute hit the top and released was totally unexpected. You were in a free fall, but not exactly floating to the ground. There was a lot of screaming from the women in other seats, as we hit the huge springs at the base of the platform. Bouncing up and down for a bit before you could regain your wits. To say the least, it was a heart stopping, adrenaline flowing ride. Being based on Staten Island, after my buddy was gone, was a memorable time for me as I had the pleasure of enjoying great food with a touch of home away from home when I visited my buddy's family and experienced liberty in the city itself. The good times in the Big Apple lasted until Nov. 1943, when our orders changed, and the PC-606 was transferred from the Atlantic theater of war to the South Pacific war zone, where our enemy would be the Japanese submarine menace.

The War Years–Aboard a U.S. Navy Sub-Chaser–1942–1945

America had been at war against the Axis powers for almost one year, and when I was waiting for my ship on the Navy base many of the sailors who were now arriving at the Navy Base for reassignment had seen action with the fleet. Full dress assemblies were called to witness the presentation of awards and medals to those who had been cited for bravery above and beyond the call of duty. Many were from the attack on Pearl Harbor, including a lanky Yoeman 2/C, by the name of Eddie Michael Lorenz, whose home was in Milwaukee Wisconsin,. Eddie had served on board the battleship USS Pennsylvania, which had survived the attack at Pearl Harbor on Dec.7th 1941, although the ship had received heavy damage and loss of life. Eddie and I received the same orders to report for duty aboard the USS Patrol Craft #606, and our friendship during the war years began. He was a regular navy Second Class Petty Officer, with four years of sea duty; I was a Naval Reservist, Third Class P.O., having only six months service and limited sea duty. We were really an unusual combination. Even though he was a bit older we became very close friends serving together on board the USS PC-606, until we parted company at Kwajalein atoll on the way to a new base assignment at Saipan in the Marianas Islands in early 1945. When Eddie left the ship he had attained the rank of Chief Yoeman, but since our little ship didn't rate a Chief Yoeman he was being transferred back to the states for reassignment. We had corresponded for many years after the end of the war. His first son was named Michael as was my eldest son. Another coincidence, he went to work for the Central Telephone Company in Minnesota, and I worked for Western Electric Co., a subsidiary of AT&T, manager of the entire bell system. Over time, we lost track of one another until I joined the PC Sailors Assoc. in 1990 and found his address among the members of the Patrol Craft Alumni. I wrote him a letter, but sadly, I was two years too late his wife answered back to tell me he had died earlier, shortly after retiring from the Telephone Co.

On that day in 1943 when both our names appeared on the assignment board, with orders in hand and sea-bags packed, Eddie Lorenz and I boarded a large Navy whale boat along with many others waiting at the Brooklyn navy yard docks. Soon it was ready to make the trip around the harbor to deliver crews to their vessels. Ending at Staten Island where our ship was moored. The stops we had made at the different docks around the harbor gave us an idea of the types of ships we might have been assigned to. There were Destroyers, Destroyer Escorts, and Wooden Sub Chasers, the SC's. Our orders had us reporting to Patrol Craft #606. Neither Eddie nor I had any idea how large a ship the Patrol Craft was, but I can say for sure that we never expected the tiny ship awaiting us. When we disembarked from the launch we saw the name "PC-606" painted on the bow of this very small metal ship sitting only 12ft out of the water. I remember the mixture of disappointment and deep concern I felt that in any combat situation we would be at a real disadvantage, to say the least. In Eddie's case it must have been an even greater disappointment, having served on a battleship and a cruiser before being assigned to the anti-sub forces.

Since the Navy had made its decision for us we had to accept our fate. We carried our bulky sea-bag and lashed up mattress and hammock up the gangway to salute the colors, and report to the Officer of the deck. There were a dozen other men gathered on the quarterdeck checking in as members of the crew as well. After being welcomed aboard by Captain Larkin, Lieutenant Junior Grade USNR we were introduced to the other four Officers, all "Ninety-Day Wonders", so called, because only ninety days of training after college gave them an Ensign's rating. Some had served long enough to become Lt. Jg., like our Captain. Having only six months service and being a short term Petty Officer, I could relate to that being a bit of a "ninety day wonder" myself. Our country had to man the ships with people who never saw a warship and we were it. After the introductions, we went to store our gear in the assigned quarters. Bunks and lockers were marked with our names; I found mine located in the forward compartment in the bow of the ship close to the deck hatch to the lower deck leading to the room with all the Sonar power and electronic equipment. I was as close to my job location as I could get.

Our compartment had the great advantage of having the forward hatch opening to the deck opening into our quarters. It was real blessing during the months to follow, when we were exposed to the oppressive heat of the tropics. Our compartment was home to many of the other members of the communications division the operators and technicians of the radio, sonar, and radar groups. I was senior Sonar Petty Officer in the Division with three other Sonar operators, and responsible for all maintenance on Sonar and Radar. Eddie had his bunk elsewhere and was second most senior P.O. aboard, with only the First Class Boatswain's Mate and a Signalman First Class having more service than he did. His position as ships Yoeman put him in control of all correspondence and ships records, including personnel files. All that had transpired before was prologue; I had now reached the ship that would be my home for the duration of the war. As it turned out it was my home away from home starting in May 1943 until Sept.15th 1945. After the war awaiting discharge I was shore based at Cape May N.J. until my discharge in April 1946 which was well into the distant future at the present time.

The keel of the USS PC-606 was laid down April 14th 1942 at the Luden Marine Boat Co. in the Stamford Conn. Shipyards, and was launched on Jan. 8th 1942. She was 174 ft. in length, 23 ft. on the beam with a draft of six and a half fathoms (naval depth measurement) beneath the bow with a top speed of 22 knots. She required a crew of 60 men and five officers. The ships armament consisted of one 3 inch 50 caliber deck gun on the bow, a twin 40 millimeter anti-aircraft gun at the stern, three 20 mm anti-aircraft guns on the upper deck, two more on the main deck amidships, one portside and another to starboard. For surface and air defense we had nine heavy guns in all. Our armament for anti-submarine attack consisted of two depth charge "K" guns, one portside, and one to starboard on the quarterdeck. Equipped with two multiple depth charge racks to roll depth charges from the stern. Our PC was well armed for its size, but it was still not very comforting considering the fact that our largest gun, the 3 inch 50 deck gun on the bow was equivalent to the nose gun of the B-24 American bomber used against Japanese barges in the Pacific. Actually our depth charges, our small size and ability to maneuver were our greatest advantage against our underwater enemies. The Three

Inch Fifty cannon could clear away a deck gun and conning tower of any surfacing sub making it close to impossible for them to function.

"The War Years", Serving aboard the USS Patrol Craft #606 From November - 1942 to April - 1946

Grand Central Station in NYC. Decorated for the war effort. It was the destination for Navy men from all over the nation.

When boarding your ship you carried everything you owned on your back.

Launching a Patrol Craft at Luden's Marine Construction Co. Builders of the PC-606.

Map of New York harbor, and the points of interest for the 606.

The crew of the PC-606 totaled sixty men and five officers most of them were just like the crew, except for their education. The majority of the crew and its officers were green as grass, only a dozen or so of the 606 crew had any Navy experience, and except for Ed, the Chief Machinist mate, the First Class Signalman, the Chief Bosun's Mate, and a few other ratings had any war experience. My limited anti-sub experience off Key West counted for little recognition; at least I was on board a Navy ship, which attempted to strike a blow against the enemy. The ages of the crew ranged from 17 to 25, except for our elderly cook, who was about 32. We called him Pops, because of his advanced age. The officers ranged in age from 21 to 30. Obviously, WW II was being fought by the younger generation as it was during World War One, when my Dad fought in the trenches in France with the American Expeditionary Forces in 1918. That first day in May 1943 when we reported on board only about half the crew had arrived. We stayed moored to the dock as other ships came and went spending our time opening crates and cartons, checking in ammunition and supplies. The time in port gave me the opportunity to brush up on my Sonar maintenance procedures; now that I actually had the real equipment available for me to work on I could perform actual maintenance.

Our Communications Division Sonar group had a head start getting ourselves organized. All of the Sonar crew had come aboard when I did, so all of our material was checked in and stored and our equipment manuals posted, allowing me to start routine tests on the Sonar gear itself. As I mentioned earlier, the equipment room hatch was close to my bunk, and normally shut down. After opening the watertight hatch there was a straight up and down ladder going down into the twelve by twelve ft. area where equipment lined the side bulkhead. A motor generator was on the side next to the hull on the left. In the center, close to the forward wall, was the shaft for the sonar dome, which was lowered below the hull allowing it to rotate in all directions. It seems I spent most of my hours in while port down in that room from May 1943 to Sept. 1945, a very, very long time in anyone's language. It was there I had to make my records clear problems and mainly to run basic routine tests each time we would return from a convoy run. There was a wall mounted desk with a permanent swivel seat where I could write out reports and my letters home as the need arose. As I will describe later, it was also a great private hideout to have a bull session, and special times when we enjoyed a few clandestine Christmas, New Year's, or birthday celebrations. With 65 people on such a small ship there were few places where one could be alone, my Sonar room was one of those few places.

We were faced with a period of pre-commissioning effort and in a few weeks we had the bulk of our crew and all of our officers aboard. The supplies were stored, and we were now ready to go ahead with the scheduled pre-commissioning testing of engines and armaments. As I mentioned earlier this crew of landlubbers had never been to sea, and on one occasion when we experienced heavy swells at dockside one of the crew was down below decks when some joker told him we were heading out to sea, and just the thought of being at sea caused him to head for topside where he lost his lunch over the rail right onto the dock. That seemed to prove sea sickness can be mental, at least in his case. Finally, we did cast off our lines for a first run out to sea, as the captain gave his commands calmly with a fine show of naval experience, although it may have been his first attempt to steer such a vessel on his own. There were numerous civilian technicians on board to assist in checkout of the engines, sonar, radar, radio, electronics and checkout of all armaments. Once we hit the heavy swells of the open sea we had one seasick crew to contend with. Most of them just tried to stay out of the way acting as if they were fine in spite of their green complexion.

The ships engines performed well and tests of the Sonar equipment checked out with flying colors. All of the Sonar operators had experienced the roll of a ship at sea during their Key West training and didn't get seasick, so they all had their try on the Sound stack echo ranging on passing ships in connection with the Radar crew to match targets. A few minor problems occurred with radio and radar, but in a short time the USS PC-606 was judged ready for her trial run to Key West Florida, where gunnery and Sonar tracking exercises would complete our war readiness. A week later with food stores re-supplied and deck drills now looking more and more professional we were assigned to a convoy heading toward Cuba where it would form up with a larger convoy group to make the dangerous cross Atlantic trip. Post war information indicated that the majority of Hitler's submarine fleet lay in wait just off the American Atlantic coastline. In May 1943, when we were commissioned, Hitler's Germany had 235 U-Boats in action against our convoys. Over 90% of them were destroyed by wars end; due to the heroic actions of the ships crews and the proud men who built the anti-sub war vessels in record time. By the spring of 1945 Hitler's subs were being sunk almost as fast as they were launched. Those who had battled the undersea menace, the anti-sub vessels, the PBY flying boats and the Lighter than Air Ships, were all part of the official American defense command. In what was defined as the American Theater of War, which was a huge area involving the Caribbean Sea and out into the mid-Atlantic ocean. A Military medal, depicting the sinking of a U-Boat, was struck to honor those who fought and died in that cause. Our PC was one of those to earn the award based on our service in the Atlantic, from May to October 1943, escorting convoys between New York and Cuba.

During 1942/1943 American efforts against the Nazi U-boat fleet were limited due to naval losses and the military's decision to protect the West coast against Japan, which left Atlantic seaboard convoys at the mercy of the Nazi U-boats. Larger anti-sub vessels such as Destroyers and Destroyer Escorts took longer to build, while the smaller metal sub-chaser Patrol Craft such as the 606, and the wooden Sub-Chasers called, SC's, could be produced in record numbers by small boat builders all over the country using the same hull design for the PC's and a new hull design for the SC's. The tide began to turn in the fall of 1943 as larger ships began to come on line in greater numbers. The German U-boats began to find it very hazardous to attack our American coastal convoys. As a result, they changed tactics and formed what they called "Wolf Packs". The subs moved away from the Atlantic Seaboard to attack the North Atlantic convoys bound for Murmansk Russia and Great Britain. South Atlantic convoys to the Mediterranean Sea were also being attacked by these groups of subs, which stalked the convoys inflicting heavy losses. In June 1943, at the time we were assigned to our first convoy duty, American waters in the Atlantic were not a very safe place and convoys stayed in view of the coastline as escort ships screened in an assigned area of the perimeter around the convoy to protect it. Our first convoy voyage south was uneventful, but our first wartime experience for the crew and myself especially, as I operated the Sonar in search of enemy subs, and wondering how I would react under an actual attack. It was our first actual sea duty of any duration, and for the first time our crew was considered seaworthy and as ready as our training and technology could make us.

Our small vessel was well supplied with the necessary armament and munitions to do its assigned mission. The personal disappointment I had earlier, concerning the capability of our small ship, had grown into an appreciation of life on board the smallest all metal warship in the Navy. We were forming a close common bond not as possible on larger ships with hundreds of men on board. We suffered the same hardships, especially during heavy weather when life on board a vessel as small as ours was at times a matter of sheer survival. We had the advantage of knowing each other well. Each of the divisions depended on the others, those men below decks in the engine room, looked to the radar, sonar, and radiomen to find and track any enemy. We relied on the men in gunnery division to protect the ship. Then too the Officers were expected to do their share of minor things like finding rare supplies of food, beverages and to find good reasons to visit interesting ports of call in which to make liberty. Actually, both officers and men had much in common, and the brass bound regulations found on capital ships was put on the back burner except for formal occasions in port.

After leaving the convoy, which went on to a rendezvous with a larger convoy at Guantanamo Cuba, we put into Miami Florida for the completion of final shakedown exercises including simulated war games on the anti-sub equipment. Similar to the equipment I had been trained on earlier at Fleet Sound School. The Sonar crew trained with Officers in anti-sub methods, while the gunners trained at becoming familiar with the use of their weapons. Later on we made practice runs on electronic targets making practice depth charge attacks, and familiarizing the gunners with the actual firing of all armaments. As I watched those target ships, which had the job of towing targets for our not so precise gunners, my thoughts were that I would rather be going into Harm's way on my sub-chaser than to be assigned some boring and hazardous duty such as they had. After completion of the pre-commissioning tests, we were officially commissioned into the U.S. Navy at Brooklyn Navy Yard, on August 7th 1943, That day was also well remembered as one of the few times our crew looked like a regulation outfit. Normally, we were a very casual group of sailors, a salty bunch as they say in the Navy.

Following commissioning we were assigned to the Eastern Sea Frontier, operating out of Havana Cuba, assigned to harbor screening duty and anti-submarine patrol in Cuban waters. When we were first assigned to the eastern sea frontier based at Havana Cuba, we had a few opportunities to visit the big city of Havana on occasion, and the Cuban people at that time had a fondness for us Gringos, as they called us. We could travel anywhere without fear, which wasn't always true in New York City. While we were on liberty pass a group of us visited Sloppy Joe's famous bar in downtown Havana, it was a very popular tourist spot owned by a champion American wrestler. The popular drink in Cuba was rum, they drank it by the glass full and to me it tasted a lot like burnt wood. They served a rum and coke mixed drink, called, Cuba Libra, meaning Cuba and Liberty. That drink was fine with the coke, since it disguised the burnt rum taste. While touring Havana we visited a Catholic Cathedral, where we saw an unusual method of dealing with unwanted babies by the unwed mothers or their relatives. There was a large ornate door in a quiet corner, located next to the convent. The door had a built-in wicker basket receptacle arranged to rotate back into the inside of the door itself. The child was placed in the deep basket then turned inward, which sounded a soft alarm. We were told later that the child then became a ward of the state to be raised according to any wishes, if any, were received with the child. The child would be taken to either a church, or state orphanage to be educated in the medical or military field. The Sisters at the convent kept foundling records in case of future inquiries. Older children were also taken into the orphanage system as well. I was really impressed that such a caring solution was taken as a normal part of Cuban life, since abortion was not considered an option in Cuba.

Havana was our port for only a short time before we were to be reassigned to the U.S. Navy base at Guantanamo Bay, on Cuba's eastern shore, as our southern terminal between assignments. There weren't any sights to see or places to visit on the Navy Base at Guantanamo just the Ships Service store for a bottle of Cuban Hautui beer. The wooden ceiling of the Ships Service hall was covered with Hautui beer labels as a result of the popular pastime of seeing if you could put one up there yourself. The beer label slid right off the bottle when wet, all covered with sticky glue. The trick was to lay it on a full pack of cigarettes with the sticky side up then flip it up into the air in the attempt to hit the roof flat. Occasionally it would stick up there among the other labels. It was just one more way to avoid boredom between convoys. Normally, the stay wasn't very long in Cuban waters, and we all looked forward to our return to Staten Island for liberty passes into the New York City, "The Big Apple". Our pier on Staten Island was in Tompkinsville at New Brighton not far from the famous Staten Island ferry docks, and a short trip to Brooklyn, Coney Island, or New York City itself.

From August 1943 until October 1943 we were part of the Eastern Sea Frontier convoy escort teams protecting convoys between New York and staging areas in Cuban waters. We also escorted ships returning home from the war zones for re-supply. Taking a convoy from cold New York to warmer waters in the south was fine duty, but we had one miserable voyage, when we were assigned to escort ships heading for Nova Scotia to join up with convoys forming for the run across the Atlantic to Russia and Britain. Sailing the North Atlantic waters in winter was a severe hardship for any vessel, even though our journey was only to a location near Newfoundland, where American, Canadian and British escorts took over. It was only October, but the freezing spray and cold wind formed a layer of ice on everything. The Arctic seas always seemed to be rougher as well, causing the crew to live on sandwiches and milk as we normally had to in heavy seas. The rough seas were probably a boon to the Atlantic convoys going east, making Nazi U-boat attacks less likely for them. As for us we learned to appreciate even more our regular trips to warmer climes.

Days on convoy were fairly quiet while on duty at the Sound Stack, as the ship would follow a zigzag course you listened to the "ping" of the Sonar transmission in your headset, and waited for the return echo of a potential target to come back. Sonar duty was a very monotonous effort, and Sonarmen had to relieve one another regularly to keep alert. While at sea on escort duty the deck gangs were the only ones involved in ship maintenance. All the rest of the ships company was assigned to ship operations on radio, sonar, radar, engine room and lookout tending to their around the clock duties. Between watches the crews slept, worked on emergency repairs, or found a quiet place to read. Dusk and dawn were always the deadliest times for a convoy, especially, on moonlight nights when the ships would be silhouetted against the night sky. It wasn't a question of, are there subs around, but when they would strike, and strike they did on many a convoy. The eastern seaboard was littered with debris from hundreds of ships and oil covered beaches. Today's accidental oil spills can't compare to the heavy environmental damage caused by the U-boats. Our convoy escort assignment was to hold our station, which was an assigned section of the perimeter around the group of protected ships, keeping alert searching for contacts ready to attack when necessary, but not to abandon the station unless ordered to do so. We had to maintain intact in the overlapping area of the screen around the convoy as a primary duty.

Almost every Atlantic coastal convoy would have some encounter with the U-boats. One encounter in which we were involved happened in Sept. 1943 off South Carolina. Just at dawn convoy escorts were dropping depth charges all around the main convoy perimeter. One contact after another was reported keeping our ship busy filling in the gaps as others laid down their attack patterns of depth charges. There were losses in among the convoy groups with known hits on U-boat's as well. There were none that we could claim any part in however. A verified U-boat sinking allowed a red stenciled outline of a sub with an enemy flag on the bridge housing, as evidence of the action taken against the enemy including, the sinking of any enemy naval vessels. When it was necessary the convoy commander would assign one of the convoy escort vessels to protect a cargo ship that was unable to keep up with convoy speed due either to mechanical or other damage problems. On one such occasion when we were heading south out of New York bound for Cuba we were assigned to a merchant ship which had dropped back unable to keep up after developing engine trouble. After a time, when it had become apparent the ship could not rejoin the convoy, we were called back to take our station in the perimeter leaving the crippled ship on its own an easy target for any prowling Nazi subs. As we left the freighter they turned toward the coastline hoping to reach safety before being discovered by an enemy U-boat.

We hated to leave them, but the main convoy had to have priority. Making such a decision was a matter of life or death for the convoy commander, but he had to go by his orders and so did we.

Since anti-sub warfare was our main purpose in the fleet the Sonar equipment was central for our ability to perform our duties of defending the convoy. The Sonar Operator tracked the submarine with the Sound Stack equipment following the direction of the undersea contact by directing sound waves to the target. Detecting the returning echoes allowed the attack officer to plot the submarine's track on a device called a chemical recorder. As the sub-chaser steered a course to pass over the target depth charge settings and firing sequences were given to the Officer at the depth charge location at the stern of the ship. The ashcans, as we called them, rolled off their racks set to explode at the depth determined by settings on the depth charge. In sequence the K-guns on each side of the ship fired their depth charges into the air then another set of depth charges rolled off the stern racks. This completed a pattern of high explosives around the submerged target. Following standard procedure the ship would turn to circle the area trying to pick up the sound of the quarry amidst the wake and turmoil our munitions had created all a part of our mission. On a personal note in my own heart, I prayed fervently for the enemy crew that may have been sent to the bottom, because of my own personal devotion to duty. Although all of our actions were done as a team effort I still had to deal with my own inner feelings against killing anyone. The young men on both sides had been required to defend the actions of their own country and its leaders, and sometimes, against their own will. The Axis powers were on the side of death, destruction, and slavery, ours was to free the world from their control. Kill or be killed was the lesson we were taught as we switched from the life of peaceful civilian to that of a fighting man in the service of our country. Gen. George C. Patton stated it best, when he said "We are asked to fight and die for our country if necessary, but primarily we are expected to make the other fellow die for his country".

Another weapon for use against submarines was a missile type firing rack on located on the bow, which could be raised at various levels to fire "hedge hogs", these were contact bombs designed to

The War Years–Aboard a U.S. Navy Sub-Chaser–1942–1945

fire from the racks. They were to be used on the approach run before depth charges were dropped to be effective. They were not used very often, and had limited effect in an attack. Depth charges, or ash cans, as we called them, were twenty five gallon metal containers filled with high explosives, and controlled by a detonator mechanism in the center. Detonators could be set for various depths before being dropped. As they sank to the set depth the water pressure set off the charge causing it to explode, hopefully close enough to the sub to rupture the hull, and bring about its destruction. One major drawback for us was the way the charges rattled the hull of our own Sub-chaser in the process. The entire ship shuddered when the depth charges exploded shallow or close to us. After an attack run the bunks and surfaces of everything below decks were powdered with falling debris from the asbestos fire insulation covering all surfaces of the ships bulkheads and overhead areas. This asbestos debris affected my lungs later in life, resulting in a loss of oxygen supply by my lungs, and a service connected disability. At the time we never knew that asbestos could cause lung damage, actually it was a necessity to prevent fires aboard ship from spreading, and many ships under enemy attack were grateful for its use in the war zones. The standard method of submarine attack had its short comings, but laying down a well-placed pattern of depth charges on a Sonar contact that was properly tracked gave the Navy its most deadly weapon against the submerged submarine. Another effective daylight weapon was the Navy's PBY flying boat. They patrolled off shore, near the convoys, to spot prowling submarines from above and then to attack them with contact bombs or depth charges. Joe Celesti, my future wife's brother, served in one of the PBY squadrons in the Pacific as an aviation machinist mate during the war. Those flying boats also helped to keep the harbors clear of mines laid down by the U-boat's in northern waters, ranging from New York harbor to Canada. The Navy also used lighter than Air Craft, or Balloon's, on sub patrol. They were used as spotters for the surface attack vessels. They were effective; however, they were unable to defend themselves against the surfaced submarine very well. In July 1943 one of the Navy Airships was shot down by a U-boat in waters off the Florida Keys.

"The War Years", Serving aboard the USS Patrol Craft #606
From November - 1942 to April - 1946

"Moonlight Convoy" Painting by Jim Kennedy of the P.C.S.A. Depicting a Patrol Craft on station with a convoy at sea. A full moon was a time of greatest danger for any convoy.

****

Depth charge attack on a Nazi U-Boat by a PC escorting a convoy.

The record of Merchant ship to U-Boat sinkings changed after 1943, as more ships came on line.

We served in the American Theater of war in the Eastern Sea Frontier for over six months, from May of 1943 to December 1943, earning the American Theater campaign medal, which covered the years from Dec. 7th 1942 through March of 1946, after the last German U-boat had surrendered. The last submarine known to be sunk off the east coast of the U.S. was in May 1945. I know of only one Patrol Craft like mine to be lost on Atlantic convoy after being struck with a torpedo. In that attack only thirteen of the 65 man crew had survived. The sinking indicated that survival on a craft such as ours was not very good. The closest encounter we had with an enemy torpedo was off the North Carolina coast while on a convoy in September 1943. Lookouts had spotted a periscope wake coming towards us some distance away, and as the bridge took evasive action the torpedo passed well in front of our turning bow. The sub was soon picked up on Sonar by a Destroyer, and several attacks were made on the sub before things got back to normal. It may have been aimed past us into the convoy, but our turning ability and speed took us into its path. On convoy we were always on the lookout for survivors of submarine attack, and in November 1943, while on escort duty with a convoy bound for New York, a lookout reported a man in the water wearing a life jacket and holding onto some debris. We were directed by the convoy commander to affect a rescue. The man was taken on board in due time and taken to the ward room. The Officer we rescued was a Lt. Elliot P. Snyder, captain of the Coast Guard escort ship Wilcox. Scuttlebutt had it that his ship had been sunk the previous day, but we never did find out the real reasons for his being in the water all alone without any major debris from his ship around him.

....

It must have been something top secret since our officers never told us what happened. Arriving in Guantanamo bay on December 1st 1943, we found it was to be our last Atlantic convoy assignment. After checking in with the harbor master the captain informed us we had new orders to proceed to the Asiatic/Pacific Theater of War via the Panama Canal. Our ultimate destination was the U.S. Naval base on the island of Espiritos Santos, in the New Hebrides Islands northwest of Australia. We were leaving Guantanamo Cuba and its "Hautui" beer behind, and also our northern home port at Tompkinsville base on Staten Island without any chance to say goodbye to anyone, in addition we were not to write home about where we were going. We proceeded through the Caribbean Sea in company with other Patrol Craft escorting a convoy, Gtmo #172, bound for Coco Solo in the Canal Zone. On the way to Coco Solo our sister ship the PC-1228 had a Sonar contact and made a run on the target dropping a standard pattern of charges. We stood by to assist, but the contact was lost and we continued on. We made an unexpected stopover at Kingston Jamaica for what we thought were minor engine repairs. Actually, it was because a young ensign, who was the engineering officer, had reported false problems with the engines. We also had two men to put ashore for medical reasons. No real engine problem was found, and later at the Canal Zone the same young Officer was found to be having mental problems. Just like all of us, he was feeling the stress of going into harm's way in the Pacific war, which may have explained why he made the false report of engine trouble. He got his wish to stay out of the Pacific war when he was taken to the base hospital for mental observation. He was replaced by Ensign William Taylor, a great replacement and very likeable man to have as one of our officers.

We had reached the Panama Canal Zone on Dec. 5th 1943, but there was such a steady stream of ships waiting to traverse the canal that we were not assigned a vacant slot in the locks until the morning of December 19th, giving us lots of time for liberty leave to take in the sights and explore what the Canal Zone had to offer. Due to the influx of ships and crews liberty was restricted to one every three days and then only until midnight. Certain areas were deemed restricted to all naval personnel. It seemed the entire Navy was out every night in the town. We were given mooring at Navy Pier #2 at the Navy Base in Coco Solo. Other Patrol Craft were moored at the pier with us, the PC-620, PC-470, PC-1228 and PC-1135, all heading to the Pacific Theater of War now that the Atlantic coast was fairly safe. We were at the Caribbean end of the canal and given shore liberty in Colon. My shipmate Eddie Lorenz, our radioman and I, went ashore together to do the town. We located a little place called Mac's Canteen, it was not as pretentious as some of the places we had been like Sloppy Joe's in Havana, but drinks and service were more our style. In the bar we met a fine young Panamanian, actually a budding business man who saw an opportunity to make a coin or two as a tour director. He offered to take us on a bus tour of the Canal Zone by crossing the Isthmus of Panama from Colon to Balboa on the Pacific side of the canal. We had the whole day ahead of us and boarded a bus for Balboa, after being assured by our tour guide that we could easily make the round trip by midnight when we had to get back to the ship since we were not allowed overnight leave.

Our fellow passengers were all plain folks, just moms, dads, and their Niño's, that's children in Spanish, they all seemed to be a bit subdued by the presence of us three Gringo's on their bus. After a time, since it was the Christmas season, we joined in a Christmas song or two, and the whole bus got involved. We sang along in English as they sang the same Christmas songs in their own lingo, they seemed to really enjoy that. The ride was mainly on two lane dirt roads through small villages along the way to drop off passengers. It was very humbling to see those people who were so very poor. Some of the towns wouldn't even qualify as slums in America; they were not dirty or trashy just poor. Finally, we reached Balboa and had our very first view of the Pacific Ocean, and all in all we had a great trip, although after having a very terrible dinner during which we decided to take the table to show our disgust at the way we were robbed. It was then we met some nice Shore Patrol Officers who thought we should change our minds, leave a big tip, and leave the table behind as well. After that event we left Balboa to head back to base. Once we were back in Colon we paid off our industrious tour director and made it back to the ship in plenty of time. Having made the trip by land we now had the distinction of also traversing the Isthmus of Panama with an all paid tour on our naval vessel by water.

While at Mac's Canteen I saw an innovation I hadn't seen anywhere else. It was a called a juke box, a coin operated record player of the times, which played your record selection and in addition there was a movie clip of the singers and the band. They were called Soundies with songs by the Mills brothers, Nat King Cole and other well-known entertainers of the forties. It must not have caught on, because I never saw one anywhere else. Panama itself was noted for servicemen getting into trouble and we made sure we stuck together when in town. Actually, our trip to Balboa wasn't too smart when you consider how we put ourselves at risk. On December 19th 1943 it was our turn to enter the canal. The day dawned damp and humid with drizzling rain. As the ship reached the south entrance to the Panama Canal we manned our stations under cover of our rain ponchos to keep dry. My station was on the bow headphones to keep communication with the bridge where everyone was keeping nice and dry. Our bow lines and stern lines were secured to the "Donkey" diesel engines, which pulled the ship along in the locks. They were called Donkey engines, because they had replaced the original live donkeys which had been used in the early days of the canal. The Donkey engine traveled along a rail track at the side of the canal slowly pulling us along. Several ships, depending on size, were placed in the lock then its giant doors were closed. Water was pumped in to raise the vessels to the next level where the process began again, continuing until we reached the Lake Gatun lock. It was the last lock at the eastern end of the canal and it opened into Gatun Lake where we proceeded under own power.

....

During the trip across fresh water Gatun lake the Chief Bosun's mate got the idea to open up the fire hoses to hose down the entire ship. We always had salt crystallized on the decks and exterior bulkheads due to flying spray. The deck crew had great fun spraying everything as well as everybody in sight and before long; all fire hoses on the ship were engaged in a common water battle. Normally salt water would be pumped into the ships water system for fire control, and now unlimited fresh water was a welcome change as we all turned out like a bunch of kids as we enjoyed the fresh water battle and taking the opportunity to do laundry and shower down. Occasionally along the channel bank we caught a glimpse of the towns and villages we may have gone through on our bus trip across the Isthmus. The entire country looked lush and green just as the islands of the far off Pacific would turn out to be. We proceeded across the lake to the channel taking us to the Pedro Miguel and Mira

Flores locks. Following reverse procedure we went into each lock as water was pumped out lowering us to sea level on the Western Pacific side. We were now at Balboa in Canal Zone where we had that terrible dinner. For the first time our ship was in the Pacific Ocean facing the open sea.

We had gone from the Caribbean Sea to the Pacific Ocean in a little over seven hours. The word Pacific means peaceful and I was hoping that was going to be true in all future respects as we headed out into it. We were assigned to moor at pier seven in Balboa West Bank, Canal Zone. We remained there at the pier in Balboa until the harbor pilot came aboard to take us through the harbor channel and the anti-submarine nets guarding the entrance. Soon we were heading west into the Pacific for a rendezvous with our single ship convoy, the S.S. Vincente, which was a Sea Going Tug, and with an Auxiliary Floating Dry-dock, AFD #14, in tow. Departing the Canal Zone was not only the last land we would see for several weeks, but it was the last bit of American land we would see until I returned to Seattle in Oct. 1945 at wars end. The Canal Zone at that time was actually American leased and governed. With our supplies and armaments replenished we were now under way to meet our convoy. The Seagoing Tug had left San Diego California earlier without escort. We made contact before nightfall on Christmas day December 25th 1943. The captain set our course for our first destination the island of Bora-Bora in the Society group of islands. The capitol of the islands was Tahiti, where the famous story "Mutiny on the Bounty" took place. At Bora Bora we would refuel and re-supply for the remainder of our long voyage to the South Pacific. The islands are just half way between South America and Australia, four thousand miles out into the open Pacific. The Seagoing Tug steamed on a direct course, at an average speed of six to ten knots as we screened ahead on a zigzag course occasionally making a periodic circle around our convoy, because of the slow pace of the S.S. Vincenti we changed our screening pattern on a routine basis to avoid any pattern which would aid an enemy sub in attacking our tiny convoy.

"The War Years", Serving aboard the USS Patrol Craft #606
From November - 1942 to April - 1946

In December 1943 we left the Atlantic war zone for a 37 day voyage of over 7,000 miles to our new station in the Solomon Islands. The photo at the right is the last lock before we entered Gatun Lake, the only fresh water we ever sailed in.

****

The island of Bora-Bora was a beautiful tropic island, but it had nothing in common with the hot jungle islands of the South Pacific. The chart on the right shows I had a twelve dollar monthly raise, by going from 3rd class to 2nd class.

Now that we were in the Pacific it would be Japanese subs we would be encountering instead of Nazi U-boats. Our voyage to the South Pacific required crossing 7,200 miles of open Ocean over a period of 37 days with the sea as smooth as glass, and the sun getting higher in the sky as we came closer to the equator. Each day was taking us further from home and country. While on duty the watch was four hours on with four hours off, but life on board during those long days at sea wasn't all that bad. We had collected lots of donated books at the USO's and Navy bases along the way. So we had lots of reading materials and a system where if someone was reading a book that looked interesting you, you added your name to the fly-leaf at the back of the book. This was done in order to establish a pecking order for reading the book. When a book was finished it was given to the next name on the fly leaf list. I'm sure I read every book and magazine on board, some several times over. We traded our library with our tug at one point to get new material. Another regular activity was the mess hall poker club run by "Doc", our medical man. Doc was a First Class Hospital Corpsman. Poker Games were played at night after evening chow when the mess hall hatch was shut. The privileged poker players assembled for an evening of cards. No money ever changed hands, but doc's records kept track of who owed what to whom. As I recall it was mostly owed to card shark "Doc" himself. To be one of the privileged players the system was to sign up for a chance to play then on a first come first served list according to Doc's book. You could buy out a place on the list if you wanted to lose your money faster. One or two games were set up to give everyone a good chance to make a contribution to Doc's retirement plan. Losing at poker was not for me, I was part of the Pinochle and Hearts bunch where you could only lose a few coins. I sent my unspent funds home to buy War Bonds for the future. All hatches on the ship were shut after dusk under blackout conditions. When a hatch had to be opened, a red blackout light would come on as the regular lights automatically went out, so we were never completely in the dark. Life on a small ship had its advantages, and the one that was most important to me was in knowing the officers on a friendlier basis than was possible on larger ships and the crew as friends and shipmates. Another thing was the low-key military regulations, which were more in keeping with a civilian Navy ship than that of the regular Navy.

 Conversation was another favorite pastime, and many hours were spent batting the breeze, as we say in the Navy, about life back home and stories about the girlfriends, the family, the girlfriends, sports, the war, plans for life after we were home again, and then too we talked about the girl friends who waited back home, or the ones we met on leave. Did I mention that we talked about the girls sometimes? The 606 crew had come from all over the eastern U.S., and each of us was sure his town and state were the best. Finding anyplace to be alone for even a little while was most difficult on a ship that was only 173 ft. long and 23 Ft. wide at the quarter deck, and populated with 65 other people. Our bunks were three deep along the bulkheads with some in the center of the forward compartment, so having your own space was a luxury few had, except for yours truly, that is. I was very fortunate to have my small hideaway to crawl into down in the small Sonar equipment compartment below our bunk area. The heat from the big glass electron tubes and the motor generator made it hot place to spend time in when I was doing maintenance at sea. It did have a big exhaust fan to vent the heat making it bearable. When in port it was better ventilated and comfortable with the equipment turned off and the forward hatch opened to the outside. We had many a bull session plus a few celebrations there in my Sonar hideaway. Other times I had the pleasure of being alone there to write my letters and work at maintaining the equipment. If asked to give a short description of my own personal feelings concerning the war I would have to say it was a time of long periods of acute boredom, followed by short periods of great stress. When the general quarters alarm sounded indicating a call to action the fear and adrenaline attacks would set in. When secured from general quarters it was back to the boredom again. Don't get me wrong! I did enjoy the boredom most of all.

We had left the Panama Canal Zone on Dec.22nd 1943 and we had picked up our convoy on Christmas day of 1943, and geographically we were on the same latitude as Ecuador South America, passing near the Galapagos Islands, where Easter Island with its giant stone heads is located. My first Christmas day, which was celebrated away from home came and went just the same as any other day standing watch with four hours on and four off. We did have a Non-Denominational Church Service that was held by our Engineering officer Bill Taylor. We took turns doing the Christmas Scripture readings and singing all the well-known church Christmas songs like "Oh Little Town of Bethlehem". Eddie and I and a few others Catholics sang the Latin version of "Oh Come All Ye Faithful","Adeste Fideles". We Spent time sharing what Christmas services were like in our own churches back home. After services we joined in singing all the popular songs like, "I'm dreaming of a White Christmas", a song that really pulled at the heart strings and brought on thoughts of home. Early in the afternoon thanks to elderly "Pop", our chief cook age 33, we enjoyed a classic Christmas dinner including turkey with all the trimmings and pumpkin pie for dessert. We would have enjoyed it even more had we known we were on the way to the land of powdered milk, dehydrated potatoes, and weevils in the buggy bread, buggy rice, and buggy oatmeal, plus all the other shortages of everything we were to experience in the battle zone. Except for the Christmas service and the great meal the crew seemed to be trying their best to ignore the season and to just let it pass, since in remembering they had to deal with a flood of past memories they couldn't handle. Several hours after we had met up with our convoy the USS Vincente had trouble with its tow line causing us to wait for hours just drifting until the repairs were completed. The delay problem gave us cause to wonder if this was going to be a much longer voyage than expected. After repairs were complete we set our course for Bora-Bora our first stop in French Polynesia near Tahiti.

On Dec.29th 1943 we arrived at the nautical location on the map of the world oceans where vessels cross 0000 degrees latitude. This is the dividing line for the Northern and the Southern hemispheres. Known as the Equator with its extreme heat it was the center of the tropics, and the Navy had a tradition of initiation for all those who are crossing the equator for the first time. They were known as lowly Pollywogs, until their initiation into the "Ancient Order of the Deep" and after their initiation they were known by all who sail the seas as Shellbacks. The initiation was to be administered by Neptune Rex, the Ruler of the Deep, and his court. Neptune's royal court consisted of the Chief Bosun's Mate as Neptune, and 15 so regular Navy types who already had their high status as Shellbacks recorded in their naval record. For a full day and for hours before the crew embarked on the nonsense of initiation. It was a bit like the hazing at a college fraternity as each Pollywog candidate had to dress as prescribed on an instruction card given to them by an appointed, personal Shellback. My order was simple, but very uncomfortable since I had to pull out my heavy wool dress blues to wear in the tropic heat and by days end I was soaking in sweat. There was a great deal of Yankee ingenuity in making the costumes which were prepared days in advance of the day of initiation. All Officer Pollywogs were included in the activities to become Shellbacks along with the rest of the crew. As the ship crossed the equator and at the exact position of 0000 degrees latitude helpless Pollywog candidates were forced down a rope ladder placed over the side of the ship by our tormentors who held harmless forked trident, which was a two pronged undersea pitch fork. We Pollywogs were forced into the water fully clothed, thus gaining favor with "King Neptune Rex" Ruler of the Deep. Our new status was recorded in our records by Yoeman Eddie; one of those nasty Shellbacks, and an official I.D. Card showing our new status was also issued for our wallets.

Our first Pacific celebration in my private Sonar quarters was on New Year's Eve 1943-1944. Eddie had smuggled a pint bottle of French Cognac, a peach flavor, on board while in Panama. For the party we invited the cook who supplied the grapefruit juice chaser and the Doc who had the Alka-Seltzer, and also the man with future access to grain alcohol for medical purposes. We gathered in the hot Sonar room with the hatch closed to welcome in the new year of 1944. It was a quiet party as we sat on the deck near the Sonar equipment passing around jug of Cognac and sipped the cook's grapefruit juice for a chaser as we told our stories of family and the holidays at home. Our cook was really feeling down, because he had a wife and family, and this was the first time in his life that he had been away from them. Not many of the crew was married, but a lot of them were engaged or had their special sweethearts back home to think about as I did. We helped one another get duly depressed and after the cognac was gone we all went up on deck to give the empty a fitting burial at sea filling the bottle with water so it would sink and not float. Any ship trash had to be disposed of properly in order to prevent giving the enemy any indication of our presence in the area. As befitting the occasion we wished a happy New Year to one and all. No confetti, no whistles, horns or countdowns on Times Square. Anyway we were pretty sure it was not going to be a very happy new year ahead only a question of how bad would it get. With the party over it was off to our bunks to reflect on the New Year's celebrations of years gone by.

With the holidays over the crew had settled down into the routine of life aboard ship. Deck hands chipped away at any rust spots on the decks and bulkheads, touching up with the yellow zinc chromate undercoat then the blue gray regulation camouflage paint. Often times their chipping would clear out so much rust at one spot that the deck had to be reinforced with metal plates, which were welded over the bad spot.

Not very comforting to know that only a thin metal plate was between us and the sea and that metal was rusting out. Our course carried us into South Pacific waters to a latitude of fifteen degrees then due west on a course for Bora-Bora our first stop. After Christmas I received a big present after muster one morning. I had been studying to increase in my pay grade, and it was now a year since I received my 3rd class rating and I was hoping for official test approval. I passed the exam and was given my Second Class Sonar stripe, joining the top rated ten percent of the Petty Officers on board. The next highest rating was First Class, and the highest enlisted rating was Chief Petty Officer. I sincerely hoped the war wouldn't last long enough for me to reach that top rating. I had no plans for a naval career having a better than average civilian life would suit me fine.

 The Chief Bosun's mate, our oldest and one of the most respected crew members, had trouble understanding how a seaman could become a Second Class Petty Officer in just one year. I reminded him there was a war on and things would get back to normal as soon as the war ended and the rating system with it. "Boats" was a fine man with fifteen years of hard service getting to the top, and although I could see his point, I had met all necessary requirements to pass the tests and the Officer Review board had awarded me the higher rating. In all humility it was only due to my great training and knowledge of the Sonar system not any magnetic personality or acute hearing ability. Also there was the responsibility of keeping the 606 operating as a Sub-chaser by keeping the Sonar and Radar operable, and I felt well qualified for my position. In reality, being only age 21 and the lead Petty Officer in the Sonar section was expected of me due to my training, but not that big deal since there were two other pretty good Sonarmen working with me and learning the equipment. The only difference was I had the headaches of keeping the Sonar and Radar gear up to snuff. To keep us in military readiness the captain had the gun crews limber up on any passing driftwood targets, and the Sonar crew manned the Sound stack around the clock protecting our small convoy. Any maintenance on my part had to be restricted to the moonless nights when darkness provided us added protection. In the Pacific we would pick up a school of tuna at times, and listening to them the Sonar they gave off fluttering sounds like a possible submarine wake or propeller noises might make. Not taking chances the captain would sound general quarters until the lookouts made verification that it was a school of tuna. If it was they would sometimes fire off a k-gun depth charge set on shallow into the school of fish. The explosion resulted in many stunned tuna on the surface which were netted for the cook and his crew to prepare as we all looked forward to a fresh fish dinner. The Tug crew also had the opportunity to net their share of the fresh fish. The fish fry was a nice change of diet plus a diversion during a humdrum day for all hands. Just about every day we had dolphins traveling with us they would swim alongside the ship then swim ahead and drop back until their tails almost touched the bow as if they were playing a game. They were a pleasure to watch and good company helping the crew pass the time. We were still far from active Japanese waters, but a Jap sub had been sunk at Pearl Harbor in the attack on the fleet, so it was possible for them to be looking for shipping heading to the war zone.

"The War Years", Serving aboard the USS Patrol Craft #606
From November - 1942 to April - 1946

The PC-606, docked at Tonga in the Friendly Islands to take on fuel, water, and supplies for the final leg of our voyage to Espiritos Santos, New Hebrides.

The dotted line indicates the route from Tonga to Espiritos Santos and the Solomon's Islands base.

A view of the Island of Tonga. The only possession in the British Empire with a queen as the ruler.

As we continued our Sonar search for potential enemy subs we did pick up one contact having all the indications of a submarine on Jan. 17th 1944, starting the process of taking evasive action. The general quarter's klaxon horn was sounded and all hands went to battle conditions. Our convoy was also signaled to follow attack procedures as we began plotting the Sonar contact to prepare for a depth charge run when suddenly a huge whale broke the surface ahead of the ship ending the attack. Our equipment gave off a solid contact, which had similar indications for a whale as it would for a sub. Unless the whale made a quick turn, which a sub couldn't make, we would still go ahead with our anti-sub attack run as if it were a submarine. Such encounters were not an uncommon event in the mid Pacific, and whale contacts served to keep us on our toes. On another instance when no whale had surfaced and the contact was on a straight course we had to follow through with the depth charge attack. The lookout didn't spot any whales and the contact was lost in the wake soon after in the wake, so we never knew whether our target was really a submarine or just one more whale caught up in wars confusion. The chemical recorder definitely showed a run on a solid contact meeting all criteria for a valid attack. For some time after the incident gunnery gang had a red whale on a Jap flag painted on the side of the bridge bulkhead indicating our victory over something, and to enjoy poking fun at us "Ping Jockeys".

Fresh water was a precious commodity aboard the ship and although we had two evaporators running continually to convert sea water into fresh water it had to be rationed if we had a cracked engine liner, or if storage tanks fell below a danger level. Before reaching our first stop at Bora-Bora rationing had to be initiated, and showers were alternated by compartment. If it got really low we were only allowed one bucket of fresh water to do our laundry and one bucket of water to take care of our sponge baths. There were times when radar would locate a heavy rain squall and the officer of the watch steered us towards it. We would be ready and waiting with soap in hand to get a fresh water shower. It was a little more of that so called Yankee ingenuity, but sometimes the rain squall ended before we were able to rinse down. Those showers in the rain squalls were fine, but if the quit too soon salt water was the only rinse available. Try rinsing in sticky salt water sometime, believe me you'll hate it. To get fresh water we also rigged a canvas tarp over the quarter deck to trap water into a drum for wash up and laundry use, in order to save the good stuff for drinking, food preparation, and the engine requirements.

Since our ship didn't have a washing machine we had to wash our clothes by hand in a bucket of fresh water. We had two evaporators to change salt water into fresh, which were working overtime when the engines needed more of the fresh water. Sometimes while screening at slow speed you could tie a working set of shirt and dungarees on a line and troll them alongside the ship for fifteen minutes or so, but if we had to pick up speed suddenly it was goodbye to the laundry if you didn't get it out in time, otherwise it could rip to shreds. The ideal laundry plan was using two sets of underwear, shirts, dungarees, and socks keeping the one set washed and ready to wear and using the other. In port we would be able to take showers and wash our duds with water from the dock supply. Our voyage to the war zone continued on a western course just south of the Equator. Now, with blistering metal all around us, dehydration could be a danger. Our seagoing doctor placed salt tablets at the water fountain, which we had to take before drinking the water. It was a ritual we performed on a regular basis during the months and years serving in the Pacific war zone, because of dehydration in the intense heat. While based in the islands we also had to take Atabrine tablets for protection against dengue fever, which was a scourge in the tropics. Medically, Doc was our only medical help available there was no one else to call and any major illness or injury was in his hands until we could reach a port which had a proper medical facility. Fortunately, our "Doc" did measure up to his medical calling of being well experienced in his trade. The decks would get so hot you could feel the heat through the soles of your shoes. Even our little mascot pup, "Boats", named after the Bosun's mate, had to wear little canvas socks on his feet to protect them from the burning deck. He was also smart enough to walk in the shadow of the super-structure when he could.

On January 11th 1944 we were forty two hundred miles, and fifteen days since leaving Panama before we arrived in Tiavani Harbor at Bora-Bora Island in the Society Islands group. The Islands are a French protectorate lying midway between South America and Australia. The largest island was Papeete with Tahiti the capitol city, and location of the movie "Mutiny on the Bounty". The islands are actually beautiful rugged volcanic lava peaks with only the peaks above sea level. To us the island looked like the storybook vision of what all tropical islands should look like. We were to be very disappointed when we arrived at our final destination. Bora-bora's twin, green peaks were truly a beautiful sight after fifteen days of nothing but sea and sky for our little convoy to look at. We were all given a turn at going ashore to look around, and we were to discover what was really meant by having sea legs. The rolling of the ship, which gave us the ability to walk on the heaving deck as a second nature, made walking on solid ground was more difficult than we were used to after being so long at sea. We all walked a bit strange for a while before we got used to walking on a level surface. All sailors, for generations, have been falsely accused of being intoxicated on land. Actually they were really poor men who's "Sea Legs" caused them walk that way.

We were scheduled to stop at Bora-Bora just to replenish our supplies and refuel. Against our will the whole process was accomplished all too quickly, and in about six hours we were ready, but still unwilling to leave. I only had two hours ashore, but I had already fallen in love again, because all the native girls looked just like movie starlets, and the island looked like my fertile imagination had always imagined tropic islands to be and the only thing missing was the movie cameras. The radio shack on the main deck had its short wave communication with the world to keep us informed of the war news. In the Pacific the battle for the Solomon Islands continued and U.S. Marines had captured Tarawa and also the Kwajalein atoll nearby in one of the bloodiest battles of the war. It was necessary to capture these stationary aircraft carriers to nullify the huge Japanese base on Truk Island in the Caroline Islands. It was all part of the Navy's island hopping campaign in the Pacific. In the plan to retake Europe North Africa was now in allied hands and the invasion of Italy was underway. The tide of war was now beginning to turn, but victory was still a long way off. For me, now heading toward the conflict, home and country were becoming more of a dream, something in the memory banks to be reviewed as the need arose.

Leaving story book Bora Bora our course was still due west with our next supply stop at Tonga Island in the Friendly Islands 1800 miles distant. We were now heading deep into the South Pacific Ocean where we would cross the International Date Line, near Tonga Island. We would lose a full day on the calendar, January 17th 1944, in the process. All clocks and records had to be adjusted accordingly. There was no formality involved in crossing the dateline other than becoming a member of the Order of the Golden Dragon by rite of passage. The dateline is at the 180th Meridian and we crossed the imaginary line at 22 degrees of latitude just below the equator. As we headed into the setting sun the ocean was like glass and the heat was now becoming a normal way of life on the equator. Life aboard the 606 went on without incident until the radar picked up the Friendly group of islands on the screen. Right on schedule, on January 16th 1944 and nine days voyage from Bora-Bora we arrived in Nukualofa harbor at Tonga-Tabu Island in the Friendly islands. The British base was just a small supply and fuel station in the middle of nowhere. We moored on the starboard side of Red Pier with several of our sister PC's, the 620 and 596 were also there giving us a chance to trade off some of our books and meet with other PC civilians in uniform like us. The other PC's left soon after our arrival on their way to Esperitos Santos to join the Pacific fleet as we were, hoping to get good future orders, hopefully convoy duty to Sydney Australia or some other fun place.

As a part of the British Commonwealth the Friendly Islands had the only other Queen to rule in the British Empire. The island Queen weighed over 300 pounds and she was carried everywhere on a shaded platform. The island was so small the bearers of her chair didn't have far to go in any direction. She didn't travel while we were there, so we didn't get a look at her. We remained at the dock in Tonga for one day and a night taking on fuel and water. The crew was given several hours ashore to stretch their "Sea Legs". As we walked down a side street Eddie and I met a native who had this large white horse tied up nearby. It had jutting bones and was very swaybacked, but he was glad to let us borrow his large mount for a few dollars rent for us to ride around and explore the kingdom. Both of us climbed up on the back of our sturdy steed, with great difficulty I might add. There was no saddle just a woven mat tied around his ample middle. His back was so broad, my legs stuck almost straight out to the side. Eddie was long and lanky and fit better on our steed than I did. We traveled quite a way around the island presenting a curious sight to the natives of Tonga as we went riding double on that big, wide bellied steed. With time running out we rode him back to the dock to show off our transportation vehicle. Jokingly, Eddie wanted to ride right him up the ships narrow gangway, but our steed was much too chubby for that idea. We tied him up to a palm tree, knowing his owner would find him eventually, and then we went back on board our floating home ready, although unwilling for the final leg of our journey to the New Hebrides and whatever the war had in store for us.

Tonga-Tabu was a very friendly island indeed. It was a little more barren than a Bora-Bora, but still a very tropical island. The ships log for the Tonga visit had several men brought up on captain's mast for punishment after being, AWOL, absent without leave on Tonga; I think their excuse was they fell asleep after taking in too much island brew, after all they were called Friendly Islands. Before we left the dock to return to our convoy some of the men threw a few coins over the dockside for some young boys to dive for. Soon there were dozens of boys as well as girls all wanting to dive for them until we ran out of coins to toss. They swam like fish as they dove deep to get the coins before they hit the bottom. Early the next day after casting off all lines we were again at sea heading west toward Japanese waters. The island of Japan was facing east and they called their homeland the "Land of the Rising Sun". Our intent was to make it their "Setting Sun", and settle their fate once and for all. With 6000 miles behind us and less than a week's journey to reach our destination we steered to the northwest passing the Fiji islands, on a course for the Esperitos Santos Naval base. The Fiji islands were one of the better places to be based being located far from the battle area and with a large town for liberty.

Finally, on the 25th of January 1944, after a record voyage of 37 days of mainly sea and sky we had taken a voyage of 7,200 nautical miles with only two points of call at pin points on the map to arrive at our destination. We were given anchorage in West Pallekulo Bay in the harbor at Espiritos Santos in the Vanuatu chain. The islands were located southeast of Guadalcanal in the battle zone and to the north of New Caledonia, deep in the South Pacific Micronesia. After we had reported in to the harbor master we bid farewell to our Tug and floating dry-dock before going to our assigned anchorage. As we negotiated the wide channel between the islands we were amazed to see the size of the American fleet anchored in the bays and coves of the many islands. With months of hands-on training and eight months of active sea duty here we were in the Asiatic-Pacific Theater of War right in the midst of Admiral Halsey's Third Fleet. There were more warships of all types than any of us had ever seen before. As small a warship as we were, we were now a part of the naval and land forces which would crush the Empire of Japan. That victory was still years away, but we now had the assets to succeed. Our berth in Secord channel was next to the USS Oceanus, a large troop transport with replacements for the men returning from the battle zone on board. We were tied up with other small ships alongside in order to get water and supplies from our big brother, the Oceanus. Our berth happened to be just off Aore Island, which also happened to be the main recreation island for the ships in our anchorage. There may have been a number of other ships recreation centers, but Aore Island must have been typical of them, I'm sure. During our stay at the base we went into a major engine overhaul, and the crew had periodic shore liberty at Aore Island. It was quite unlike anything we ever experienced.

"The War Years", Serving aboard the USS Patrol Craft #606 From November - 1942 to April - 1946

The First Marine Division invaded Guadalcanal to secure the air base at Henderson Field. It took six months, in a battle fought on land and sea, to defeat the Japanese and stop their conquest of the South Pacific, and their plan to invade Australia. Giving America its first major land victory over the Japanese Empire.

Natives of the New Hebrides on the Island of Espiritos Santos. There was a native war going on up in the Hills, according to the base news.

Solomon island natives going from ship to ship to sell fruit. We were glad to get fresh fruit.

The War Years–Aboard a U.S. Navy Sub-Chaser–1942-1945

Upon arrival you were issued three tickets good for an American brand of 3.2% beer, and before you could leave the dock there were thirsty sailors offering a dollar or more for them. Those few who didn't drink were way ahead since snacks and soft drinks were free. The beers were National brands with a low alcohol content of 3.2% rather than the stateside content of 8%. Because of the temperance lobby in Washington, who thought 8% beer was a bad influence on our young boys overseas. It was dumb logic; since 3 beers at 3.2% is equal to 9.6%, it was just a matter of volume. The Seabees had palmetto log benches scattered around for seating, but the big eye-opener was the large number of gambling devices. They had blackjack and poker games, ring toss, roulette wheels and any gambling game you could imagine. It was all run by the Seabees, who were based on the island and had built up the Las Vegas style set-up. All of it could be folded and stored away quickly in case the Shore Patrol Police came by. "Sea-bees" was the nickname of the Naval Construction Battalions, "C.B's", who cleared the rubble of war and built airstrips, port facilities, and docks once the major islands had been taken from the Japanese. Very ingenious types those CB's, they sold souvenir Jap swords, helmets, flags, guns, handmade jewelry and anything else to make a profit. I'm sure they all made it big time when they returned to civilian life! When my son Michael joined the Navy during the Viet Nam war he was in the Seabees, but as far as I know they were a different breed not given to getting rich selling souvenirs of war.

When Doc, who was our own big time gambler, saw what was going on at Aore Island he brought along his poker deck and his heavy square canvas playing surface to get in the game. He kept his poker games going as long as possible since liberty ended at sundown, and locating our ship in the darkness of blackout conditions was next to impossible, so we always had to get back well before dark. Our stay at Esperitos Santos included two weeks of engine overhaul and to fix some cracked cylinder liners. Now we could have our fresh water again without rationing. All repairs were completed on Feb. 13th 1944 and we put out to the open sea for a trial run on the engines returning after successful completion of tests to berth #16 Seacord channel. We were moored port side to USS PC-620 and were now ready and available for assignment.

Hopefully, we would get a nice convoy to Fiji, New Caledonia, Australia, or New Zealand, or in some other nice safe direction. False hopes ended when the Captain returned after receiving our orders. As expected, they were to the northeast not south to join up with task unit #35.1.7 consisting of three cargo vessels bound for Guadalcanal in the Solomon's Islands, which was now the major base in the ongoing effort to drive the Japanese back to New Guinea, and eventually to Japan. One freighter in the convoy was carrying a cargo of poison gas bound for an isolated island where its deadly cargo would be stored. Scuttlebutt had it that, in case the Japanese resorted to chemical warfare we could threaten to respond. On Feb.15th we filled our fuel and water tanks and loaded our food stores. Soon we were underway to a rendezvous point just north of the islands where we took a position at the port bow of the convoy. The captain had brought some photos of Espiritos Santos natives and their primitive life. His information included the news that up in the rugged hills there was a native war being fought with bows and arrows and spears. That primitive war was presently in progress as we proceeded into our own high tech war.

Another bit of scuttlebutt, the navy term for gossip, concerned Mrs. Roosevelt, the wife of our president, F.D.R., and the first lady of the land. It seems she had preempted an entertaining USO show at the Marine base and was giving a long speech when she was roundly booed by the Marine veterans of the Solomon's who wanted to see the show. Her angry remarks inferred that they were unfit to be among civilized people and should be rehabilitated before going home. She almost caused a riot after that statement. When the story came out in the American press President Roosevelt apologized to all of the armed forces because of the incident. As we headed out to sea through the anti-sub nets protecting the Secord channel we could see a large billboard on the hill high above the supply base. On it there was a message in huge letters: "Kill Japs, Kill Japs, Kill more Japs and it was signed by Admiral Bull Halsey. That message brought the war home with a bang as we were heading out ever closer into Harm's way. We joined our small convoy just north of the New Hebrides base where Espiritos Santos was located and settled into a basic convoy screening pattern. Beginning our operational duties and getting back into wartime readiness activities on board the ship. The fact that we were getting closer to the war zone had a quieting effect on the crew. We had faced potential conflict in the Atlantic war zone, but here it was different with invasions and land battles still in progress and planned. All hands concentrated on their jobs and it seemed even the normal conversation was subdued. I suppose everyone had their own thoughts to deal with just as I did. By muster the next morning things had begun to return to normal and the crew became more at ease.

Details of our assignment contained in his orders were shared with us by our Captain, D.F. Larkin and the executive officer W.J. Norton, Lieut. Jg. The orders revealed that our convoy was headed for the island of Guadalcanal, Solomon Islands. We would be based along with many other ships in what was jokingly called "The Donald Duck Navy", because of the small size of the ships. It was all in good humor, because our fleet of convoy vessels consisted of SC's, PC's and other small escort vessels. We reached our destination February 20th 1944 early in the morning and we dropped anchor off Lunga Point Guadalcanal and the captain went ashore to make his report to the harbor master. We were being assigned to ship escort and port protection duty among the islands of the Solomon chain escorting troop and hospital ships to and from the battle fronts, and escorting supply ships to and from the newly established bases where the Japanese had been driven out. In many places the islands were just by-passed, which left stranded Japanese troops to either surrender or starve. Our permanent anchorage was to be Purvis bay at Tulagi just off Florida Island and across "Iron Bottom Sound" from Guadalcanal. It was named, Iron Bottom Sound, because of the ninety or more warships from both sides on the bottom of the bay, which were sunk in seven major battles. They had all been fought in the open waters between Guadalcanal and Florida Island during the dark days of 1942 and 1943, when defeat was not just a possibility, but a commonly held opinion. Thanks to those brave men who had fought and won those battles the war would end years before it would have otherwise. The battle for Guadalcanal was the real turning point in ending

Jap expansion giving us an airfield from which to attack Japanese bases in the Solomon's and the major bases at Rabaul on New Britain Island.

The largest island of the Solomon chain was Guadalcanal and its capture began the strategy of island hopping to cut off Japanese forces, and to isolate them from their supply bases rather than take each of the hundreds of islands then occupied by the Jap conquerors. The campaign plan under Gen. Douglas MacArthur was to capture the main islands of the chain to neutralize the enemy stronghold at Rabaul in the Bismarck Archipelago off the New Guinea coast. The capture of the Admiralties Islands permitted a giant leap to the Palau Islands, in preparation for the recapture of the Philippine's. Gen. MacArthur had escaped from Manila in 1942 when Japanese forces invaded the American governed islands. His departing message to the Pilipino people was, "I Shall Return". The recapture of the Philippine's was his constant personal motivation throughout the war and to restore the islands back into American control, and incidentally with him to be American governor, as he had been before the war. It was in August 1942, eight months after the Pearl Harbor disaster, that the First Marine Division went ashore on Guadalcanal. The Jap's had started building an airbase from which cities in Australia could be attacked in preparation for the invasion of that country. The task of the First Marine Division was to take the small airstrip and neutralize the Jap forces on the island. It would be the first step on the road to defeat for the Japanese Empire. After six months of bitter fighting, where allied forces had to battle not only fanatical Japanese, but also the natural tropical enemies of malaria, dengue fever, leeches and razor sharp saw grass as well.

American losses on Guadalcanal were costly in blood and treasure, over 7,000 Navy, Army and Marines were wounded or killed in action with the loss of many ships and planes as well. Japanese losses in the Solomon's were high, with 25,600 troops, 3,500 navy men and their ships, 645 pilots and their aircraft were also lost. Over 13,000 Jap troops escaped in barges to other islands without hope of rescue or getting supplies. They were attacked again and again by the Americal Division, which had American

The War Years–Aboard a U.S. Navy Sub-Chaser–1942-1945

and New Caledonia army troops in operation until they ceased to be a viable threat to the war effort, but still a dangerous nuisance to survivors of ship sinking's who made it to shore. The campaign for the Solomon Islands continued up through the chain of the main islands. The larger islands were, Tulagi, Florida, Gavutu, Russell, Rendova, Vella-La-Vella, and Choiseful being secured first. The next largest island with an airstrip to capture was at Bougainville. Officially, the Solomon's campaign lasted from Aug. 1942 to Aug. 1945 at wars end. We were part of that campaign in convoy escort duty until the spring of 1944 when we were reassigned closer to Japan, based in the Marianas Island's. The final Japanese end to the Solomon's conflict was in the 1960's when the last Japanese holdout came out of the jungles. They were left to die among the many islands, and constantly being hunted down and captured as native reports came in to military authorities. They had hiding places in the hills and caves where they lived like animals for so many years. When we arrived at Guadalcanal in Feb. 1944 the island was secured and the Seabees had constructed living quarters, permanent docks and supply depots at Guadalcanal and other bases. There was a fuel and water depot on Florida Island across Iron Bottom Sound for our fleet to use.

On that first day of arrival we were anchored off Lunga Point waiting for the captain to return to the ship with our first assignment. For many months to come we were to anchor at Gavana Inlet on Florida island when in port, with Carter City, built by the Seabees, as our supply depot for food, ammunition, and supplies of fuel and water. Near our anchorage in Purvis bay on Florida Island at Lyon's point, was our assigned recreation area. It was a far cry from the Aore Island facility, being just a stretch of deserted beach littered with empty oil drums, where we beer drinkers were permitted to go in our wherry boat at times to enjoy our 3.2% beer among swaying palms in the hot tropic sun. More about how we spent our recreation hours later on in this happy tale. Florida Island was to remain our home base from Feb. 1944 to May 1945 when we moved closer to the coming battle for the Japanese home islands. Our convoy duty would keep us at sea for a day, a week, or even longer depending on our convoy orders. Primarily we were

The Life & Times of "Himself" ... The War Years

part of the anti-sub fleet which was to protect the supply convoys and hospital ships traveling up and down the Solomon's chain. Jap submarines were based at Jap installations at Rabaul and in the islands of New Britain and New Ireland. They still operated in the Solomon Islands chain looking for likely targets, and our little fleet was in the first line of defense against mini subs or their big deep sea attack subs.

In July 1944 one such mini-sub attack came close to putting the PC-606 out of the war. We had returned to base for re-supply and refueling after completion of an escort assignment to Treasury Island in the Admiralties group. We had escorted USCG Serpens, USS Horace Greely, and USS Zelphinius in convoy with PC-589. On our return we were tied up to the dock at Guadalcanal while the captain had gone to report to the harbor master. At the dock while waiting for him to return with new orders we watched the unloading operations nearby from the Coast guard ship, SS Serpens, which had been part of our earlier convoy. The cargo contained ammunition such as depth charges and other flammables, and a steady stream of Ducks, those water going trucks, which were taking the cargo from the ship onto the beach for storage. The unloading area was a beehive of activity as we waited and in a short period of time the captain returned and we were soon heading across Iron Bottom Sound on our way to refuel and re-supply for our next duty assignment.

We had only traveled for a short distance when the entire dock area exploded. We felt the concussion and saw the ball of fire as the Serpens went up in flames. Later we found that the pier we had left shortly before the explosion was now gone. At the time we could see debris falling in the water and near the dock the Serpens was a burning hulk. Later we were told that a midget sub had somehow entered through the anti-sub nets and had torpedoed the ship. We then immediately went to general quarters and headed to our pre-arranged stations to cut off any escape. All available PC's and SC's joined in the search and within a short time it was reported that a mini-sub had been captured after depth charges forced it to surface. In the excitement of the search one of our SC's began to sink when it accidentally collided with a partially submerged superstructure, or reef. Later, it was towed to dock as the crews were working frantically to remove their own possessions before the ship settled to the shallow bottom beside the dock. When the excitement of the attack was over we returned to anchorage. And after we had dropped anchor we joined with the Captain as all the crew silently said a quiet prayer of thanksgiving considering our close call at the dock. We were also thankful the skipper hadn't stopped at the officers club on his way back to the ship. Earlier in this tale I made the statement that war could be expressed as long periods of extreme boredom, or short periods of high adrenalin and stress. This occasion was a (10) on the stress scale.

A typical day for our ship as on Feb. 20th 1944, as usual we had taken on water and fuel at Purvis Bay on Florida Island and we were moored with PC-585 and PC-1125 waiting for a new assignment. Many of our orders were for short runs around the islands or manning the sonar buoys on the nets around the harbor. It was difficult to protect such a wide area with so many small islands by using nets, so we had to be the prime method of protecting ships in our local war zone. On one occasion the captain had orders to up anchor and make contact with the PC-1127 serving as convoy commander assigned to escort a merchant ship, SS Mormac-Wren, to Munda on New Georgia Island. We arrived at Rendova Harbor where we were then assigned to harbor screening duty. Later we resumed escort for SS Mormac-Wren in company with PC-1127 for return to Lunga Point Guadalcanal. While on convoy the ship went to general quarters concerning an aircraft contact on the radar, which was identified as friend by its, Identified friend or foe, IFF signal. We secured from G.Q. and after returning to base we were assigned to harbor screening duty off Lunga Point Guadalcanal. This event was typical of our duties as a member of the "Donald Duck Navy". Yes, it was boring to a large degree, but in the back of your mind was a reminder that a sudden call to general quarters or an event like the Serpens would change it drastically. Think about a year or two of this kind of life on board a small anti-submarine vessel during wartime, but it was something that had to be done to win the war, and I honor all those who served with me in doing it. To relieve the seemingly endless days out on the open water as well as to keep up the crew's efficiency the navy saw fit to rotate escort duty with other ships in the squadron.

"The War Years", Serving aboard the USS Patrol Craft #606 From November - 1942 to April - 1946

These maps show the area of convoy operations by our so called, "Donald Duck" Navy. From our base on Iron Bottom Bay at Tulagi, to the Gilbert and Marshall Islands, and in the Solomon's group.

The PC-606 on Sonar Buoy station off Guadalcanal island in the Solomon's. In addition to convoy duty we patrolled the harbor entrances on screening duty, while in port.

Some merchant ships from Australia needed to be escorted to the other islands than those in the Solomon's. Further to the north were the Gilbert and Marshall Islands in the Central Pacific, so our screening and convoy duty also covered a range of territory miles to the west of Guadalcanal and 2000 miles to the north. One such voyage assignment was north to Tarawa in the Gilberts, which stands out in my mind. On May 8th 1944, in company with PC-585 and pc-461 we escorted task unit 11.1 from our Tulagi base to Tarawa. It was our first convoy away from the Solomon's for a long period of time, and well over 1500 miles to the north. Tarawa had been taken from the Japanese about the time of our arrival at Esperitos Santos at the end of 1943. The victory came after fierce fighting lasting for three days. It resulted in 3,100 American Marine casualties, more than the attack on Pearl Harbor. Out of 4800 Jap defenders only 148 survived the battle, the rest decided to die for their Emperor rather than surrender. The destruction by the Naval air and sea bombardment prior to the invasion gave Tarawa the appearance of a weird land of shattered palm trees, which looked like splintered telephone poles with deep shell holes everywhere. That's what it looked like when we were there in April 1944. A Quonset hut base had been built in the area carved out by Seabees and its new airstrip was now in operation. Each of these captured islands was like adding a new unsinkable aircraft carrier like those in the sixth fleet of Admiral Halsey. The fifth fleet of Admiral Spruance continued on with a campaign of island hopping across northern Micronesia. Seizing key islands, by-passing others, and neutralizing the Japanese installations too costly in lives and materiel to be worthwhile invading. Truk Island in the Caroline's group was the best example of the by-passing operation, which was heavily defended by suicidal Jap forces and almost impregnable to invasion from the open sea.

In by-passing Truk then establishing bomber bases around it to destroy its facilities saved many American as well as Japanese lives in the island hopping process. Our voyage to Tarawa was interesting in another way, because by coincidence, Bob Hope and his USO entertaining troupe were scheduled to perform at the Tarawa movie area that evening. Afternoon rains were coming down in buckets when we left the ship to go ashore to see the show. We wore our Navy ponchos to ward off the soaking tropic rains. A poncho is like a waterproof tent with a head hole and hood with side slits to poke out your arms. It is one of the most practical rain gear ever invented, and kept us dry as a bone except for our feet, which were in the water puddles. The Seabee movie area was an amphitheater with palmetto logs in place of benches, and not built for comfort as you can imagine. We found a few front row center seats and waited for the show to start. The rain slowed somewhat, but never did stop entirely, and puddles had formed between the logs. We were pretty sure the show would be cancelled, because the stage was only a 25Ft. by 25Ft. wood platform covered with a canvas top, and the canvas was bulging in the center as it filled with water. Everything was soaked including the audience. About several hundred service men had been waiting there for hours hoping for an announcement of some kind, whether to cancel or go on with the show.

Finally, Bob Hope and his troupe of twelve arrived and Bob first introduced Jerry Colonna, who was a well-known comedian and then attractive Frances Langford, the popular singer. With the troupe were a combo of five musicians, but the most appreciated were several very attractive young dancers. While Bob kept us in stitches with his jokes Jerry Colonna was poking a hole in the bulging canvas and jokingly pretended to be taking a shower as the water drained out of the canvas on his head. He was a riot, but the water on the stage made it difficult for the girls to do their tap dance, but they made a great attempt at it in spite of the wet stage and their efforts were really well appreciated. You had to admire them for trying to entertain us under the most adverse circumstances. During the war that is what made Bob Hope the legend that he was, as he went into harm's way himself to entertain the troops. That show on Tarawa was the first and only USO show our ship's crew ever attended during our tour of duty. Many USO shows came and went, but we were seldom in port to enjoy them. On our return trip to our Solomon Island base we gave a wide berth to the Caroline Island chain. The islands were well fortified and were still actively under Japanese control. Truk Island, the largest island in the Caroline chain, was their most heavily defended stronghold in the Central Pacific. At Truk the Japs maintained a base for submarines, planes, and ships. Truk was a thorn in the side of the Americans until the capture of the Marianas chain of islands far to the west.

Our next voyage north was to the northernmost convoy destination, the Marshal Islands of Eniwetok and Kwajalein. The largest island atoll in the central pacific was Kwajalein with a natural harbor for ships re-supply operations to serve ships on the supply route between bases in the war zone and the U.S. It was also used as a base of operations for the Navy Island hopping campaign. These islands were taken from Jap control in February 1944, and provided the next stepping stone to the Marianas Islands further to the west. Their capture would put our huge B-29 Super fort bomber squadrons within range of the Jap home islands. On Nov. 26th 1944 we made our rendezvous with USS AK-108, an attack transport with U.S. Army troops bound for the invasion of the Marianas Islands and the USS Rotanin-Prione, which was en-route to Eniwetok Island in the Marshall Island chain. Our voyage was short and uneventful arriving at Eniwetok on Dec. 1st 1944. After being detached from the convoy we refueled for our return to Lunga Pt. Guadalcanal traveling independently. On that trip there was an entry in the ships log for Dec. 6th 1944 mentioning a Sonar contact picked up by the duty Sonarman sending the crew to general quarters. I was on the stack during the attack and it appeared to me as a classic sub indication. With the Captain at the chemical recorder following the track, a six depth charge pattern was dropped on target. After regaining contact in the wake and turmoil of the water, another pattern was dropped. After a final search I was unable to relocate the target. It was recorded on the chemical recorder to be a potential submarine attack, so without any visible results in the water to show a sinking the ship secured from general quarters and life went back to normal.

    The episode was typical of the anti-sub policy of reacting to any worth-while Sonar contact, due to the way sound waves were distorted by inversion in the warm Pacific waters. In October 1944 the island of Pelélieu in the Palau Islands was captured. This was the western stepping stone in Gen. Mac Arthur's campaign to retake the Philippines. It was one of the most costly Marine victories of the Pacific war. The part that escort vessels played in the operation was protecting the movement of troops and supplies to establish a forward base and airstrip in preparation for the campaign to fulfill Gen. Mac Arthur's promise to the Philippine people when he said "I Shall Return". To the troops who fought in that fatal campaign it seemed to be a personal ego trip by the otherwise great general that he was.

There was lots of negative scuttlebutt about his misuse of Seabee battalions and materiel to construct his homey personal compounds on New Guinea behind the lines. In keeping with his promise US army forces landed on Leyte Island in the Philippines on Oct. 20th 1944, beginning a campaign which lasted until February 6th 1945. Also, in late October 1944, the U.S. Pacific fleet crushed the bulk of the Japanese fleet in the battle of Leyte Gulf. Only its dwindling undersea fleet of submarines remained a major threat to American forces in the Asiatic/Pacific Theater of the war. The remaining Japanese warships now remained hidden in Japanese ports unable to confront the American Navy, and left to wait the coming American invasion forces when they would reach the Japanese home islands. Some capital ships had been run aground to use as shore based artillery in the battle for Okinawa. Information after the surrender found that the largest submarine ever built by the Japanese was equipped with midget subs and was able to fire banks of torpedoes without using a periscope. It was a deadly weapon and could have caused a great deal of damage to the American cause. It was three times the length of our small 173 foot sub chaser and could sink us before we even knew it was around. It is believed to be the sub which sunk the USS Indianapolis, but it came too late to help the Japanese against the American Navy.

A note in the ships log for Sept. 20th 1944 shows that Captain O.C. Spencer, Lieut. Jg. was now in command of the USS PC-606, Becoming the third skipper of our P.C. and Lieut. W.J. Norton was now detached from command and J.E. Searight Lieut. Jg. became our new executive officer. Also a new Ensign, J.J. O'Keefe, came aboard to fill in our officer's complement at five. Later, in Dec. of 1944, after our fifteen days of leave in Sydney Australia for rest and rehabilitation, Capt. Spencer was relieved as captain for some medical reason. He left the ship in Jan. 1944 for observation and reassignment at Guadalcanal Medical Center and Lieut. Searight became our new captain. When the invasion of the St. Mathias Islands was underway In Sept. 1944 we escorted the USS Sterope from Guadalcanal S.I. to Emerau Island. The trip was uneventful going to the island, but not so on our return trip. We were underway traveling independently at standard speed and our course took us to the north of the Jap base on New Ireland. The Captain was alerted when the radar operator detected several aircraft on the scope. We went immediately to general quarters since we were in Japanese waters. It was difficult to identify them at first and it appeared as if they coming in for a low level attack, but as the planes came within range the radar finally picked up their IFF signal, which gave off the identification as a friendly aircraft. The planes pulled up after what seemed to be the last second before we would have opened fire. It left all of us quite a bit shaken over what might have happened. Then with a waggle of their wings the two Army Air Force Mustangs turned and disappeared into the dusk. We were very thankful for the excellent eyesight in our Air Force, and their ability to identify their own flag at such a great distance.

That wasn't the end of our trials on that trip, because shortly after dark when we were geographically opposite the Jap base at Rabaul on New Britain our radioman picked up a general message from fleet command informing all ships at sea that a Jap cruiser had left port and was somewhere in the straits of the Bismarck sea. Being in that area the Captain ordered the ship to general quarters immediately. We were all praying that we could get to home waters before any contact was made with such a warship. Within minutes both the Sonar and Radar made a simultaneous contact. It was large and moving very slowly and in the blackness of night totally invisible. I was in the radar shack, assisting an apprentice Radar man and as we observed that large contact on the scope he quietly asked me if I would say a prayer with him and we began to say the "Our Father" together as we watched the huge contact on the scope. One thing that most service men would tell you, there weren't very many atheists in the war zone. There seemed to be no hostile response to our presence from the huge target, indicating something other than a vessel. The Captain ordered an AA flare round from our three inch battery. The flare exploded short of the target blinding the gun crew and the lookouts momentarily. When a second flare arched out over the target we were all filled with relief as the bright flare illuminated our much dreaded enemy. It was an immense floating mass of natural and war debris including trees, many oil drums, wood planks and masses of seaweed, which created a floating island of junk. With all the metal drums mixed in it did appear on our Sonar and Radar screens with all the indications of large vessel. The Lord answered our prayers in a big way that night, and the Captain used our full 22 knot speed capability to get out of the area as soon as possible before a real target showed up. Before long we were back at our anchorage in Purvis Bay at Florida Island looking forward to boring picket duty for a welcome change.

"The War Years", Serving aboard the USS Patrol Craft #606 From November - 1942 to April - 1946

All ashore for liberty on a deserted beach at Gavana inlet, with swaying palms and 3.2 beer, chilled in a fuel drum using a Co2 fire extinguisher for cooling. Standing second from the left is the author, enjoying the fun.

Further up the Gavana inlet, was a partially sunken, Japanese Destroyer. On board I found a metal box containing Japanese postcards and occupation money from the Philippine Island's.

Reading the ships log shows our routine didn't vary much day to day. The ships log contained the entry of "Steaming as before" more often than any other entry, except for the many times it recorded "preparing to take on water" at Kukum Dock, fuel at Purvis Bay or food supplies at Carter City. All those places were built by Seabee's who built the docks and Quonset Hut storage buildings, which contained all the articles for conducting the war. Our guns were used constantly to blow up mines, sink the floating hazards we would encounter while on convoy, or gunnery training, so food and ammunition needs had to be met. The movement and delivery of supplies was next in line to combat action itself. The next most used phrase in the log was "getting underway with the captain at the conn" usually en-route to a convoy rendezvous with a hospital ship, troop or merchant ship. During a period of seventeen months, from January of 1944 until May of 1945, that was our routine in the Solomon Islands. Take on fuel, food and water immediately after returning from a convoy and prepare to go out again on another escort mission or to screen at the nets in the harbor entrance. As mentioned earlier we escorted convoys to Tarawa in the Gilbert island chain to Eniwetok and Kwajelein Atolls in the Marshall Chain. In the Solomon's chain we escorted troop ships, hospital ships, and merchant vessels to Russell Island, to Vella la Vella, Munda, Bougainville, Treasury in the British admiralties and other ports close to Japan's New Ireland and New Britain.

When arrival back in port after an escort assignment we had to refuel and resupply and perform maintenance of the weapons, engines, radio communications and Sonar equipment, and in general prepare the ship for our next duty assignment. The base at Carter City was a cluster of Quonset huts, those prefabricated metal buildings which could be taken down and reassembled as the bases moved closer to Japan. It had barracks for the Seabee crews and Navy Port Authority personnel. They had a movie area as well and half of the ship's crew had liberty each night when we were in port. Liberty was divided into port and starboard sections, so the ship always had enough personnel on board in case of an emergency callout. The movies were only black and white and were usually recent releases, but whether old or new they were a welcome diversion from the days of sea duty. Cowboy movies were always very popular with lots of hooting and yelling from the audience when the good guys shot up the outlaws or Indians. War movies about the Navy were always classed as a type of comedy by veterans, because of the way Hollywood exaggerated the portrayal of Navy and Army life and they usually brought a lot of laughs. Movies were only shown on outdoor screens made to be collapsible to drop on pulleys during air raids. Benches were made of two by ten boards not like the uncomfortable, round palmetto logs they used at the Tarawa movie house. The shows always went on in rain or shine, and we used our rain ponchos as seat cushions if it didn't rain. Early in 1944 an occasional air raid still occurred, but when the Jap strongholds at New Ireland and New Britain were neutralized and the air strip on Bougainville Island everyone was taken we could look forward to movies without any interruption.

There was little else in the way of recreation for us at our home base except for a few misnamed "beer parties", which were not really parties at all, merely an opportunity to get off the ship for a time and have a cool 3.2% beer with your shipmates. The parties had to depend on the availability of the ration of beer, because the navy, in its infinite wisdom, allowed our supply officer to obtain a ration of beer amounting to so many cans for each man per month. Those interested in a beer party signed up for beer chits and saved them until their turn for liberty came up. On the day of a party we loaded the beer ration in the wherry boat along with a CO-2 fire extinguisher, which was used to cool the beer. Ashore we had a clean fuel drum to hold the water and the cans of beer. By discharging the contents of the fire extinguisher into the drum of water we were soon provided with ice cold beverages, or frozen beverages if the CO_2 was used excessively. Several boatloads of party-goers proceeded by wherry boat to Lyons Point beach. This was in no way compared to a Miami Beach, but a deserted stretch of shoreline at Gavana Inlet with its empty oil drums and a few scraggily palm trees. I would like to say how great it was, but being an honest person I must be truthful, the heat ashore was suffocating, the nearby swampy, bug filled jungle had an oppressive smell of decaying vegetation to go with the fishy smell of the slack water in the cove.

You couldn't go for a swim without wearing your shoes, because the coral rock was sharp and dangerous, and a cut could cause many serious infections. One disease caused by coral rock was called elephantitus; an infection causing extreme swelling of the limbs, which remained enlarged. I recall seeing one native with his leg twice the normal size because of the disease. Then there were the big attack flies during the day and swarms of super mosquitoes if you went ashore at night. Diseases such as malaria and dengue fever were a common enemy for everyone in the tropics. To combat it we had to take our daily dosage of Atabrine, a vile tasting yellow tablet along with our regular salt tablets to ward off the diseases spread by the mosquitoes. Bringing up the question, why would we, or anyone for that matter, go ashore to drink 3.2% beer under such conditions? Considering the alternative to stay on board the ship where the decks were even hotter, and do all the things you did to pass the time during the weeks or months at sea since your last shore opportunity. So the answer was that even a small change was a welcome change. Life was what it was, and we did volunteer for this didn't we? Looking at the good part, at least we were not in the Army or Marines crawling through these stinking jungles.

On one more interesting occasion, when we were ashore at Lyons Point to party, we took the ships wherry boat and went exploring on up the Gavana Inlet into a small river. Near the end of the navigable waterway we discovered a partially sunken Japanese Destroyer. The water was shallow and the ship was partially under water only to its lower deck. We went aboard to explore for quite a while, checking the bridge and the above deck compartments. In one of the bunk areas I discovered a rusted strong box hidden way under a burned bunk. For all its rusted looks, it was in fair condition. The strong box was not locked, just rusted shut. After a few minutes with my navy knife I was able to pry it open. To my amazement it contained money from Japan, a picture post card, and Japanese Occupation script from the Philippines. There was a blank book made from rice paper, and Japanese war bonds as well. A very surprising find since it was evident the ship had burned out completely. I have the money and a page of the rice paper in my WW II record. The ship had a huge hole in the deck where it had taken a bomb hit, which caused it to sink in the shallow waters of the Inlet with most of the superstructure above the waterline. Someone in the crew found a burned Jap helmet among the debris. I didn't find a helmet myself, but I do have a photo wearing the one they found. It was a tight fit, Japs are small people!

There were a number of episodes of life aboard ship that helped to make our dull lives more interesting. It is commonly believed in the old Navy that a woman on board a ship was considered to be bad luck. On this particular occasion it seemed all too true, but only from my observation, that is. It all began when the Executive officer went ashore on ships business and met a nurse at the Guadalcanal base medical unit, who was from his home town. He arranged for her and two other nurses to come on board for a spell. Once they were aboard we headed across the bay to follow our in port routine going from place to place as we prepared for our next assignment. To pick the mail, take on fuel, water, and food supplies as we always did. This day there was a definite change in how the crew reacted when these three attractive young ladies came on board. Even though nurses were all Officers they were still women and the center of attraction for the crew, who had not seen a member of the fairer sex for at least ten months. The officers planned to have their guests spend some of their time on the flying bridge above the main deck to enjoy the breeze and the view of the ship cutting through the water. Chairs were arranged for them and the Captain ordered coffee to be brought from the wardroom. It was a minor request; however the request became the first reason why women on board can be bad luck. The ship suddenly heeled over as the helmsman turned the wheel over sharply trying to avoid a channel marker. It seems something had distracted him from the set course and as a result the poor ships steward, who was bringing the hot coffee, lost his grip on the ladder to the flying bridge. Fortunately he only suffered minor burns on his hands, arms and chest as the hot liquid spilled on him.

You could look at the bright side and say we were lucky to have not just one, but three nurses on hand plus our own good "Doc" to attend to his injuries. As we crossed Iron Bottom Sound heading for Florida Island the crew attended to their duties, and for some reason the Gunner's mate decided it was time to check out the 20 millimeter anti-aircraft guns on the flying bridge. Soon he was presenting a short armament course for the three attractive young ladies. After his lecture he replaced the gun covers, but for some strange reason he forgot to lock in the gun barrel in place to keep it from swinging free. When he had finished he casually rested his arm on the weapon, which caused it to swing outboard. He held on to it for support and overboard he went for a predictable, but unexpected swim. That was number two on the bad luck parade. The Captain rose to the occasion and circled back as they tossed the gunner a life preserver to hang onto until he was able to climb up the rope ladder put over the side for him. With our gunner back aboard the Captain could say he had made a great impression on the gals with his expert rescue of a man overboard. It was just a minor accident totally unavoidable of course, but no one ever fell overboard before or was scalded by coffee in performance of their duty. It only happened when our attractive female guests came aboard.

It was not over yet, because on the day we became a cruise ship we lost our precious ration of beef over the side. Australia has a lot of sheep, in fact they have many, many sheep, and really an abundance of sheep and the neighboring country of New Zealand also raised lots of sheep. In order to get meat we had to take a certain amount of plentiful lamb and mutton to be able to get a much smaller ration of beef. As food supplies were being brought on board at Carter City the section of beef our supply officer had obtained for us was somehow dropped into the drink. The normally adept crewmen had their minds on something else beside their main job of bringing supplies on board. Our loss was felt for weeks as our taste buds had to wait for another time before getting a taste of ground beef again. Of course it was just one more unavoidable bit of bad luck, and in no way related to the attractive female passengers who came aboard. At day's end we returned our three visitors back to the dock at Guadalcanal grateful to the skipper and the exec. for their reminder of what we were out there fighting for, home and country and the girl we left behind. We were so grateful that nobody ever voiced the opinion that our unusual troubles were in any minor way connected with having women on board. That was just a Navy myth. Or was it??

On March 10th 1944 we were to escort an American hospital ship in company with USS PC-555, from Lunga Point, Guadalcanal to Reynard Sound, Russell Island then Cape Torakina at Empress Augusta Bay, Bougainville to bring back the wounded to the medical center at Guadalcanal. We arrived on March 11th 1944 in the harbor anchorage at Bougainville. The second Japanese assault to recapture the American perimeter around the airstrip was still underway. The attacking enemy forces were some of the tall Japanese Imperial Marines. The very same animals that was responsible for the terrible "Sack of Nanking", when the Japanese Empire was engaged in the conquest of the Chinese nation. Men, women and babies were brutally murdered in the attack. American newsreels and newspapers showed the slaughter by the Imperial Marines. The Americal division was composed of Australian and many native troops from places like New Caledonia, and other Australian island protectorates along with the US Army's 37th Division who were engaged in the ongoing battle for control of the island. The airstrip had been captured from the Japs in January 1943, but many of the Japanese forces were still at the end of the island and had been reinforced in an attempt to take back the airstrip and harbor.

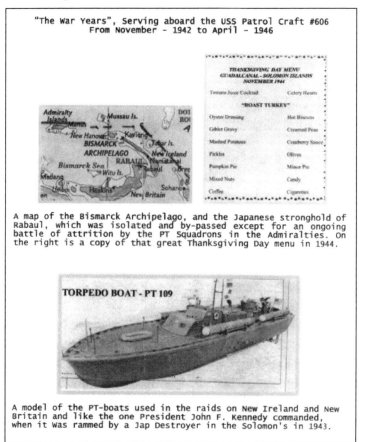

"The War Years", Serving aboard the USS Patrol Craft #606 From November - 1942 to April - 1946

A map of the Bismarck Archipelago, and the Japanese stronghold of Rabaul, which was isolated and by-passed except for an ongoing battle of attrition by the PT Squadrons in the Admiralties. On the right is a copy of that great Thanksgiving Day menu in 1944.

A model of the PT-boats used in the raids on New Ireland and New Britain and like the one President John F. Kennedy commanded, when it was rammed by a Jap Destroyer in the Solomon's in 1943.

The War Years–Aboard a U.S. Navy Sub-Chaser–1942–1945

Bougainville was one of the largest of the islands in the Central Pacific. It was the scene of bitter fighting from November 1943 until March 1944. By the end of 1943 the central region of Bougainville had been controlled by the 21st Marine division leaving both ends of the islands to the well-entrenched Japan nese, but by years end the enemy realized the allied airbase on Bougainville was too much of a threat to their naval base at Rabaul on New Britain Island, and decided to retake the airstrip and its natural harbor. The Japanese had a force of 12,000 men on the southern tip of Bougainville. Facing them were 27,000 troops of the 37th infantry, the Americal division, and a Marine contingent assigned to protect the base from infiltrators. March 1st when the enemy attacked the defending Americans they had air and naval support, unlike the original invasion when the enemy had total air support from its huge base at Rabaul. The battle lasted for three weeks ending on March 23rd, when the enemy was pushed back to the ends of the island. The remaining enemy forces that were unable to escape remained in place planning for another attack, which never came. By avoiding further engagement with the enemy countless allies and Japanese lives were saved. The importance of controlling Bougainville was emphasized by the Japanese Commander of the enemy forces, who said "If Bougainville falls Japan will topple". Thank God he was right.

At the time we arrived there on March 10th 1944 American forces still controlled the single airstrip and five miles of shoreline north and south, and the Japanese controlled the rest of the island. As the battle ashore continued the hospital ship was anchored well offshore inside the anti-sub nets, and the casualties were taken out by landing craft and taken aboard. We were anchored closer in to shore as other Patrol Craft had the responsibility of protecting the harbor area. We were the only ship close in to shore resting at anchor. To pass the time I found myself a spot up near the bow and settled down to do a little reading. My book was one I had read before, one of the wacky Thorn Smith novels all about the roaring twenties. As I was reading and laughing out loud at times I could hear a few explosions near the closest end of the small air strip. Each explosion was preceded by a puff of white smoke high up on the highest mist shrouded hill. The island was covered with tangled bougainvillea vines, a very tropical thick vine full of sharp thorns. It was very beautiful in full bloom making the hillside look like a solid floral mat. We were told later on that the puffs of smoke came from a Jap gun on tracks, which ran back into a tunnel in the hill. They would run the artillery gun out to the entrance to pick a target and fire. The smoke puff gave away their position for a time and Air Force planes dove on the spot dropping bombs or napalm. Then the sequence would start again, the gun would fire, hitting or missing a target and the planes would attack then circle for another telltale puff of smoke to attack again. From my vantage point on the bow it didn't seem real, but rather like a movie. Fighter planes were taking off and landing on the air strip to refuel and reload, as they tried to eliminate the Jap artillery piece.

As I continued to watch, another puff of smoke appeared on the hill, but this time it did not hit on the air strip as before, instead a geyser of water went up about 1,300 feet away from our anchored position. Since we were the only possible target nearby it appeared we were the sitting duck they might be aiming at. I ran to the ward room port hole and alerted one of the Officers. He reacted quickly calling the engine room to get underway and had the anchor winches start up immediately to move out of range. Before the anchor had even cleared the surface we began to move slowly when another geyser went up close to our former position, proof enough who their target might have been. Shortly afterward we were notified to return to base with the hospital ship, ending our minor involvement in the Bougainville campaign. The next time we returned to Empress Augusta bay those guns in the caves had all been eliminated although; the battle to drive the japs off the island was still going strong. Actually, the army never did capture the entire island, mainly the airstrip, the main native village, and several miles of harbor shoreline west and east of the air force base. The jungle was almost impenetrable and the island was now considered secure. The third marine defense battalion and the US Army 37th division remained to deal with those by-passed Japanese army groups, which were now isolated and without supplies, in the jungles of Bougainville and the adjacent islands.

March 20th 1944 we were on convoy escort in company with PC-1127 as escort for the USS Jack London going from Lunga Pt. Guadalcanal to Cape Torakina Empress August Bay at Bougainville,

The War Years–Aboard a U.S. Navy Sub-Chaser–1942–1945

where we anchored overnight. It was here I must admit to the strangest thing that ever happened to me, that of being captured during WW II, which occurred on Bougainville Island. It may sound really strange, but two of us American sailors were captured by the also American, U.S. Marines, when we had the opportunity to go ashore to explore the now secure area. Our custom when visiting strange ports of call was to go ashore to see what there was to see, a simple desire. For some reason I don't remember we had taken one of the officers ashore in the wherry boat leaving my buddy Eddie and I to go exploring. East of the army base we found some abandoned fox holes containing some extra K-rations, so we took time out for lunch. Also left behind in the foxhole were some hand grenades in a pouch. We hung several of them on our Forty Five side arm gun belts and continued on. When we came to a secluded lagoon we decided it was a good place to toss a few grenades just for test purposes. We used some palmetto logs for cover as we took turns tossing a grenade out into the water hoping we could stun some fish to take back.

After about ten minutes or so we were surprised by a few curious natives coming out of the brush with machetes thinking the Japanese may have returned, because of the explosions. Seeing we were just tourist Americans they soon left to go back to their village. Visiting a native village sounded like a good idea, so we decided to follow them into the jungle a bit going along their native trail. As I walked I was looking down to pick my way over tangled roots and logs. It was a good thing I looked up, because I was about to come face to face with a huge hairy spider. Tip to tip he was as large as my hand and I had stopped just short of its huge web strung across the trail. The thing was multi-colored and scary looking, nothing you would ever want to come face to face with. Whether it was poisonous or not I don't know, but it sure makes my skin crawl when I think of it. Irrational fear of spiders is called arachnophobia the term biologists use. I'm glad I don't have that, but I don't like spiders. Another unusual discovery was a buffalo head nickel dated 1937 I found shining there on the ground. It was a fairly modern coin back then, but a big surprise to find it in such a place. We found the biggest souvenir in heavy brush just off the trailwhen when we discovered a burned out

Japanese tank. It was very small, and maybe just a two man vehicle. Naturally, we began to search the tank for any Jap souvenirs.

We must have been making lots of noise in the process, because behind us we heard a lot of swearing and angry orders in English telling us to put up our hands. The command was followed by a string of such nasty cuss words they could have turned the air blue. Comments about stupid swabbies being let out of their cages while in port. It turned out to be a squad of army grunts who had apparently crawled through swamps and jungle crud because they thought Japs were back in the perimeter. The sergeant continued calling us pet names in an angry manner. You could say he was very upset, because we were told to put our hands on our heads even though it was obvious we weren't Japs. They marched us back to the dock where our ships duty Officer was waiting with our wherry boat for us to return. As it turned out our Lieutenant outranked the army Officer in charge and he knew that his crewmen had to be innocent, so he stuck up for us. We did know better than to make fun of an army Sergeant, so we just kept quiet. You would think they would have been happy to discover it was only us peaceful swabbies infiltrating into their territory instead of the Japs. Those grenades we found came in handy for fishing later on, when we got to a good fishing lagoon or ran into a school of tuna at sea. The liberated K-rations were also good to snack on during midnight watch, but as for the tank we didn't even get a photo of it.

We were often assigned to monitoring the numerous Sonar buoys, which protected open harbors. The Sonar units were placed around the entrances in addition to the submarine nets to give an overlapping electronic protection to main harbors. This was in addition to our electronic screening and submarine detecting. There was also a joint system called, JASA Search, and we were involved in one that was called into action on July 7th 1944 at 0800 hrs. A submarine was sighted off Leru Island in the Russell Island group and PC-606, in company with an Australian Patrol ship, the HMZ-Q-108, and several assigned aircraft formed a sub killer group giving the best chance to locate and destroy an enemy submarine. We operated for over two days in a systematic search of the many coves and inlets of the islands in the Russell Group. Our low draft made it possible for us to go into coves the larger ship could not.

Another sighting of the submarine was reported north of Russell Island, and the search moved to that location without any positive results. We secured from the JASA Search operations after two days of unsuccessful underwater and visual effort to locate the contact that had been sighted. That was our first and last effort in that type of a sub search and it was quite a change from normal operations.

The Solomon's island duty of our PC-606 was mainly convoy and screening duty at our base islands of Guadalcanal and Florida the two main islands of the Solomon island chain. We operated there from Jan. 1944 until March of 1945 when we were reassigned nearer to the central war zone. We were to be located at Tanapag harbor on the island of Saipan in the Marianas chain of islands, which were formerly held by the Japanese. During the many voyages on convoy we spent a lot of time on the open sea and there were many nights when I would lay down on the uncomfortable depth charge racks on the stern looking up at the heavens filled with super bright stars in the pitch black darkness, and as I watched the wake of the ship with the bow cutting through the water the effervescent wake would glow with a like a billion fireflies. I learned later on that it was caused by tiny micro-organisms peculiar to Pacific waters. It was so hypnotic to watch as I lay there in the blackness of a moonless night when even the stars seemed to be close enough reach up and touch. The peacefulness of it all was an opportunity to be alone with your thoughts, trying hard not to dwell on the fact of just how vulnerable our small vessel was. I prayed hard that we would go home safely knowing God was the only one who could bring an end to a war that just seemed to go on forever.

Above the Solomon Islands chain are the Admiralties Islands in the Bismarck Sea due north of the New Guinea Japanese stronghold. Emerau Island was a main base for the American Patrol Torpedo Boats, "PT", squadrons. They operated between the islands of New Ireland and New Britain where the Japanese had a strong presence. On our first trip to Emerau Island in Hamburg bay we were given permission to take on fuel. The dock was narrow with only pilings for docking, and as we approached the dock an Australian soldier was assigned to jump into the water to tie up our docking lines to the pilings jutting out of the water. It was probably a normal procedure for him, but as he did so someone spotted a shark fin some distance away and called out a warning to the man in the water. I happened to be at the main entrance to the radio shack where several Sub-Thompson machine guns, like the ones used by gangsters and FBI men in the 1920's, were stacked for emergency use. The deck of the radio room had been painted and ropes were tied across the hatch to keep out any traffic. The paint was now dry, so thinking I could intervene in the shark attack, I climbed through the lines to get one of the heavy sub-machine guns. I climbed back through the tangle of ropes to the outside passageway in less than a minute, but on the way out of the radio shack I tripped over the ropes on the hatch with my finger resting on the trigger and suddenly the gun fired stitching a nice neat row of holes in the tarp over the quarterdeck as my shipmates dived for cover. Meanwhile our Aussie friend was swimming for his life and I recovered in time to open fire into the water where the shark seemed to be spraying a pattern of bullets in front of the dark shadow in the water hoping to hit it. The shark wasn't seen again, but I sure did take a lot of ribbing about my "G-man" shooting ability. The Aussie soldier did come aboard to thank me later on. An entry in the ships log of Aug. 8th 1944 shows that Ens. A.V. O'Keefe reported aboard the PC-606 for duty.

As I mentioned before, Emerau Island was a Patrol Torpedo Boat base and future President John F. Kennedy's PT-109 helped to make the Patrol Torpedo Boat very well known. The PT squadron at Emerau Island was often involved in raids against Jap troop and supply barges moving in the straits between New Ireland and New Britain in the Bismarck Sea. The small Torpedo Boats would go out when information from intelligence reported Japanese troop movements in that area. The purpose of sending the PT boats into the waterway was to destroy the Jap barges. The method was to locate the enemy on radar fire a flare and destroy as many barges as they could leaving at high speed as quickly as they came. There were times when non PT-boat sailors were able to get permission to trade off with PT crew members to go on these search and destroy missions in their place. I decided to go along on one such volunteer mission as a PT boat radar operator, while the regular man enjoyed a day off at the base. It was a regular thing among the PT boat crews and a novelty for a lot of us crackpots who lost their common sense for a time. The PT boat is a plywood craft with two Chrysler engines powerful enough to lift a good sized plane into the air. On the long bumpy ride to the straits the kidneys took a real beating and holding on for dear life was a requirement at all times and one patrol was plenty for me. After arriving in the straits between the two large islands the radar showed up a number of targets up ahead moving between the islands. Once in range flares were fired to illuminate the barges and the 37mm bow gun opened up along with the 20mm AA guns. In less than a minute we were high tailing it out of there. In the darkness we could hear the japs yelling as their barges were sinking to the bottom. It was a war of attrition against the Japs and the PT's kept up the pressure on the by-passed Jap forces remaining at the enemy bases.

Also on Emerau Island the Seabee's, as the U.S. Navy construction group was called, had their own base where an underground souvenir and jewelry business flourished. You could buy a silver Cat Eye ring made from hammered out silver dimes for the setting, with the stone as a semi-precious Cat-Eye, from rare sea shells all real works of art. You could also buy a genuine homemade Japanese flag, or ash trays made from spent steel artillery shell casings. Even Japanese Samurai swords were available for a large sum, and there were a number of smaller war souvenirs to send home. They were able to do all of this when they were not building airfields or supply depots, quite ingenious those Seabees. Another incident concerning our visits to Emerau Island was when one of the crew was able to a get a lot of raisins from the supply base through a friend. He said he knew the recipe for Raisin Jack, a bootleg whisky from the Kentucky hills. They made the mixture and put it into jars so it would ferment and hopefully reach the required potency. They stashed the jars in a hidden place on the island, and all they talked about was how great it would taste when we were able to get back to Emerau. Unfortunately, by the time we came back the jugs had exploded and the mixture was all over the hidden place ending the bootleg episode. A good rubdown or an ear cleansing with medical grain alcohol made lots more sense than Raisin Jack. It was August 8th 1944, on the second anniversary of our official commissioning at the Brooklyn Navy yard; we were assigned to escort a single ship convoy the merchantman USS Alcoa Pegasus en-route from Lunga Point Guadalcanal to Treasury Island located at the north end of the island chain then to Empress Augusta bay at Bougainville.

Once we were anchored in Empress Augusta bay we decided it was a great place to hold an anniversary party. We had been preparing for this anniversary party to be held in my personal hideaway down in the Sonar hold well ahead of time. Doc was able to requisition small supplies of medical alcohol as long as he had his records to show how all the medication had been dispensed. For example, the grain alcohol, which was 180 proof, was commonly used by Doc's medical department for cleaning wounds, for cleaning out ear canals, for rubdowns of stiff muscles and other necessary medical purposes. For weeks before the party the participants had experienced cramps, muscle aches, pains, and minor lacerations. In my case both of the ears had to be cleared and cleaned to be better able to hear those sneaky Jap submarines. Thus Doc was able to account for one totally empty small bottle of the clear medicinal liquid. Doc used simulated alcohol, somewhat like plain water for use on our aches and pains so as not to waste the good stuff whenever our small group signed up for sick call. Another permanent member of the party was the Cook, who was able to provide ample orange and grapefruit juice to water down the alcoholic content and to increase the volume of our adult beverage.

My contribution to the celebration was the hidden accommodations in the Sonar hold and Eddie, another permanent member, helped by signing up for those rubdowns attended the party as well. At the appointed time we went down into my hideaway and shut the hatch to spend a quiet time of friendship enjoying a grapefruit spiked punch containing one small bottle of grain alcohol. Having been shipmates from the time of the ships commissioning our lives had changed quite a bit since the day of our first party on New Year's Eve of 1943/1944 when we were heading across the Pacific to the war zone. We still had our sea stories to tell and each of us talked about what was happening back home with our families and those good times on liberty in Australia and back in the states. It wasn't a happy thought that we might have to spend still another year in this God forsaken place. We had finished another year at war and we all wondered how many years we would have to share together before it would end. We spent an hour or so enjoying our illegal pastime until the Kicka-Poo Juice was gone. We ended our nice quiet celebration by going back to our duties, none the worse for the small amount of alcohol in the large amount of grapefruit juice we had imbibed. Before ending the party we laid plans of future rubdowns and ear canal cleansings to save up again for another wild party down in the Sonar hold.

There were other party occasions when we were able to tap into the stores of warm beer. The beer supply was stored below deck in the forward hold next to the Sonar hold. Fortunately, the cook had the key, because other food supplies were stored there too. To ensure the inventory of the beer would not be changed we simply removed cans from a case in the pile then replaced the empty cans back in it after emptying the beer by turning the can over, puncturing it with my navy knife then to drain the beer into a jug for consumption at the party. The empty case was put on the bottom of the pile to keep the case inventory intact. The beer was cooled down by using the standard method of a CO_2 fire extinguisher. We often discussed the time that at some later date the evaporated suds would be a quite a shock to somebody opening an empty can. It was times like this at our parties that we could laugh at ourselves and the efforts we used to somehow put a different spin on an otherwise grim life in the war zone.

We were ordered into dry dock on the 30th of September 1944 to make repairs to our port side propeller shaft, which was experiencing excessive vibrations while underway. The repairs were to be done on the Aux. Floating Dry-dock #13, which was a sister ship to the AFD #14, the one we escorted from Panama across the Pacific towed by SS Vincennes the seagoing tug back in Dec. 1943. It had now been almost eighteen months since the PC-606 was launched, so we were overdue to have our barnacles scraped and get a fresh coat of navy blue-gray paint. It was a very messy operation to remove the rust and undercoat the hull with zinc chromate rust protection before the final Navy blue-gray finish coat was put on. My personal assignment during dry-dock was to refurbish the Sonar Head unit. Unfortunately, that didn't take very long and I had to join in with all hands in scraping, chipping and painting. One thing we were all grateful for was that we were not on a larger vessel to do this chore. After the completion of the dry dock operations, on Oct. 7th, we put into the supply docks on the island to fill our requisitions, top off water and fuel tanks in preparation for our return to sea duty.

Thanksgiving Day 1944 was spent safe in the harbor anchorage at Florida Island. We didn't even have Sonar duty at the harbor entrance. It was a lucky day, because Thanksgiving dinner was available for everyone at the Guadalcanal base mess hall, and our captain got base permission for the 606 crew to participate in the generous offering by the base command headquarters. Nothing against our cook Pops, but the opportunity for Navy base chow was hard to ignore. The Guadalcanal base had been turned into a fine base by the Seabees, and their mess hall was second to none. Early that afternoon we headed across Iron Bottom sound to Guadalcanal anchoring in the harbor at Lunga Roads with only a skeleton crew left on board. The rest of the hungry crew made their way to the chow hall to join the long lines, but the wait was well worth the array of food available to us. There was roast turkey with all the trimmings with all manner of vegetables and desserts. It was a sight you wouldn't believe. They even had real hard boiled eggs; all we ever saw in our mess hall were those scrambled dehydrated eggs along with the dehydrated potatoes and gritty powdered milk.

Needless to say we ate until we were stuffed. As always with the Navy there was a prominent sign above the serving line, which said "Take all you want, Eat all you take". We even got back into the line after a short walk around the area to let the main meal settle down in our stomachs. One thing that didn't change, no matter how great the chow was there were weevils in the bread. All types of flour had the ever present weevils from the tiny black adults to the white invisible grubs. The white grubs matched the bread when cooked, but it was a common sight for us to hold a slice of bread up to the light so we could pick out as many visible weevils as possible. They were as well cooked as the grubs and were 100% protein, but it did take some getting used to. The same was true for corn meal, farina and other grains. The only cure for weevils was to have enough freezer space to store the flour for a time. The weevils crawled to the surface of the flour and hid in the folds of the paper wrapping of the bags where they soon became "frozen" weevils. Then with a little care in opening the bag you had fewer weevils in the bread flour. We had very little freezer space on our ship, which made us a bunch of weevil pickers from way back. It was either pick out the weevils or skip the bread. A case of choosing "The lesser of two weevils", you could say. Excuse the pun!!

"The War Years", Serving aboard the USS Patrol Craft #606 From November - 1942 to April - 1946

Sydney Australia for R & R in December 1944

Our visit to Australia for Rest & relaxation after 18 months in the Pacific. View of Sydney harbor and bridge.

I went by ferryboat to this beach, and learned to do the Hokey Poky, in company with Rose, my personal Sydney tour guide.

Sydney Australia for R & R in December 1944

Mail call on return from Sydney brought mail from new friends in Australia.

The PC-606 moored to Woolamaloo dock in Sydney harbor.

With Christmas coming up very soon everyone had a chance to send one of the new V-mail letters to the folks back home to insure that our families would have at least one Christmas letter from their boys in overseas. The V-mail was a legal size form letter sent in lieu of a Christmas card. Each one had different graphics and space for a personal message. The V-mail was microfilmed at the base and the microfilm was sent to a Fleet Post Office in the United States where it was changed to a four by five letter all ready for delivery to the address of the recipient. I was able to mail two different ones home in 1944. Earlier in the year my good friend Eddie had been promoted from First Class to Chief Yoeman. As a Chief Petty officer he was able to check out a jeep at Lunga Point allowing us to tour the historic island of Guadalcanal. We saw Henderson field, which had been won from the Japanese at such a terrible price. We visited many of the former battle areas now being reclaimed by the green tropical jungle. We also had the opportunity to see the prisoner compound where Japanese prisoners were being held before their transfer to a permanent prisoner of war concentration camp. They all seemed so little and so relaxed. Some were playing basketball while others just lay around looking sullen. Hardly the fierce warriors I had pictured them to be, at least their war was over. At Bougainville there had been some of Imperial Japanese Marines who were much taller than most Japanese. At Nanking China these same animals had slaughtered an entire population. We considered them a very nasty, brutal bunch and I couldn't help being a bit angry seeing them treated so well after what they did to our own men when they were held in captivity by them at Bataan other places in Asia and Japan.

    Concerning the brutality of the Japanese soldier against their prisoners, after the war I read a book called Banzai. The book was about the life in the Japanese military and the indoctrination of the men who joined that army. The brutal treatment of a recruit was so bad that it is no wonder the front line soldier in the Japanese army treated his enemy so terribly. It was because of the normally brutal way he was treated by his own superiors. A sergeant could beat a private with a baseball bat for even a minor mistake at any time. The punishment policy of the Japanese on their own men was such that they didn't have any reason to be compassionate with their enemies. Here again it is not necessarily the attitude of the soldiers, but the indoctrination by their superiors that made them brutal soldiers and individuals, and the drastic difference between them and the American fighting men may have been a factor in winning the war.

After the tour it was back to the ship, and by days end the entire crew had their turn to head for the chow line to get their share of turkey and all the trimmings. Our officers came back from the Officers Club filled with good cheer and with the ships company back on board after our memorable turkey dinner we headed back to our anchorage where the Radioman went for the mail at the Post Office in Tulagi. After his return we had mail call, and many early Christmas packages were arriving containing Christmas cookies, mostly crumbled in shipment, but still edible. Some received candy all sticky and melted in the heat. A side item about that melted candy from home. Hershey Chocolate Company had invented a tropical chocolate bar, which became part of the "C" and "K" field rations. These were a type of food ration for troops in the field, and also used by the Navy during stormy weather or under combat situations when meals could not be prepared. The new chocolate wouldn't melt no matter how hot it got. You just had to keep chewing it into crumbs before swallowing it. Like chewing up chocolate sawdust might be a good way to describe it. However, it still had a chocolate taste and reminded you of what real chocolate was like in the chocolate bunnies at Easter time back home.

The best part of mail call was mainly the letters from friends, girlfriends and families back home. I wrote quite a few letters to people I had met in New York and the Bronx, in Key West, and from home in Pittsburgh, so I would usually get some mail. I did have my own girlfriend back home who wrote to me often. She was my little five foot blonde, Lois from Mt. Washington in Pittsburgh. I had given her a ring on my last trip home after a short acquaintance, but as we had become better acquainted through our letters my feelings about marriage were fading and it was becoming obvious to me that we had made a mistake. Regrettably, in late summer of 1944, I had to write and tell her as best I could about my own changed feelings in hopes she would understand. It was a "Dear Jane" letter you might say, to receive a "Dear John" letter meant the girl back home was in love with someone else, but in my case it was the boy telling the girl he has changed his mind. After sending that letter to Lois I began to receive poison pen letters from her older sister, who never did approve of me very much, so she started writing me nasty letters. She continued sending them for some time after the breakup, which I thought was very unpatriotic of her. I was sure she would be happy over my decision. Actually, her letters became a welcome diversion for me at mail call, until she couldn't think of anything else to say. Lois never did write me again, but after the war ended I did meet her accidentally in downtown Pittsburgh and we enjoyed some time together. She even gave me back the ring I had given her during the war. She had kept it on a chain around her neck as a reminder to pray for me, which was nice of her helping bring me home safe and sound with her prayers.

With the great Thanksgiving dinner becoming a nice memory we were back to normal, and soon underway as convoy escort for a troop attack transport AK-108 en-route to Eniwetok in the Marshall Islands, which was a round trip voyage of eleven days. On the return trip to base at Guadalcanal, on Dec. 6th 1944, a strong submarine contact was made when the Sonar picked up an echo with the strong indication of a submarine. As required we went to general quarters preparing for an attack, but Just before making a final run to drop a depth charge pattern a sperm whale surfaced ahead of the ship ending the attack. General quarters was secured and another whale went on living a while longer. Many whale contacts had all the qualities of a sub, and unless the whale surfaced, or turned in a sudden manner that a sub couldn't do an attack run was made. It was a relief to see the whale, but we Sonarmen took a lot of good natured ribbing from the crew about being "ping happy". On our return to Guadalcanal after the convoy to Eniwetok we received the best news since we came to the war zone. The PC-606 was ordered to proceed to the port of Sydney Australia for the purpose of 10 days rest and rehabilitation. We had been in the Pacific Theater of War since Dec. Of 1943, and after spending a full year in the battle zone a rest for all hands was definitely in order. Relaxation we didn't need, but the R&R was a welcome prospect. All refueling and preparation for the trip were completed for our scheduled departure date of December 21st 1944. We would spend the Christmas season in a large city instead of at sea.

Following orders we proceeded on our way independently with our engines turning at twelve knots cruising speed, spending six days at sea with no slow moving convoy to hinder us. The brightest constellation in the night sky of the South Pacific is the Southern Cross. A perfect cross formed by stars with the upright pointing north to south and guiding our way like a beacon. Our course took us through the Coral Sea where the first sea battle fought entirely by carriers and their aircraft gave America her first naval victory in the South Pacific, thwarting the planned invasion of Australia by Japanese forces. Heading toward the South Pole from the equator it was winter back home, but it was actually spring in the Southern Hemisphere and those cooler temperatures were a welcome change from the heat of the equator. We spent Christmas day at sea with the thought of the great Christmas present awaiting us in us in Sydney Australia. Even though we had the feeling we were leaving the war behind we still operated under blackout conditions until we reached Sydney harbor. However, we discovered soon after in peaceful Sydney harbor the war had followed us even there.

We entered Sydney harbor on December 26th 1944 and we were given dock space at berth #10 at Wooloomaloo dock in the Navy section of the harbor. As we slowly made our way into the harbor the beauty of its white houses with bright red tile roofs covering the hills right on down to the edge of the harbor, and the sight of large buildings and vehicles again meant civilization was nearby waiting for us to enjoy. The ship bustled with activity; those with immediate leave were getting ready to go ashore even before we tied up to the dockside. Others, like me who had chosen to take the first duty period would remain on board ship to stand watches, handle any emergencies and help to store food supplies. There had been lotteries held in each division to decide the days we would have duty and which days we would have liberty. My choice was duty for the first watch with the notion that the others would locate the great pub's and places to visit and thus save me a lot of time exploring on my own. This logical thinking on my part paid off, because the fantastic food was an important benefit to standing the watch. There was a standard delivery for the ship daily with a five gallon can of milk, fresh eggs, cheese, bacon, lettuce, tomatoes, steaks, hamburgers, and excuse me for drooling, need I go on?? Our cook remained on the first watch to handle food requisitions for all the food items not available to us up in the war zone. He did a fantastic job of providing us with the supplies to make up great meals for weeks and months to come in place of our normal dehydrated meals.

My on board duty assignment was as Petty Officer of the watch on the gangway with a seaman as my watch messenger. We were to spend four hours duty and four hours off during days of duty and the delicious aroma of frying bacon, hamburgers and rare steaks was continuous in the galley. We were able to eat our fill of all the food we had not seen since leaving the Canal Zone in December of 1943. After the first day of liberty a few crewmen returned to the ship to spend the night. We listened with much interest to their stories of what a great port Sydney was and made a note of the places to investigate when our turn came. Earlier I had mentioned how the war followed us to Sydney harbor. It was very early on the second day and Eddie was the watch Petty Officer when we were alerted by the duty Officer who ordered general quarters conditions due to an order to put to sea. Only about one fourth of the crew was on board, including some of those on leave, who had spent the night on board. The engines were started up our lines were quickly taken in and we were heading out to sea. Some of the deck crew was lashing down all supplies and boxes loose on the deck. There was a report of a sub being sighted by a freighter off the harbor entrance, which had triggered the alarm and we were the only available anti-sub vessel to answer the call. As Sonar operator I did pick up a possible contact after leaving the harbor entrance and we attempted several runs in spite of the heavy swells dropping several depth charges from the stern racks since the k-guns were not available for use. We followed the contact further into deeper water, but the seas soon became too rough and the sound waves were erratic so we never regained any contact. After a fruitless search the harbor master instructed us to return to port. On the way into the harbor we screened back and forth in case it had gotten by us somehow, but the echoes in the harbor were too numerous to be of any use. A Japanese sub this far from their base on New Guinea would be unusual, although convoy escorts to and from Australia and New Zealand were still in effect to protect the supply lines to the forward battle zone.

To hear the story at a local pub later when I had my turn ashore, a Jap sub had tried to sink a ship and a small Yank sub-chaser with only a handful of men on board was locked in a battle with it. I tried to set them straight on the story, but after all, we did have a contact of sorts and we did drop a few charges and we did have a small ship and crew so I guess a lot of the story was true except for that locked in battle part. During our stay in Sydney that story of the PC-606 was enough to break out the welcome mat for us. After returning port we returned to our enjoyable duties for the remainder of the day consuming extra portions of steak and eggs making up for our lost time. At noon we were relieved of duty and off we went to see what Sydney had to offer us sailors in search relaxation and fun. Eddie and I heard that many of the crew had rooms at a hotel in Kings Cross in the heart of the town. We hailed a cab and went there to check out Kings Cross for ourselves. The location was similar to Broadway and Forty Second Street in New York City where all the action was taking place. We checked into a room then went looking for our wandering shipmates. They had scattered for the day and the desk clerk thought they were headed for Bondi beach, Sydney's favorite water spot across the harbor by ferryboat. I went in one direction heading for Bondi beach and Eddie decided to go off in another direction. On the way to the ferry dock I located a pleasant looking pub to have some Aussie stout beer. An Aussie soldier saw the rating badge on my arm and asked if I was with that sub-chaser in the news. I told him I was and after an hour of free stout beer and lots of sea stories I had to leave while I was still able to walk. Only one of those potent Aussie stout beers was equal to several regulation 3.2% Navy beers.

"The War Years", Serving aboard the USS Patrol Craft #606
From November - 1942 to April - 1946

"The B-29 Super Fort Bomber"

The huge B-29 Bombers of General Le May's 590th Air Group, forced the Japanese War Lords to accept total surrender on the USS Missouri.

The Mariana Islands, and the B-29 Bomber bases.

Guam in the Marianas Islands. The B-29 bombers runway ended at the end of the cliff.

View of the cliff at the end of the B-29 runway. Watching them takeoff with a full Bomb load was something to see, as we patrolled offshore.

Map of the Mariana Isl. The dotted line shows our area of convoy and Air Sea Rescue duties.

After boarding the ferry I explored its double decks and picked a spot up by the bow to better enjoy the scenic trip to the beach. The boat filled up quickly and soon we were on our way across the harbor. After a while I heard loud laughter and singing from the main deck area, so I went down to check it out. The sight in the open area of the deck was so unusual I still have a vivid memory of it today. As I recall it there were many types of people gathered around, men and women civilians, American and Australian military, young and old they all formed a large circle. They were singing and doing a dance called the Hokey Pokey, which goes like this; you put your right hand into the circle then out, then your left, then your feet, backside, head, etc. all the while singing a simple little song called, doing the Hokey Pokey. The dance began in Australia and came to America with the returning troops after the war was over, along with another Australian song called, Waltzing Matilda. I was standing by the rail just watching the fun when I was suddenly pulled into the circle by one very cute Aussie Sheila, which is the name for a girl in Aussie slang. Her name was Rosie and she had reddish hair and a personality to match. From then on she took over the job of educating me in how to do the Hokey Pokey. She also became my regular tour guide while I was on leave in Sydney. She was on her way to Bondi beach for a swim and invited me along. Personally, I had no desire to go swimming, in fact; I would rather get as far away from the water as possible. At the beach we found a shady spot for me while Rosie had her swim and I just watched. When I first came ashore I had wondered if I would meet someone just like her. We talked a lot getting to know all about each other and that day she was on her way to visit her family in a nearby residential area north of the Sydney. After she had enough of the swimming she invited me to go along to meet them. I had made only a very halfhearted effort to locate my shipmates who might be at the beach and now I really had no interest in finding any of them for a while, because Rosie was a lot more interesting. She worked as a housekeeper for a U.S. Air force Officer and his Aussie wife, and on her time off she made periodic visits to her home to see her close family.

Here I was after only just a few hours ashore in the company of a nice attractive young lady, and on my way to visit her folks. Those Aussie girls were real fast workers. Actually, it was a great opportunity to observe a bit of Australian home life and I was very interested in the prospect, but I really wasn't prepared for the wonderful treatment they gave me or the welcome I received. Americans were considered very special to the Australian people. An invasion had been almost certain, and the Japanese were preparing their assault forces at the time of the great American Naval victory in the Coral Sea. American and Aussie forces were beating back the Japanese in New Guinea and in the Solomon Islands saving Australians from a destructive war in their homeland. You would have thought a celebrity had come to town as friends and neighbors of her family dropped in to share a beer and listen to my stories about the progress of the war and tales of life in America. It was the dream of most Australian girls to marry a Yank and go to the United States with its imagined streets of gold that was the belief of many parents and relatives as well. Rosie had let me know she had a child and I got to meet her infant son there at her home. He was the pride of her life and the child of her American intended husband. They had applied for marriage permission from the military, but he had been transferred out before the permission came through. He had left for active duty suddenly and his letters had stopped soon after that, possibly due to military secrecy. Since then the Air Force Officer she worked for had been trying to locate the father, and since her son was considered to be the dependent of a service man she could go to the United States as soon as ship transportation became available.

    I was the first American Rosie had gone out with since her future husband had left and she wasn't interested in romantic entanglements, which suited me just fine. My visit with the folks lasted quite late, well past the time to catch the last bus back to Sydney, so some kind family member gave up their bed for the night and after a few more hours of great conversation we all turned in. As I lay there in a comfortable Australian bed I reflected on the day's events. I felt very much at home somehow and it was a good day to tuck away among my other fond memories for later on during the down times of the war zone. Rosie's red hair had its Irish origins going back to the deportation days when the nasty British courts exiled many Irish and English people to servitude in Australia for trivial crimes. They served as indentured servants of the upper class business men, cattle ranchers, and farmers and became the early settlers of the land down under. The following morning I awoke to the smell of steak in the air. The Australian breakfast of choice consisted of steak and eggs and not a tiny cube steak, but a thick sirloin or a T-bone steak with four fried eggs. No grits or spuds just steak, eggs, toast and a hot cup of black tea. Rosie's mom made me most welcome and although she didn't talk much she asked me what I wanted quite often. She did say how glad she was that I met Rosie, because she was pleased to see her daughter laughing once again. Apparently her situation had put her through a depressed period in her life; as well it could for any girl. That afternoon Rosie had to be back at her employers home where she worked and we had to leave for Sydney. We said our good-bye to all the folks and I thanked them for their wonderful hospitality. On the bus we traveled a scenic route riding through residential areas to the city limits then we changed to a cab for the rest of the way to the home of the Air Force Major.

Gas rationing was in effect in the country and some taxicabs ran on steam with a glowing hot charcoal fire burning in a trunk firebox while others used compressed gas with a tank on the roof and it was quite strange to see cars with a gas bag on top. Rosie introduced me to the employer she worked for and we spent some time getting acquainted. The Major wanted to know all about the encounter of the PC-606 and the sub incident, which had been a topic of conversation at his headquarters. Later on as he gave me a ride to my hotel in Kings Cross, he let me know the facts about Rosie and he just didn't want to see her hurt. I assured him all was well and Rosie had a mind of her own. Anyway, she was firm in her plans to be reunited with her soldier boy and go to America with her infant son. The last thing on my mind was any romantic relationship with a girl in a war that seemed to go on endlessly, and under the circumstances I couldn't see what the future had in store for me anyway. Rosie and I enjoyed our present companionship to suit our situation. On the face of it I guess she should not have been going out with me or any other man while engaged to marry, but I was enjoying my time with her. Later on when I was back in the war zone I wrote home to Dad telling him that if a girl with reddish hair and a baby stopped by for a visit that she was just a friend. Rosie knew all about me and my family and we had each other's home addresses, so if she ever did come to visit in Pittsburgh she would at least know someone there.

Back at kings Cross, I eventually caught up with Eddie and many of the crew. Based on their activities and the stories they told me later there was one continuous party going on. There were even local bootleggers who delivered watered down whiskey, and there were lots of Australian gals who always seemed to know where the next party was to take place. I joined in on a few of those parties meeting other Aussie girls and having a good time in the hotel ballroom, where you could dance to the popular American songs. During my days on liberty I enjoyed the time I spent with Rosie touring Sydney the most. We went to English style pubs and night clubs and visited points of interest around the city when she had time off during the day. At times we went out in a group with Ed and some of the others, but most often it was Rosie who planned what to do and where to go and I just followed along. It was a fine recipe for enjoying my leave and I almost forgot about the war we would have to return to all too soon. The Christmas season was still in effect and most of the time while on leave the city of Sydney was in a party mood. We enjoyed many of the activities provided by different local organizations. The time went by all too swiftly, but we managed to enjoy the days we had on leave. We had to serve our three days of duty on board the ship enjoying the good food and comparing notes to plan our next tour ashore.

Australians seemed to have a holiday every other day, but we were still members of the U.S. Navy and each day we were required to check in either by phone or in person at the Navy dock station in case of any emergency. I had three days duty to serve with the remainder to spend ashore. On my last 24 hours of watch duty with my messenger on the gangway the galley still well supplied and available. Those bacon, lettuce and tomato sandwiches were just waiting to be consumed along with the steak and egg breakfast. My last watch looked like a breeze with very little activity except for logging men in and out, but one small problem occurred when the Captain came aboard during my watch. He was accompanied by a young woman he had met on shore and was obviously in a party mood. He proceeded to give the young lady a grand tour of the ship and at the end of his tour he used the messenger of the watch to help him demonstrate the use of weapons and depth charges. He decided to show his date how to simulate a depth charge attack. Instructing the seaman to stand by the depth charge rack he gave him orders to set the charges for three fathoms. The seaman went through all the motions of preparation and said "charges ready sir", the captain said "roll one", and the seaman pretended to drop the ash can. The Captain told him; "I gave you an order to roll one". The seaman said "Captain, you don't mean that we are at the dock". The messenger came back and told me what happened. As the Captain was leaving the ship a bit later he told me to put the man on restriction for insubordination and for refusal to obey a direct order. Deciding he would not remember anything about it considering his condition and his strange actions I ignored his order to restrict the seaman, but I decided to notify the deck officer as to what happened for the record. I found out later on that when the Captain was asked about the incident the next morning he was relieved that I had had not obeyed such an order. Maybe if the seaman had done as he was told, we might have had a nice extra-long stay in wonderful Sydney for repairs.

When my last day of leave arrived I had been invited to the home of Rosie's employer for dinner and a farewell get together. The Major and his wife were great people and they made my last night in Sydney very memorable by giving me a good chance to say goodbye to my Sydney tour guide Rosie. I spent the rest of the day back at Kings Cross paying my bills and spending the rest of the time in the ball room dancing with some of the girls I had met and having a few last drinks with my shipmates. That night it was back to the ship with our rest and relaxation accomplished. Early the next morning, as with all good things, the time came to depart. Our last day in port was hectic; supplies kept coming aboard as the cook filled in every vacant space with hard to get canned goods of all sorts. We would eat well for a few months at least. New girl friends came down to the dock for last minute good-byes and lots of tearful hugs were exchanged. As for Rosie and me, we had said all our last good-bye the day before after dinner at the Majors home. I had given her a letter I wrote while on watch for her to read later on, nothing romantic just an honest expression of thanks for making my stay in Sydney better than I had imagined. Looking back on our stay, I guess it was a good thing we didn't stay in Sydney much longer, because some of the crew were making serious promises to new sweethearts and wedding requests might be coming next. By midafternoon Jan. 14th 1945 the Sydney Bridge was passing astern and the open sea was ahead and my last look at Sydney was one of regret, but not sadness we had gone there for rest and rehabilitation with good results. The rest I had found was minimal, but I did feel quite rehabilitated.

We had our orders to return to our base at Purvis Bay, Florida Island in the Solomon's 1,700 miles to the north. Our average speed was twelve knots during a voyage of six days, from January 14th to the 19th. New Zealand was a short trip from Sydney and was the R&R base for the Marine Corps. A visit to Auckland was said to be memorable with the peaks of seven extinct volcanoes making up the wide horizon. New Zealand is about the size of California, uncrowded, unpolluted and with an ideal climate. The summer in the southern hemisphere lasts from December to February and the winter is from June to August. Maybe a future R&R visit would be great at Auckland, although I hoped the war wouldn't last that long. All departments began sharpening skills to work out the leisure kinks caused by R&R in order to regain our wartime footing. It was as if those days in Sydney had happened in a dream and we were all navy again.

Those stories of Sydney were told and retold on the trip back to base. Some stories, when told separately by crewmen who had been to the same party sounded as different as day and night, stretched a bit in the telling. Arriving at Purvis Bay letters had piled up in the mail bin with Australian addresses including a few for me. I wrote to Rosie until July of 1945 when the Air Force Major had written to me with the news that she was heading stateside for a reunion with her soldier boy who was O.K., and I was glad she now had her family intact. We had made life a little happier for one another during a difficult time in both our lives. Back at our bay anchorage the ships Officer complement had undergone several changes. The first was the departure of our Captain, Lt. Jg. O. C. Spencer on Jan.16th, who was detached to Fleet hospital #108 on Guadalcanal for observation and treatment and transport back to the states. It could be that his actions in Sydney or other actions while Captain of the ship may have had something to do with his transfer. Whatever the reason he was like all of us, serving his country honorably as was expected of him. Lt. Jg. J. E. Searight was now our new captain serving until June 27th 1945 in the Marianas. The ships log of the time indicated that on Jan. 19th 1945, Ensign H. N. Swanson reported on board for duty to fill in the compliment of five Officers.

"The War Years", Serving aboard the USS Patrol Craft #606
From November - 1942 to April - 1946

Iwo Jima in the Japanese Volcano Islands

View on the left of Mount Surabachi, site of the famous flag raising, where 7,000 marines died in the five week battle to secure the island. The cemetery at the base of the Mountain held most of the casualties. Over 20,000 Jap defenders also died in the battle. Right photo, offshore view of the eight mile long volcanic island. It was captured to have a base for fighters, to protect the B-29's to Japan and return, also a base for disabled bombers to land, saving lives and planes.

The PC-606 on Air Sea Rescue for B-29's offshore from Tanapag harbor, Saipan in the Mariana Islands.

After the long voyages to and from Sydney we were in need of an engine repair overhaul and to do so we put into the Carter City repair dock. We were there from Jan. 19th through Jan. 26th for a major engine overhaul by the black gang of the engine room. Of all the 606 crew these men deserve special recognition for the work they had to do under adverse conditions. Spending our days and months right on the equator was bad enough, but these men performed their duty down in the extreme heat of the engine room. Our lives depended on our speed and they were the ones who kept the ship's engines running. Then too, during any general quarters alert, hatches were closed to the engine room keeping them below decks at their posts. In those instances when a PC went down due to enemy action the black gang was likely to go with it, and personally I had the greatest admiration for them. Once our repairs had been completed we put to sea for engine operational tests then it was back with the fleet. We operated in company with many PC's, SC's, and other vessels going thorough gun firing exercises to improve anti-aircraft and surface firing abilities of the gun crew. During that time scuttlebutt had it that the brass knew some of us would be heading for the Marianas Islands closer to Japan very soon.

Widening the area of submarine screening of the sector around the harbors of the Solomon's was ongoing. PC-606 in company with PC-1228, PC-597 & PC-1589 among others, would relieve one another as screening commander remaining moored to the Sonar Buoy station. From there the other ships were dispatched to investigate any Sonar contacts or unknown radar contacts. Occasionally they would check on any floating debris or loose mines destroying them as hindrance to navigation with their deck guns. There was always something happening to give a little spice to an otherwise boring chase from one point to another. There was the live "man overboard" drill when a young signalman striker fell from the starboard signal bridge. The ship went to man overboard conditions while the bridge executed the standard Williamson Turn procedure in order to recover the soaked crewman. The previous "man overboard" drill was the result of having attractive nurses on board that distracted one of the gunners causing him to hit the drink. The signalman involved in our man overboard drill, told me how he made contact with the PC-606 after receiving orders to report to Florida Island. He told of traveling from one island to another in a native boat wearing a coolie hat in case they were checked out by any Japanese aircraft making his arrival by canoe a first for anyone on the ship. When we were anchored in the harbor at Purvis Bay or at the dock the local natives paddled their canoes from ship to ship selling fresh fruit, pineapples and other exotic fruit, including a tarantula spider one time in the bananas, One other sale item was the native made grass skirts not at all like the Seabee fakes. They would sell or trade for cloth or cigarettes rather than money. These were not like the natives of Bora Bora they had the look of people who had suffered much. The Japs were not friendly to their conquered subjects and often used them as slave labor or worse. Life under normal island conditions had to be difficult for them judging from the look of those natives we saw. We did enjoy the fresh fruit though and the cook would take up a collection to buy in a supply of fruit for the mess hall when available.

After several weeks of in port screening duty we were assigned to escort the USS AK-75 attack transport on its voyage from Guadalcanal to Emerau Island of the St. Mathias chain of islands some distance to the west of our base. On our long voyage we ran continuous screening operations at sea and during its scheduled stops, and while in port protecting the AK-75 during its loading and unloading operations. Our first port was at Green Island screening the south channel during port operations. We remained until March 24th 1945. The only major activity came on March 21st when a solid screening Sonar contact was made. General quarters were initiated and an immediate attack on the Sonar contact was made dropping a spread of six depth charges. Attempts to regain the contact failed the contact lost and we secured from general quarters. Our voyage with AK-75, took us from Green Island to the next port of call Emerau Island. While there we screened off Cape Ballin in Hamburg bay. After a month long assignment escorting AK-75 we were released to return independently to Tulagi. Arriving back at our anchorage three days later on April 10th 1945 we put into Renard sound in the Russell Islands for minor repairs at a small craft repair barge. When repairs and trial runs were completed we topped off fuel and water and filled food supplies and requisitions in preparation for our next voyage. At that time we observed a mock invasion exercise going on near the beaches of Vella la Vella Island just north of Florida Island. At the time we were not aware of the future invasion target, but a large number of landing craft and army personnel took part in the exercise.

. . . .

Living on the smallest all metal ship in the Navy only 173 feet in length and 25 feet amidships living in a compartment which is home for 26 other sailors must never have been a serious consideration by the builders of the ship, and in addition we had the heat of the tropics to deal with. Having exhaust fans to keep the hot air moving was fine at night with the deck hatch open, but in the daytime if you had a night watch the tropical heat made sleeping next to impossible during the day. A damp towel over your head helped for a bit until it dried out on your hot temple. Other bunk areas were also crowded and uncomfortable. Somehow fights were minimal by the crew in spite of the poor living conditions. My own conclusion is that the very nature of our mutual daily exposure to ever present danger and hardship had a tendency to suppress petty differences, because of our constant dependence on one another. We were not like the movies, where crews were always getting into fights. The record aboard ship of Captain's Mast disciplinary action indicated that minor transgressions by crew members were at a minimum. only the crime of being Absent without leave, was the most common crew violation in the record for some unknown reason.

In April 1945 we received our orders for a drastic change in our wartime duties. We were to leave our tropical paradise in the Solomon's and to proceed to Guam in the Marianas Islands where we would be much closer to the Jap Home Islands. The Solomon's Island war action continued until wars end and the battle for the Japanese homeland was just beginning. The Marianas Islands were the first Japanese territories to be captured in the war. By July 1944 they were being used by our huge B-29 bombers to strike at the heartland of Japan. From our new base on Saipan at Tanapag harbor we would be stationed within 1500 miles of the Japanese Empire itself. 600 miles from its nearest possession was the island of Iwo Jima, in the Volcano Islands. Iwo was a small almost barren island covered with volcanic ash from its volcano Mt. Surabachi. Besides the welcome orders to leave the Solomon Islands we enjoyed another fine improvement in our living conditions. Since we were now leaving our Tulagi base one of the officers made a great trade to provide us with a washing machine and a movie projector as well. Somehow during our two year tour in the Solomon's the ships

Officers had acquired their own personal shore transportation, which was a total surprise to the crew. And since we wouldn't be coming back to Guadalcanal a trade was made with a base officer and we no longer had to hand wash clothes. With the projector we could now show movies in port when blackout conditions would permit. The Officer Corps gained a large measure of gratitude because of their trading ability. Also we were able to be a much cleaner crew due to our new second hand washing machine.

By May 11th 1945 the ship was in readiness for the long voyage to Guam. We were assigned for escort duty with convoy Task Unit 11.1, consisting of three Landing Ship Tank invasion vessels, the LST's #624, #923, & #1026, bound for the Army base on Guam in the Marianas. We were to travel in company with escorts PC-461 & PC-585 by way of Tarawa in the Gilberts. After an uneventful voyage we arrived at Tarawa on 5/17/1945 then on to Eniwetok atoll in the Marshalls. When we arrived at Eniwetok my two year companionship with Eddie came to an end. Now a Chief Yoeman, Eddie was detached from the PC-606 for duty in the United States. I was happy for him, but we had been almost like brothers since May 1943 enduring danger and hardship and many good times together for over two years. There was still a long war ahead as far as we knew then and I would sure miss him. When the Navy says it's time to go, off you go with seabag, hammock & mattress on your shoulder to your new duty assignment. As I Look back on the length of the war, when it did come to a final end on Sept. 5th 1945, I was rotated back to the states for discharge myself just four months after Eddie. I left the ship on Sept.19th 1945 after 25 months aboard the PC-606. Three days after my 23rd birthday on the 16th of September.

Prior to the invasion of the Marianas Islands our 7th fleet had surprised the main Jap fleet in what became known as the Marianas turkey shoot. Over 500 Japanese planes were downed; three aircraft carriers and numerous support vessels were sunk. Only one American was lost in combat due to the quick rescue of the downed pilots by Navy ships. Then in June and July 1944 the Army's 27th Division fought their way ashore on Guam and Saipan after days of heavy naval bombardment and air attacks. Future Pres. G.W. Busch was a fighter pilot on air support at Guam and was shot down during the battle. Saipan was only 85 square miles in area, but it was ideal for the huge B-29 Superforts which would bring the war to the Japanese home islands. The largest Japanese suicide, "Banzai", charge during the war took place on Saipan when 3,000 Japanese troops made an attack on American positions in suicidal waves. American soldiers on the line said the enemy bodies were piled so high the Jap troops coming in behind them could not advance. By July 1944 all of the Marianas Islands, Saipan, Tinian, and Guam, were in American hands. In 1944 the first B-29's hit Tokyo beginning around the clock bombing of the enemy home islands. The airstrips had been under construction before the battle for Marianas ended. Runways had to be 1 1/2 miles long and double the normal airstrip thickness to support the heavy B-29 super fortresses. By May 1945 when we arrived at Tanapag harbor it was being converted into a forward supply base with an airfield complex to serve the bombing effort. The 509th B-29 bomber group under General Curtis Le May was in full operation by then and our duty assignment as part of the Ninth Fleet Service Squadron Two was on Air/Sea rescue and submarine screening of Saipan's Tanapag harbor and the area around Tinian, sister island of Saipan. We were also called upon for convoy duty Iwo Jima in the Volcano Islands and to Guam Island to the south. We were also available for convoys to Okinawa south of Japan, but were never on convoy to that very dangerous place for Navy ships. American losses of men and ships were even greater there than the losses sustained at Pearl Harbor.

By the time of our first convoy to Iwo Jima the battle for Iwo had ended. The battle had begun on Feb 19th 1945 and continued through March 16th and the signs of war's destruction were everywhere. Our small convoy had one troop ship with several supply ships and as escorts there was one "DE", Destroyer Escort and another Patrol Craft. Iwo was the largest of the Volcano group of islands and was only 750 miles from downtown Tokyo, Japan. It was the first Japanese territory taken in the war so far and the Jap defenders were ordered to fight to the end and 20,000 of them died in the five week offensive. The terrain and hidden enemy positions made it one of the worst invasion conditions faced by the Marines. The Marine's had suffered a higher average casualty rate than on D-day in France and

7,000 Americans died in the five weeks campaign. A thick covering of fine volcanic ash and grit covered ground of the island. Smoke that smelled like rotten eggs rose from fissures in the ground in places.

At one end of the eight mile long island was Mt. Surabachi, a dormant volcano which the Japs had honeycombed with tunnels and bunkers. It was here that the flag was raised on the Surabachi summit on Feb. 23rd 1945. The sight of the American flag waving on the top of Surabachi gave the men pinned down on the beaches added incentive to win the battle, a famous statue of the event is now in the WW II Memorial in Washington. After the battle ended and the island was well secured the Fifth Marine Division casualties were buried in a Memorial cemetery at the base of Mt. Surabachi where so many of them gave their lives. The sight of the row upon row of white crosses was testimony to the cost of taking that tiny bit of volcanic land so crucial to winning the war against Japan. At the time our convoy was offshore at Iwo Jima, even though the battle was over, I was able to watch some young Marine replacements climb down the cargo nets into the Higgins assault boats to take them ashore and I was grateful that my Dad insisted I join the Navy. Victory at Iwo Jima was a costly victory, but necessary to provide an air base between Japan and the main bases in the Marianas allowing disabled B-29's returning from bombing runs to Japan to make emergency landings. Also it was now possible for Air Force fighters to fly cover for the B-29's all the way to their Japanese targets and return saving many planes and crews. As months passed we made numerous trips back and forth to Iwo Jima on convoy runs since Japanese submarines were still considered a menace as we came nearer to the home islands. A book about the sinking of the cruiser Indianapolis by the largest submarine ever built by the Japanese was prowling the waters off the harbors of Saipan and Guam. The book tells how it followed the cruiser and attacked it after it left the harbor in the Philippines. The cruiser Indianapolis was sunk with the greatest loss of life for any naval engagement in history. The sub was operating in the Marianas where we were on duty protecting the harbor from sub attack. I didn't know this until years later and it gave me the shivers to think about meeting up with that monster sub.

"The War Years", Serving aboard the USS Patrol Craft #606 From November - 1942 to April - 1946

The July 1945 Typhoon almost ended the war for the 606

An LST, like the one we were escorting to Iwo Jima, when we were caught in a typhoon.

The Cruiser Pittsburgh, which broke in two during the same storm, further to the south.

On June 8th 1945, VE-Day, the Axis powers surrendered in Europe, and on August 10th 1945 the Japanese surrendered. The official end to the Pacific war came on September 2nd 1945, on board the battleship, USS Missouri.

Our new base on Saipan was much different than the primitive life we lived in the Solomon Islands at Florida Island. Not that it was just like back home, but the shore base did have better facilities, including an army post exchange. It was actually a combination store and a recreation hall area with ping pong and pool tables and seating tables to enjoy a beer or a coke on shore liberty. We had greater opportunity to go exploring on the island to see how the Japanese lived and to visit Shinto shrines and invasion sites where shattered Jap bunkers still stood. We were much further away from the equator now and it was more semi-tropical and comfortable weather-wise. It also meant we had to look more like regulation Navy instead of a looking like a group of Barbary pirates. We were able to visit the bomber base to see those giant B-29's up close. They were so huge it was a wonder they could get off the ground much less fly with the bomb load they would normally carry. They had a list posted in the recreation hall where volunteers could place their names to go on a bombing raid over Tokyo. The basic idea of the list was to allow mechanics and bomber support personnel the opportunity to participate in the squadron's job of bringing Japan to its knees. A number of our crew put their names on the list to take a trip including yours truly. There were lots of names ahead of mine and fortunately before my turn came up the brass stopped the practice due to the fact that so many tourists were being lost when a bomber went down. Why would I endanger my life by going along on such a trip? All I can say is that it seemed like a good idea at the time. At that age one can do some pretty dumb things!!

When the B-29 's were taking off for Tokyo or returning from a mission we were on air/sea rescue duty offshore with a sector assigned for us to cover the rescue of downed bomber crews. Air/sea rescue had sectors with names like Nursemaid, Housemaid, Parlormaid and Chambermaid. As if we were on a cleanup detail. Our job was to screen in these sectors for days at a time putting into port at Tanapag harbor to refuel and prepare to go out again. The routine was broken up on occasion with a convoy assignment to Iwo Jima, or a short one to Guam. Those trips to Iwo were of three or four day's duration depending on convoy speed. At times things got a little more exciting as on June 20th when we went to general quarters to participate in a joint air and sea search to investigate a surfaced submarine report. The target was determined to be an allied submarine out of its safe zone and under escort into port. The submarine search was secured and we returned to screening in our sector. We had regular news reports on the progress of the war on all fronts and one of them concerned one greatest naval battles of the Pacific war. It was also the last battle for the main Japanese fleet in the Suragao Straights just north of the Philippine's. General MacArthur's invasion force was moving against the Japanese conquerors at Leyte and a Jap fleet led by one of the greatest battleship ever built, the Yamamoto, was coming south to destroy the invasion force.

The Leyte invasion site was protected by a small American Naval force consisting of three converted Aircraft Carriers and a small number of Destroyers, Destroyer Escorts and a squadron of Patrol Torpedo Boats. The Yamamoto was equipped with 18 inch guns which had a range of 25 miles. It could wipe out any of the naval force without even getting close, but the carrier planes and heroic Destroyer Commanders and PT's attacked again and again forcing the superior Jap Naval force to turn back. The Americans suffered severe losses, but inflicted such damage on the Japanese ships that they believed they were being attacked by the main U.S. Fleet of Admiral Bull Halsey. It was the last confrontation with the Jap fleet until the invasion of the island of Okinawa. Had the Jap fleet reached the invasion force at Leyte they would have set the end of the war back for years. The bravery of the PT's, Tin Can Destroyers and their crews is recorded in naval history as the greatest David and Goliath naval battle of the war. When we heard the news of the battle our prayers of thanksgiving were many. The invasion of the Philippines would have been doomed with terrible losses and it would have been many more years of conflict ahead to defeat the Japanese.

The Saipan airstrip ended at a sheer cliff and the planes seemed to just drop off the cliff as they reached the end of the runway then to pull up after a heart-stopping drop toward the water below. During the battle for the island Japanese soldiers as well as the civilians leaped to their deaths from these same cliffs. The local people would rather die than to be captured, believing the Japanese propaganda about American brutality. When taking off for a raid the big bombers followed each other down the runway continuously one behind the other until the sky was filled with them. They came from the air strips at Saipan and Guam joining together for the mass raids over the Japanese home islands. On the return trip the toll was high when Jap fighters and anti-aircraft guns caused a lot of damage to surviving planes. As they would pass over us on their return landing approach you could see blue sky through holes in the wings and openings were visible in the sides of their fuselage as well. Some had engines with propellers feathered, but were still able to fly while others ditched offshore unable to land. That's where our Air/Sea patrol group came into service going out to bring in survivors and the bodies of casualties. There were grave registration personnel on board to handle personal identification of those killed in action. Later on there were times when bodies would surface from sunken planes and we had to hold burial at sea. This was done by using heavy netting weighted down with rounds from our deck gun to carry the bodies into the depths. Identification of the bodies and getting finger prints was a somber duty, but a necessary one.

During return flights we were always a welcome sight to any crash survivors waiting for rescue. Bomber losses remained high until Iwo Jima was taken and secured. After that Fighter escort planes were able to fly cover most of the way to Japan and return. Crippled bombers now had a place to land or to ditch with rescue help nearby. There were Air/Sea rescue ships on patrol at Iwo Jima at all times and our ship served at both locations. On the occasions when we went ashore on the island of Iwo Jima during our Air/Sea patrol assignment offshore we had obtained use of an army truck to pick up supplies and were able do some exploring. As we visited the Fifth Marine cemetery at the base of Mt. Surabachi I recalled an earlier visit ashore when burial details were still finding and burying the fallen, but now all recovery was complete. Looking at the stark white Crosses and Stars of David in what seemed like an unending row upon row of white you felt compelled to stop and offer a fervent prayer for those brave men who had made the final sacrifice for their country and saving all mankind for that matter. Praying also, in gratitude that you have survived the conflict so far. We climbed to the top of the volcano to visit the site where the famous flag raising took place on Feb. 23rd when the Marines reached the top of the lava mountain. The Japanese had turned Surabachi into a fortress of bunkers and tunnels. Smoke still rose from fissures down inside the volcano cone and the smell of sulfur, much like the smell of rotten eggs, was overwhelming. There was very little in the way of vegetation and the ash covered everything. To even walk in the ashes was a problem and the cinder like ashes got into our low cut navy shoes making walking difficult and painful. It was a hellish place indeed for those Marines who fought and died on that miserable little island under such conditions, and I have the greatest admiration for them all. There was a cartoon in the stars & stripes military newspaper which showed a Marine who had died on Iwo standing at heaven's gate with St. Peter telling him to come on in he had already served time in hell. Amen to that!

As we patrolled off Iwo Jima on submarine screening duty on May 8th 1945 the news came over the army radio station that the war in the European Theater was over. They called it "VE" day a term for Victory in Europe. We also heard the news reports from radio Guam about the wild celebrations going on all over America and the plans to shift all of our military might to the Pacific in what was called Operation Olympic the plan for the invasion of Japan itself. The news gave us greater hope that now it would be our war that would end soon as well. We really didn't do a lot of celebrating over VE day, but it gave us the great feeling that now all efforts would be turned to the Pacific war. Okinawa was the southernmost island of Japan proper and had been invaded in April 1945 with the battle still underway. The American invasion fleet was under attack by suicidal Kamikaze planes, or the "Divine Wind" in Japanese! The planes were actually flying bombs manned by young men and teenagers who had been trained only how to take off and fly into American capital ships. They were committed to die for their Emperor who they considered to be a god. In the final count of the Navy's losses over 300 American ships had been hit and 36 were sunk with 3,000 navy casualties. The Kamikaze's had caused a greater loss than that suffered at Pearl Harbor. By the 21st of June Okinawa fell to American forces and the battle for Okinawa turned out to be the last land battle of WW II and one of the costliest naval engagements along with Pearl Harbor.

....

It had taken from December 1941 until August 1945 to get into position for the full invasion of the Japanese home islands and now the worst of the Pacific war was yet to come. Plans were to invade and capture a nation where every man woman and child had been trained mentally and physically to defend it to the death. The invasion plan was called Operation Olympic and the time of invasion was planned for November 1946, according to the war archives. That was in the future the war was still on and now we had greater opportunity to go on liberty and explore Saipan. On our first liberty ashore we roamed along the beaches and along U.S. Hwy #1, which was a two lane black top road between Tanapag and the Air Base. As we walked along the beaches we could see high up on the dunes the thick concrete bunkers which were strong evidence of the Japanese resistance to the invasion. In one location there were Shinto shrines in open air pavilions with a symbolic set of posts with a bowed top cross piece over it. Japanese worship ceremonies, which were a form of ancestor worship called Shinto-ism, took place here, Clumps of sugar cane grew wild along the roadway and in the fields. I had never chewed a sugarcane stalk before and it was sweet and tasty. The most surprising find ashore was a common nuisance everywhere; it was the great abundance of large snails that had been brought by the Japanese as a table delicacy called Escargot, the French name for a cooked snail in its shell. In spring the breeding snails were so numerous that the road became as slippery as ice when jeep and truck traffic ran over them and walking on them was no fun either. They had no natural enemies on the island except for those who liked to eat them, so they just multiplied to become a major problem over time.

 Further up along the shoreline was a rusting, beached Japanese freighter, which had been taken over for living quarters and storage by a squadron of PBY's. Those Flying Boats also assisted in Air/Sea rescue looking for survivors of downed aircraft out beyond our patrol sector limits. They were able to set down on the water to pick up and return survivors to base. On our exploration jaunts we were also warned not to stray too far inland from the base area, because there were still stray Jap soldiers known to be hiding up in the hills, and even though they were regularly hunted and caught our white navy hats made too good a target for a Jap sniper. There was an All Faiths memorial chapel on Saipan, so we were again able to attend mass on the Sundays when our ship was in port. The church was used by all religious groups both Christian and Jewish services. Attendance was always high; atheists were pretty much a rarity in the war zone. Most men were not ashamed or shy about the need for prayer and Divine guidance.

• •

The Pacific was subject to Typhoons, those cyclonic storms like the Hurricane of the Atlantic which we experienced while on Atlantic convoy early in the war. There was little warning when one hit our single ship convoy in mid-July of 1945 until the wind and seas grew in power creating our worst experience in the war. We had been assigned to escort LST #646 a Landing Ship Tank, which was carrying replacements for the campaign on Okinawa 1500 miles to the northwest of Saipan. Our voyage was by way of Iwo Jima where the convoy would be escorted by other escort ships to Okinawa itself. A voyage to Iwo Jima was just a breeze normally; little did we know what nature had in store for us on this trip. As we set out from Saipan the seas were getting a bit rougher than normal, but there was no radio report about a pending typhoon. As the day wore on the swells became higher and the winds increased to gale force with the waves becoming so much higher and deeper we had difficulty keeping in contact even by radio with our convoy. After dark we couldn't use the signal lights due to blackout conditions so all that night and most of the next day we were out of contact with our convoy vessel the LST #646. The seas had become so high that as we rode to the crest they were down in the troughs and for quite a good while we each thought other had been lost.

    I couldn't help having a great deal of sympathy for those poor soldiers on that flat bottomed LST they must have all been seasick throughout the voyage. Later we learned that the concern aboard the LST was for our tiny 173 foot ship being tossed around like a cork, and what it must be like for us in the storm. We had a list meter on the bridge bulkhead in front of the helm, which indicated how far over the ship would roll in the swells. A ninety degree list would put our mainmast yardarm in the water and the gunwales on the deck would be partially under water. In that event it would be very questionable that we could recover from a list that serious. The highest degree of actual roll recorded was sixty, and a very close call by any degree. The cook lost the majority of his cups and plates and all gear not bolted down was in danger of rolling on the decks and washing over the side. Down below decks we stayed tied into our bunks as seawater filled with debris sloshed back and forth in our forward compartment splashing the guys strapped into the bottom bunks. As the ship rose on the mountainous swells we braced for the drop into the trough far below becoming almost weightless during the drop to the bottom, as close to weightlessness as I have ever been. At times it seemed you were closer to the bunk springs and mattress above you than to your own bunk. There were dangers even in visiting the head during any storm, but in this case a visit to the head could endanger your life. The crew incurred a number of minor injuries as we bounced around in our sleeping compartments or on duty. Food and sleep were out of the question and the Officer of the deck only had a skeleton crew manning the bridge and engine room to control the ship as best they could. For the rest of us we thought only of survival and divine intervention as the ship pointed its bow into the swells to ride each giant wave to the top of the crest as we braced for the heart-stopping drop. All that could be done to keep from capsizing was to keep headed into the waves as they broke over us knowing that a turn into the trough would roll us over bringing final disaster.

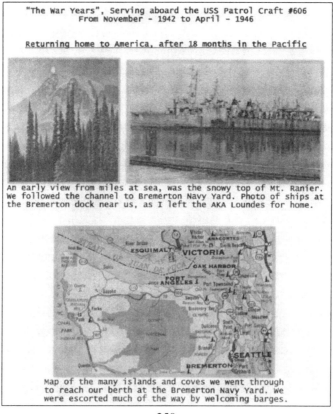

"The War Years", Serving aboard the USS Patrol Craft #606
From November - 1942 to April - 1946

Returning home to America, after 18 months in the Pacific

An early view from miles at sea, was the snowy top of Mt. Ranier. We followed the channel to Bremerton Navy Yard. Photo of ships at the Bremerton dock near us, as I left the AKA Loundes for home.

Map of the many islands and coves we went through to reach our berth at the Bremerton Navy Yard. We were escorted much of the way by welcoming barges.

By nightfall of the second day the winds began to lessen and we gradually returned to some degree of normalcy with waves under five feet. Apparently we had been caught on the fringe of the typhoon and not in its center, thank God for that. The storm went on to hit northern Okinawa and Japan. Our missing LST #636 reappeared on radar and after radio contact they reported everything shipshape with no casualties, but for us the cleanup took a bit longer. The same typhoon caused the light cruiser Pittsburgh to break in half when it was hit by the center of the typhoon further to the south. For us to have survived in the center of such a storm would have been a miracle, actually it was a bit of a miracle to have survived as it was. With the storm to the north of us we were again in visual contact with our convoy and when seas subsided we were able to return to our anti-sub screening. The seas were still quite high for us to have any effective Sonar screening, but we were now entering Japanese home waters where their subs were most active and high seas were a hindrance to them as well. Our fourth day out of Saipan on July 10th 1945 we were in sight of Iwo Jima and once inside the picket line LST #636 with its troop replacements was turned over to the harbor master and we received orders to return to Saipan as escort for the USS Beagle but not before we had refueled and replaced stores and the broken crockery for the cook. Thanks to the use of the Atomic bomb the Japanese War Lords were forced to sue for peace on Aug. 10th 1945. Although many people today feel the atomic weapon was too destructive to use due to the number of lives lost in the nuclear attacks those losses are dwarfed by the estimated millions of American military and Japanese civilian lives which would be lost in Operation Olympic the land invasion of Japan.

    President Truman's decided to use the Atomic weapon and the War Lords who controlled the Emperor were forced to face the fact of possible total annihilation, unless they officially accepted the unconditional terms of the surrender required by the Allies. Radio Guam had announced the final surrender on Aug. 14th and it seemed that a suicidal craziness had set in on Saipan. Even some B-29 pilots seemed to be buzzing the ships in the harbor where we were anchored. With their huge size they seemed so close you could almost feel the downdraft. Fighter planes were the main ones doing all the buzzing until I began to wonder that if having survived the war would I survive the peace? Launches roared in and around the anchorage of ships raising rooster tails along the shoreline. There were a many outhouses built out over the water's edge and as the launches pushed waves ashore the occupants had to abandon the facilities in a hurry. Just a sad case of being in the wrong place at the wrong time!

Throughout the base and harbor every ships horn, whistle, or general quarter's klaxon horn created one continuous symphony of noisy joy. There were sixty men and five officers aboard our ship and some of us had been together since May of 1943 along with those who came aboard over the years, so we were a classic example of what shipmates could be. Having been aboard our 173 ft. Vessel for two years plus, our greatest reaction to the news of surrender was nothing less than delirious. We danced around like fools hugging, punching and pounding on each other over and over. Sitting at anchor in the harbor and away from the shore made us a good target for every pilot who wanted to see how close he could come to the flag on our masthead. It had been four long years plus eight months since Pearl Harbor and the war in the Pacific was now ended. The actual official victory over Japan, "VJ" Day came on September 2nd 1945 when General Douglas Mac Arthur accepted the formal surrender of Japan aboard the battle ship Missouri in Tokyo bay. The celebrating on "VJ" day was a repeat of Aug.14th, but much more subdued and those pilots who were willing to risk their necks in crazy flying were now looking forward to going home all in one piece. Our waking hours and all of our conversations were now of home and what it would be like after the years of escorting supply, hospital and troop ships over ten thousand miles of tropic oceans sailing to hundreds of islands from Guadalcanal to Iwo Jima. Finally it was really over and the prayer every night for months on end had been answered, the war was really over, it was ended. The joy in that realization is so difficult to explain to anyone that I always found it easier to keep it to myself rather than to try to explain the unexplainable. Anyone who endured those years must have experienced that feeling in the same or greater degree depending on their own war experience and circumstances at home or in the warzones.

···

Our Air/Sea rescue and anti-submarine screening in the designated sectors went on as before all through the month of August including another convoy #IWS-71 on Sept. 5th 1945. We were to escort for four LST's #631, #1269, #1031, and #1393 for use at Iwo Jima, which was now occupied Japanese Territory. After an uneventful voyage we received our return orders back to Saipan harbor escorting LST #669. The anti-sub fleet was still on full alert although the war had officially ended, and we were to continue wartime practices as part of the occupation of Japan force until all remaining Japanese submarines could be found or accounted for. It was possible that individual sub captains may refuse to surrender as some Nazi sub captains had. Orders issued on Sept. 10th declared the seas to be considered safe for all ships and for the first time we were able to operate without wartime blackout conditions while at sea. Now we could use our projector to show our movies, but on the first night as we tried showing movies on the quarter deck the wind blew away our screen and movies had to wait.

It was difficult getting used to having lights at night again after years of blackout conditions. Another final job on my part was shutting down the Sonar gear to be used now only for operating in shallow waters to find reefs instead of submarines. Thank God for that too!! Sept.15th 1945 we returned from an escort trip to Iwo Jima and that trip turned out to be my last voyage to that God forsaken place. We were beginning to follow normal ship routines and our feelings had settled down to a waiting game as "VJ-Day" day passed into history. Thoughts of going home were uppermost and according to scuttlebutt discharges would be based on points and how soon orders might come for transfer to stateside. The news came by on our return from Iwo. A navy directive to the fleet ordered those with the highest number of points to be the first ones rotated home for discharge. Points were calculated on length of Navy service the amount of time on overseas duty and other factors. All of us who were part of the original ship's crew were in the first lucky group to be notified for processing at the new point of departure area at Saipan Air base. I was in the first group getting orders to report to the Saipan debarkation center for transport back to the states. That welcome news was a birthday present coming on Sept. 16th which was my twenty third birthday, what a birthday gift!!

I had a few days to bring all my Sonar records up to date pack my possessions in my seabag for the trip home then to lash up my seabag, hammock and mattress for the Navy to ship to my discharge destination. After that it was simply saying good-bye to the crew and waiting. A number of other long time crew members had their orders as well and we were scheduled to leave on the 19th at 1200 hours. As bad luck would have it, on the day before I was to go ashore I was on my way down the hatch ladder to the mess hall to get myself a last cup of jo. Now this was something I had managed to do even in the roughest weather, but this time I wasn't so fortunate. I had empty cups in one hand as I reached for the hatch handle with the other when my foot slipped on the wet ladder steps. As I fell forward my nose caught on the metal handle inside the hatch and it was almost torn from my face. I landed on the mess hall deck, amid broken cups. The mess cook saw me bleeding all over his newly scrubbed deck and having only his clean deck in mind he shoved a messy slop bucket under my nose to catch the blood. My luck wasn't all bad; because the Doc was right on hand to stop the bleeding. When he got through with his bandages they covered up half of my face and I looked like a mummy. When the captain saw me he indicated I might have to delay my departure until the bandages could come off. I immediately went to see Doc and had him remove everything except a section of plain adhesive tape across my nose to keep it in place then I went back to the captain to show him it was just a scratch with no need for any delay at all. He laughed and saw it my way telling me to see the medical group on shore when I got there. The injured nose actually had a good purpose later on at the departure center.

After the longest two days in my memory here I was with orders in hand ready to do what I had longed to do for years, I was heading home! It sounded so great I kept repeating it over and over mentally, but leaving my ship and the shipmates I had served with for so long, some of them since pre-commissioning days beginning in May 1943 in Brooklyn seemed unreal somehow. After a fond farewell the whale boat launch pulled alongside to take us to ashore to be processed as the crew lined the rail to see us off, knowing that their turn would soon come as well. The launch stopped at a number of ships to picking up all those heading for processing. After that we proceeded to the Navy section of the B-29 bomber base, which was now in use for processing returnees. On our arrival at the barracks we found we had to wait for the next troop transport and it could be up to three weeks for another one. I knew I was back under control of the same old Navy policy of "Hurry up and Wait". In the barracks we were assigned bunks and the system of alternate duty for four to six hours each day was in force. There was a big "Make Work" project on Saipan involving a huge lumber pile which was a mass of 2x4's, 2x6's, and 2x12's. There were all sizes and grades of lumber which had been dropped in a jumbled pile after the invasion of Saipan. Supply ships had a priority to unload as soon as possible then return to the states for resupply so there wasn't too much care taken during the unloading process. The brass figured they had a ready pool of manpower available to rectify their mistake and decided that we could spend our spare time waiting for our return ship by helping restack those giant toothpicks. Because of my nose injury, I had attended sick call and was excused from the work details until it healed. The guy in the next bunk had worked on the lumber pile for about a week and I was assigned to join the same crew he was on after my nose had healed. After a few days I had to join the work force and his advice to me was to stick with him and bring along some reading material.

    I was aware he had a plan in mind and now that my light duty was over I was going to join him. We boarded the work bus and arrived at this unbelievable mass of tangled lumber waiting to be reclaimed by sailors who thought they were just going home. The lumber was to be used for reconstruction later on. There were also mountains of fuel drums filled with jet fuel and other war supplies which were to be destroyed according to post war government policy. The idea was to destroy perfectly good supplies to avoid flooding home markets with tons of war surplus goods and materials. It seemed such a crime to see boxes of flight jackets and other air force wearing apparel being burned. Brand new watches and sun glasses were being crushed by bulldozers with the idea to protect stateside companies from government competition. The area around the huge lumber pile was surrounded by a fence and at the entrance gate we were checked in by the Chief Petty Officer in charge who just pointed to the big pile and told us to have fun! Sailors of all ratings were working in two's taking each end of a board then carrying it to the appropriate pile for its size and then returning for another one! There wasn't any difficult thought processes involved here, just a strong back!

"The War Years", Serving aboard the USS Patrol Craft #606
From November - 1942 to April - 1946

View of the many docks in the Bremerton Navy Yard.

After docking at the Navy yard we received our tickets home by train. Crossing the country from Washington state through eleven states to Pennsylvania and home. Riding in a train similar to the one below, I arrived at Pennsylvania station in Pittsburgh Pa. After an absence of many months, since my last leave in 1943.

Pennsylvania station in Pittsburgh, where I arrived, after my cross-country ride of 2,200 miles. Ready for 30 days leave, and then on to Philadelphia for final discharge from the U.S. Navy.

My new associate picked a large 2x10 as our first effort I would have favored a much smaller, lighter 2x4, but I picked up my end and followed him to the 2x10 stack, which was quite a distance away from the main lumber pile. I stayed with him even though I still wasn't sure what the purpose was, and after we stacked the board neatly on the correct pile I followed him to a crawl space at the end of the stack. It led to an opening into the lumber pile itself, well hidden by undergrowth and leading into a low open room. The place was also populated by a few other workers. Make that goof-offs, and was apparently well used. Someone with construction ability and experience had braced the stack with a support framework as the pile grew up around it. I imagine it was probably some clever Seabee's who decided not to sort lumber earlier. As time went by others who knew about the hideaway came in to join the gathering of goof offs. There were peep holes to look outside to watch for the work bus and possibly to sympathize with those poor souls working at hard labor. We read for a while and shared personal sea stories of our experiences in the war. We stayed in our hideaway until it was time for the return bus to arrive then we gradually mingled with the work force, and even went so far as to pick up a small board now and then as we waited for the trip home after our hard day's work. It was the first time for me to meet with experienced, professional goof offs and I must say it was very impressive. They say that an expert goof off will gladly work twice as hard to get out of work rather than work on something he doesn't want to do. I could see my education had been limited in that field and I wondered how many other hideaways there were in that lumber yard. One day they would be found and chalked up to the old Yankee ingenuity!! Once again my uncanny ability to meet the right people had saved me from a gross injustice in the Navy's attempt to make the former honcho of the communications division do servile work such as stacking lumber.

Another make work project was to clean up at the base Officers club. This was quite a down grade for us high ranking Petty Officers, but not totally without benefit. Because, while cleaning up the club tables there were numerous cans of unopened beer, cokes and unused alcoholic drinks to be disposed of. We made a punch of the drinks left behind by the patrons from that last call for alcohol, which caused patrons to over buy their drinks. With a little ice added to the beer, coke or punch we sipped away on the sly as we took our dear old time cleaning up the mess made by our Officer corps, and also keeping an eye open for stray coins of the realm dropped by drinkers. Nine days after arriving at the base and only three visits to the famous lumber yard with my non-work record intact. My name appeared on the base bulletin board to report to the Chief Yeoman's office for my orders. They were welcome orders with transportation aboard a fast "AKA", Attack Transport, to Seattle Washington then by train to Pittsburgh Penna. for 30 days leave and a final train ride to Philadelphia Navy yard for processing and discharge. Now that was a set of orders anyone would approve of, but little did I know at the time that the word "Snafu" would become a part of my life. "SNAFU" means situation normal, all fouled up, and it was waiting for me in Philadelphia Pa. as I shall explain later.

....

Those with their orders cut were taken by bus to the main dock to board an LCVP, Landing Craft Vehicle Personnel, to take us to our AKA transport, the USS Lowndes anchored just offshore. The troop transport was the biggest ship I had ever been on since joining the navy and as we came aboard a crewman was assigned to groups of twenty or so passengers. Our guide led us down ladders and long passageways to our assigned tiered bunk compartments. Mine was just below the main deck and also close to the mess hall with easy access to the open deck area. After exploring the ship, which had three decks of bunk space I was grateful to be just one level below the main deck. Even then I still had an uneasy feeling being down below decks even though the war was over. At times we brought our blankets topside to sleep in sheltered areas around the gun shields able to look at the stars dreaming of home and letting the roll of the ship rock us to sleep. Any Attack Transport like the Lowndes could make 30 knots easily and the 7,000 mile voyage to Seattle was possible with ten days of good weather. However the weather didn't cooperate very well and three days out we hit rain and heavy seas. Nothing like a typhoon, but lots of GI's, Marines and landlubber sailors were turning sickly green. Meals in good weather were no problem and each deck had its hour on the serving line. The breakfast was basic, very good with nothing dehydrated. Breakfast consisted of fresh eggs, sunny side up or scrambled, with bacon, ham, sausage and pancakes. You could take all that you wanted, but you had to eat all you had taken. When the seas were rough eating wasn't as popular by many of the passengers leaving lots of opportunity for us salty sailor types to enjoy that great chow.

The second meal was the heavy dinner meal with several different entrees plus dessert and beverage. After six p.m. sandwiches were available for snacks and coffee was on tap at all times. There were no tables and you had to eat standing up with wide shelves to rest your tray on. When you finished your meal the trays were emptied into a barrel then had to be dipped in another barrel of detergent water. Now imagine the picture of confusion when bad weather hit on day seven during the dinner meal. The slop barrel and wash water sloshed all over even though those barrels were anchored firmly in place. Soapy water on the decks and the rolling action of the ship caused many slipping, sliding bodies to create total chaos. During those messy times it was better to eat in the ships service hall where you could live on candy bars, coke and crackers. Until the seas calmed down only sandwiches and canned drinks were available for those who had an appetite. Seasickness must be a very miserable feeling, but I was fortunate in that respect and I never suffered that illness. One more blessing I had received to help me deal with my life as a sailor in the American navy.

As we came in sight of land, on Oct. fourth 1945, we could see the high mountains of Washington State with Mt. Rainier being the most prominent. America looked so wonderful as the passengers lined the rails to see the land we had sacrificed years of our young lives for and many others who had died for our freedom. The only way to describe the excitement on board is to say it was euphoric. Seeing war hardened young men all around you with tears in their eyes, punching and slapping each other like a bunch of bears was a sight to behold. I was no different with such a feeling of joy compared to my feelings back in Dec.1943 when the PC-606 left Panama for the South Pacific and the war zone. The future then was so uncertain and filled with potential danger. My own personal prayers had been answered and I had returned safely. The future was bright and now I could make up for those lost years of my youth, which had been given up, but not wasted in service to my country. I joined up shortly after my 19th birthday and I was now a 23 years old adult. Thank God I had only sacrificed a part of my life and not all of it, as many men my age had done.

It was now October and there was a chill was in the air and warm dress blues and navy Peacoat were called for. At Saipan my sea-bag and hammock had been packed with shipping tags made out for delivery to my next duty station which was to the Navy Yard in Philadelphia Penna. Everything I needed was in my well stuffed ditty bag, and I had carried my warm Peacoat for the train ride home. No more nights on the rolling deep for me I was ready to hit the gangway as soon as we docked fully prepared to become a landlubber again. As our transport slowed to pass through the Straights leading into Puget Sound we were able to see the Canadian shore on our port side and Washington State shores on the starboard side. It was a beautiful sight in spite of a light drizzle, so typical of the Seattle area. Our biggest surprise came as we were entering Puget Sound when we saw two tug boats each pulling a barge decorated with bunting and flags positioned on each side of the ship. Riding on board each barge was a high school band with loud speakers blaring and cheerleaders leading a group of the home folks in cheering our homecoming. It was a good idea having a separate one on each side or the ship would have a dangerous listing problem as the returning military men lined the rails to see the excitement. VJ day was on Sept. 2nd and I thought by now all the shouting would be over, but the folks in Seattle continued to celebrate for every troopship as they arrived. It was a wonderful gesture on their part and one I will never forget. There were horns and whistles from the many boats and ships we passed in the harbor on our way to Bremerton Navy Yard and our berth at pier 90. During our approach to Seattle we had lined up at the ships administration office to receive orders for leave and the rail tickets to our various destinations, so we were all set and prepared to head for home with tickets in hand ahead of time.

After docking was completed those who had trains to catch were the first ones off into waiting busses for the Seattle train station.

The day was chilly with a damp drizzle falling and after being in the tropics for so long I seemed to be susceptible to the chill and I was starting to feel quite puny as they say in New York. Riding through the city I felt worse and by the time I boarded my train I had become hoarse and had a slight fever as well. The antique railroad car was something out of the early 1900's with a potbellied stove at one end. It had reclining seats which wouldn't recline very well and windows that didn't shut tight allowing cold air to enter creating a real problem, since it was quite cold during our entire trip across the top of the country. Thank God the engine and the wheels were working fine and before long we were out of the snow covered Rocky Mountains and heading across the open plains to our first stop in Chicago Ill. On my journey home I would cover 2,200 miles across the states of Washington, Idaho, Montana, South Dakota, Minnesota, Wisconsin, Illinois, Indiana, Ohio and then home to Pittsburgh Pa. This would be a much quicker trip than the forty days we spent crossing the Pacific as convoy escort with a forward speed of only six knots per hour.

Many of my fellow travelers were service men who came on the USS Lowndes and I had come to know some of them quite well. One of them was from Philly who became my voice while I had the laryngitis. I could hardly speak and my sore throat lasted until we reached Chicago. My aunt Marcella lived in Chicago, but I wasn't able to talk to her. My friend Bill made the call for me and passed on my comments to her. At Chicago we were scheduled to change to another train on the way to rail stations in Pittsburgh and Philadelphia. The new train had many more civilians traveling with us, and when the word got around that there was a sick sailor on the train people kept coming by with cold pills, throat tablets, food and best of all a heavy blanket. As time went by I began to feel so much better and the train was also a lot more modern and warmer. We had a homier atmosphere as people gathered around the groups of servicemen seemingly hungry for first hand news about the far away war zones. Many had family or friends coming home to be discharged and adult beverages seemed to appear from nowhere and soon a party of sorts was in full swing as we sang all the new and old songs of the 1940's. We were still familiar with popular songs through the armed forces radio services, which could be heard in almost every part of the globe. I believe all of us on that train would agree that we had been truly welcomed home.

"The War Years", Serving aboard the USS Patrol Craft #606
From November - 1942 to April - 1946

Assigned to Shore Patrol duty at Cape May N.J.

Map of the Cape May, Wildwood area, where our duties were as Shore Police on the base, at the brig, the wave barracks, in the towns, and along the shore during early Cold war days.

1941 WILLYS ARMY JEEP

we used a Navy Jeep like this one to operate along the beaches, while on duty as Shore Patrol officers in Wildwood and Cape May. My discharge was made possible by the Congressman I voted for.

It was late at night when my train arrived at Penn station in Pittsburgh and I had called home from Chicago letting Dad know my schedule. Because of how unreliable train schedules were I had planned to take a cab home on arrival. A few cabs were lined up at the curb next to the station and I picked the first one for my ride home. The cab driver spent most of the trip explaining how he was classified 4F and the army wouldn't take him and how he was truly grateful to those who served. It was nothing new, during the war many men couldn't meet the military requirements for service or had deferments as I could have had, but I was more interested in seeing all the familiar streets and places of my prewar years and filling in the memories of that time. Finally, here I was back at 2110 Plainview Ave. home again in Pittsburgh. Pa. I still couldn't shake the feeling that this was just another of those dreams I had experienced before when I would soon wake up back on the PC-606 at my duty station on the bridge. The cabbie wished me luck and as reached for my wallet the driver tooted his horn and drove off giving me my first and last free cab ride, ever.

    The toot on the horn brought Dad. Charlotte and Brother Jerry out on the porch and the hugs were plentiful. Dad's hugs were special as he stopped just short of cracking your ribs, with dad you knew you had been hugged!! We gathered around the kitchen table with a cold bottle of good old Iron City beer, nothing like the 3.2% beer of the navy days. We talked on into the early hours. I had slept quite a bit on the train from Chicago to Pittsburgh and I wasn't the least bit tired. Charlotte and Jerry finally went to bed, but Dad and I kept on going until the dawn. Dad was so happy to have his two sons safely home that he spent half of my thirty days of leave taking us to visit friends. The anguish of a parent with sons in harm's way must be a heavy burden and for Dad it was now over and time to rejoice. It was a time to get reacquainted again with all of the friends from the neighborhood from school and all the relatives. Things were different than before I went overseas, everyone was much older and we had been apart too long, dramatically changing our lives. It seemed many of the things we once had in common were now lost and maybe forever. We had experienced difficult unfamiliar events and now it was time to forget them as best we could, but putting them out of your mind isn't as simple as people would believe.

    During my leave at home the fall November elections were in progress and I was now able to vote. I was old enough to vote while overseas, but no polling places were available out there. I went with Dad up to the Brookline American Legion hall to cast my vote for the Democrats, of course. Dad worked for the city now and it was best for you to be a Democrat to hold your job so I registered as a Democrat. I personally met and voted for Jim Fulton, who was an army veteran running for the congressional seat from our district. His ultimate election was a big asset to me later in the year when he helped me to finally get home and out of the navy!! There was no great urgency on this leave since I would be on my way to Philly for processing and discharge so I just enjoyed life and the first Thanksgiving Day home in years. Charlotte had a wonderful meal prepared, and no weevils in the bread. At times I would still hold the bread to the light by force of habit to inspect for the little critters to the surprise of all until I explained about the bread in the Pacific. Looking forward to my discharge I was glad to head for Philadelphia, and soon after Thanksgiving with my leave ended and I was traveling east by rail. In doing so I was completing a giant circle from New York in 1943 to the Pacific and return with 3000 miles across the northern tier of states from Seattle to Philadelphia in 1945 in addition to an estimated 20,000 ocean miles not including the many side voyages to Australia and the Pacific islands while on convoy duty. Now I was looking forward to one last journey from Philadelphia to home for good with my Navy discharge in hand.

My train arrived at the Philadelphia Navy Yard was right on schedule and I reported in as required according to my travel orders. My name was logged in and I was assigned to a bunk and a locker with instructions to watch the daily roster for my name to appear. It all seemed simple enough I had a liberty pass and duty was not required by those awaiting discharge. After I spent a week of sleeping and taking in the sights around Philly and staying out as late as I wanted I became quite bored with it all. My navy seabag had not yet arrived from Seattle and all those around my bunk area had come and gone a number of times. When I checked with the base office to see what the problem was a Wave Officer checked out my orders and record file and told me to wait. She returned in about a half hour with the news that all my personnel records from the USS Lowndes had not made it to Philadelphia. Everything I owned, all of my belongings, my seabag, hammock and mattress had vanished. They assured me it was a common problem and I was to check back in a day or so to fill out papers so I could be discharged.

There is only so much one can see in Philadelphia or any big city and I never thought I would tire of going on liberty, but I wasn't getting paid and without money it is next to impossible to enjoy oneself. The base had a recreation area and I began to spend more time there. They had movies, pool, shuffleboard and tables just like any local pub with beverages available. On the bulletin board there were all kinds of notices to go to dinners, dances and church suppers, which I really enjoyed attending. That was all very nice, but I was really looking forward to being a civilian again and not a lonely sailor in port. Finally, after my third time reporting back to Administration Desk they had some papers ready for me to sign for pay purposes, clothing allowances, and other necessary items. The only trouble was that if I signed them it would also delay my discharge by six to eight weeks. The question for me was; what if my original records turn up in the near future? Their answer was; I would not need the new records. When I asked what would happen if I didn't sign they said I would be assigned to a shore base until my records turned up then I would be discharged as soon as possible! Since I fully expected my records would soon be found I decided to refuse the offer to sign new papers hoping mine would be discovered in the near future. After I made that decision the Navy was quick to make theirs. The next day I had orders to proceed to Cape May N.J. for shore patrol duty at the US Naval Air Station. Once again I had been reminded of the Navy's own Murphy's Law, which states; everything that can go wrong will go wrong. In the Navy it's called "SNAFU", meaning situation normal, all fouled up!

Cape May is about 100 miles to the south of Philadelphia Pa. at the entrance to Delaware Bay jutting out into Atlantic Ocean. The U.S. Naval Air Station was close to the tourist towns of Cape May and Wildwood N.J. Being located right on the seacoast it seemed like an attractive assignment for me to finish out my naval career while awaiting discharge. The bus ride to Cape May Naval base was a pleasant trip along the Atlantic coast through the small summer tourist towns all boarded up for the winter. The entrance gates of the U.S. Naval Air Station on Cape May were just north of the town of Wildwood. It was mid-December and the wind off the Atlantic reminded me of Lake Michigan at the Great Lakes Naval training station back in Nov. 1942. Here I was ending my career as a frozen swabby just as it had been when my navy service began. After reporting in to the Deck Officer I was assigned to my "living quarters", a navy term usually referring to a space for Officers only. The shore patrol barracks had individual units for each man including a soft bed, desk and wardrobe. Very plush compared to the tiered bunks hanging from chains or hammocks which were my normal sleeping spaces in the past. My duty schedule was great with two days on duty and three days off and five days leave every other week, including Christmas week. Our duties consisted of guarding the navy brig and the Guard Station at the WAVE sailor's barracks. We also rode shore patrol by jeep in the tourist towns of Wildwood and Cape May. Our main Shore Patrol duty was to keep check on military personnel taking liberty in the tourist towns. By the end of 1945 the Russians were becoming a threat to peace in what came to be called the "Cold War". It was now a part of our Shore Patrol duty to ride our jeep up and down the isolated beaches looking for signs of communist infiltrators. The Navy was very serious about the job and we had to make reports on a regular basis. One war had ended and now another was just beginning and I was part of the new war on a small scale.

 We operated as a six man squad and we had free rein in arranging our duty days with one another. Since my discharge was being delayed this was an ideal way to put in the waiting time by spending only short periods on actual duty' Being part of the navy police force had some other advantages. Visiting all of the bars and lounges up and down the coast as a Shore Patrol Officer you became well known to the proprietors and bartenders. Later, when we visited while off duty they were often generous with free food and drinks hoping to gain some advantage. They knew we could actually put their place off limits if they didn't conform to navy rules. One rule that we strictly enforced was drunken sailors didn't get served. One local bar in particular had an influence on my future working lifetime. It was called the Steel Bar and it was right on the beach in Wildwood. It had a black combo on the stage with lots of jazz and big band sound and also a Honky-Tonk piano for singing along. Singing along at the piano was just my speed and I spent a lot of time there. One night while on duty, I made a stop at the Steel Bar on my rounds. The piano player greeted me by name and at the piano bar was an attractive young lady who also said hello and repeated my name. The piano player introduced us and after getting acquainted we made a date for later that week. Her name was Ellen and her family owned a fancy restaurant on the nearby beach. They also had a large home right on the ocean. Her folks were not rich, but they were definitely well to do by my standards.

Ellen was the oldest daughter and the apple of her daddy's eye. In a short time I became well acquainted with all of her family. Ellen and I started to spend a lot of time together, and one afternoon at the Steel Bar we were at our table when three men came in for lunch. They were local men and Ellen had gone to school with one of them. He came to our table to say hello to Ellen and we asked him to join us. He had been discharged from the Army Signal Corps and had been hired by the western Electric Co. installing telephone equipment at the local Bell Telephone office. I told him about my navy electronic training and he said Western would hire me on the spot and I could start work right there after my discharge. First I wanted to know if they had an office in Pittsburgh and he promised to find out. On my next liberty he gave me the phone number of the Western personnel supervisor to contact in Pittsburgh. However, if I wanted to sign up before my discharge his boss wanted to meet me. As fate would have it, because of those lost records and my shore patrol assignment in Cape May and my acquaintance with Ellen I found out about the opportunity to work for the Western Electric Co.

As a result of my delayed discharge I was to begin my thirty five year career as a technician in communications with Western Electric a subsidiary of AT&T Co. Through all this talk about a job in Wildwood or Pittsburgh Ellen was determined to have me to take the job locally. She had been making matrimonial noises off and on for some time. Even showing me the neat little bungalow her dad had built for her close to the big house on the ocean. Her father spent some time in the hospital because of a mild heart attack and on one of our visits to see him in the hospital he spent a lot of time explaining what he would do for Ellen when she married. Other members of the family were also acting as though it was a forgone conclusion that wedding bells would be soon around the corner. This was happening in spite of my own personal denials to Ellen and her family. My constant thoughts were of those lost years during the war and all of the wild oats I wanted to sow before any lifetime commitment would be considered.

"The War Years", Serving aboard the USS Patrol Craft #606 From November - 1942 to April - 1946
Department of the Navy Cold War Certificate & Military Award.

Certificate of recognition & award to all those who had served during the cold war, which had lasted from Sept. 22nd 1945 until Dec. 26th 1991.

The final mark of a former service man. The discharge button.

The official document declaring I was now a First Class civilian, and not a Sonarman 2/C.

That was my mental state then, but it was changed sooner than I had planned by a girl named Peggy who I was destined to meet after I got home. One of our shore patrol duties which our group covered was guard duty at the WAVE barracks where our female sailors lived. We were on hand to take care of intrusions on the grounds only. They had their own WAVE Petty Officers to handle any problems within the barracks by themselves. Most of the problems came after midnight when the lady sailors were returning from liberty and our orders called for eviction of any males who tried to get in a few last hugs and kisses. The WAVE grounds were extensive and we used our jeep lights and a search light to find any bush dwellers. There were lots of hiding places and we knew them all. Spoil sports that we were we had to send the gals one way to their barracks and the guys toward the bus stop or the cab stand. Once the barracks settled down we were off for a check of the base perimeter along the ocean side and the Cape May hotel area.

The plush hotel was rented for the duration by the Navy for Officers serving at the base and the Air Station. After the base was closed down in 1947 it cost the government millions of dollars to refurbish and recondition the hotel back to its original state. We patrolled the housing area for high level Officers and VIP's assigned to the base. One of the officers had a rebellious daughter and we were constantly getting calls from headquarters to find her and take her home. We usually knew where to find her, because most often she would to go a favorite local pub and finding her was not the problem it was after we found her that the fun started. While trying to get her to return home we couldn't hurt her of course, her father wouldn't like that. We would shut off her drinks and keep her in check until she reached a point where she believed us when we promised to take her to another bar for one more drink. Once we had her in the jeep we would take her home instead. She was only nineteen years old and really had a serious drinking problem, not to mention the lack of parental discipline.

Three months had gone by and still had no word about my lost seabag and records. I wasn't getting paid since I had no pay records and I had to survive by cashing in the savings bonds which I had accumulated while overseas. The Red Cross had this emergency loan program, but they would not give me a loan unless it could be taken out of my pay which I wasn't receiving. I couldn't convince them that if I was getting paid I wouldn't have needed any loan. Scratch the Red Cross from my list for future support. My only apparent solution was to sign the navy papers and accept six to eight weeks then look for discharge soon after. My situation was getting bleak and I had almost made up my mind until one evening while on guard duty at the base brig the navy jail. We often played cards with the prisoners by putting a long table against the bars so two prisoners could play with two guards. During the game and one of them mentioned he planned to go into politics when he got back home. That reminded me of Congressman Jim Fulton, the ex-GI I had voted for while on leave in Nov. 1945. He had won his seat and was now a Congressman. In desperation, I decided to write a detailed letter concerning my situation and remind him of our meeting during the campaign for his seat in Congress. It was near the end of March when I mailed my letter, but I didn't really expect any help from him about something so personal and I considered it to be a bit of a long shot. Still, I decided to give it a little more thought before I signed any papers, I would just wait and see.

    Being assigned guard duty at the brig was a breeze; the navy jail was in a separate building and just like a small city jail. Most of the prisoners were usually base personnel who had been sentenced for minor infractions of some navy rule or regulation. We had to take our prisoners out for exercise and work details such as cutting grass or policing the grounds and doing make work projects in general. It was also a good time to catch up on sleep or do a little reading and letter writing. One of the prisoners was in for punching out a mean civilian on a bus, for not giving up his seat to a pregnant woman, thought that he knew me and he in turn looked familiar to me. After a bit of remembering it turned out that he and I were in St. Paul's Orphanage together when we were children. We weren't close friends at St. Paul's, but I knew him fairly well then. We went out on liberty together after his release and along with three other sailors to make a night of it.

    About that time, due to the Russian threat, the Navy was heavily recruiting those scheduled for discharge and the base was a main target of their recruiting drive. Two of the sailors with us that night had decided to sign up and to reenlist for another four years. They explained to us about all the great advantages being offered, like choice of duty, re-training and pay incentives. By dawns early light, and after an excess of beverages, all of us had made a pact to re-up for four more years in the United States Navy. Now the navy has no conscience when it comes to re-enlisting and when five sailors reported back from liberty asking to sign up their only question was, "Can you hold a pen and write your name"? The other four sailors signed happily without any problem, but my head had cleared on the taxi ride back to base and I decided against making such a decision. My shipmates called me chicken of course, but thank God I was clear headed in time. Two days later all four were shipped out with new orders. No indecision on the Navy's part, but then they all seemed happy with their decision as they departed. If I knew anything about the navy the personal choices they were offered wouldn't last very long.

My relationship with Ellen and her family had come to a mutual end due to the arrival home of a former admirer who showed the proper matrimonial interest in Ellen. My visits to Wildwood diminished not wanting to interfere in the reunion. I was sure I had handled the situation quite well avoiding the snare of matrimony. I did get to meet Ellen's ex-GI and I found him to be a fine man. I wished them both all the best in their future life together knowing he would wind up as manager of the family restaurant. His position was probably unpopular with the Ellen's siblings, but a great opportunity for a returning veteran to have and a loving bride like Ellen to help him. I was glad to be second best in the race. Time for my decision was close at hand I was getting tired of riding trains back and forth across Pennsylvania riding three hundred miles each way. I had made the trip at least one day a month for five days leave. It got so at home that everyone wondered why I was still in a uniform even thinking I had reenlisted as so many men had done. Because of Russia now acting more like an enemy than a former ally it was necessary to keep up our military strength, but that was not for me. My plan was to sign up with the Western Electric Co. in Pittsburgh then to file the required navy papers for my separation from service by accepting the six to eight week delay. It was on a Thursday that I had mailed the letter to my new Congressman Jim Fulton and the following Friday I went home for another four days of leave at home. On my arrival I was surprised to find my Dad waiting for me there at the depot with a Navy telegram with the words; leave cancelled, return to base immediately for discharge.

It was hard to believe that my letter to Rep. Jim Fulton was responsible for the telegram, maybe my missing records had turned up. I was tired from the long trip, so I spent the night at home. In the early morning I boarded the train back to Philly then by bus to Cape May. When the bus arrived at Cape May Naval Air Station I presented the telegram to the Officer of the Deck in the administration office and he directed me down the hall to the executive officers desk. There were several base officers in attendance as he quizzed me about how the Bureau of Naval Personnel had become interested in my discharge. They had received orders to estimate my back pay and discharge me from service within the week. I told the Executive Officer my Dad was much involved in local politics in Pittsburgh, and that Rep. Jim Fulton was a personal acquaintance. That letter had such swift results that on Monday, April 5th my bags were packed and I had a nice big pay check in hand. There was a personal Navy van waiting to deliver me to Philadelphia, where I would catch a Navy bus bound for Lido Beach, Long Island, N.Y. The main Navy discharge center on the east coast.

The process was very simple, mainly involving paperwork to be completed. At the last stop in line you received a going away packet with your honorable discharge, record of service and a lapel pin to go with your campaign ribbons. It looked like a chubby eagle and indicated to all concerned that you were now a civilian in uniform. I also received a destination train voucher for use at the train or bus station for a ticket or cold cash if you desired. All that remained was a bus trip to the Long Island train depot and a "One Way" ticket for the three hundred mile trip to Pittsburgh and home. It was four months from the time when I should have been discharged until now and I had gained a lot more experience in my young life. I had avoided early matrimony and had experienced the first steps in what became known as the "Cold War". Because of my time at Cape May I had gained the information for a job I would hold for a lifetime. Fate does have a way of shaping your life in ways you never dreamed. It was now early spring and the trip was drastically different. On those previous trips home I always had a return trip to make back to

The War Years–Aboard a U.S. Navy Sub-Chaser–1942–1945

somewhere, but this time I was homeward bound for good. The train traveled around the famous horse-shoe curve west of Altoona Pa., which was built in the 1850's when railroads entered the steam age. My Great Grandparents had looked at this same scenic view as they traveled as immigrants to a new life in Pittsburgh in 1860. My father came this way in 1917 during WW I on his way to NYC bound for France with the A.E.F. I first saw the horseshoe curve in 1943 on the way to board my ship at the Brooklyn Navy Yard, and now I was having my last look at the same spectacular view of Horseshoe curve heading home from WW II in April 1946. History has a way of repeating, but I hope and pray that no more of America's sons or grandson's will have to travel to or from any future war.

My final arrival home five days after receiving that historic telegram was no more than just an ordinary event, since the family had been expecting me home for so long they gave up asking me when. My sister Jeannie was now married and had a young son, my brother Jerry had a job and was on his own. Now at home in the old homestead on Plainview Ave. it was only Dad, Charlotte and me. My settling into civilian life wasn't much of a problem, mainly it was mainly shedding the life of regimentation and returning to the way of life that had been suspended for a time, but not quite forgotten. My first shopping trip to town was for some new civilian clothes, so I could not only feel like a civilian, but could look the part. My sports jackets still fit me and were still in style, since the war had suspended any style changes in men's fashions and clothing materials were in short public supply. My navy uniform was used by my seamstress sister to make her son, Skippy, a sailor suit. I was now ready to get back in the mainstream and start a career with the Western Electric Co. as an equipment installer. The first step was to contact a Mr. Mulligan, whose name and phone number I had received from the supervisor in Wildwood. After my initial call he gave me a date and the time to come into Pittsburgh's main Bell Telephone building on Seventh Ave. for an interview. Not long after I went in to see him with my Navy records and a list of training schools I had attended to show him my experience. We met in his fourth floor office and after reviewing my records he said he was ready to hire me, contingent upon a standard six months trial period. My job description was to be an installer of telephone equipment with a pay rate starting at .50¢ per hour, as the base rate, plus an additional amount because of my specialized training skills in electronics. It would be a whopping .88¢ per hour or $35 weekly with annual raises of .02¢ or.03¢ per hour. It was an attractive offer for those times and I was well satisfied.

My start to work would depend on when the supply of copper cable and steel for equipment manufacture were available. So although, I was hired by the company my going to work depended on the future arrival of equipment and cable sometime in the near future. Fortunately for me, and other unemployed veterans, the GI-bill had been passed by Congress providing twenty dollars a week for fifty two full weeks for all veterans. This was to tide them over until a job materialized, or they started back to school. Veterans called it the twenty/fifty-two club. It was the perfect start for this former sailor with twenty bucks for incidentals and a good job waiting in the wings. This gave me the spare time to enjoy my new freedom as a civilian "first class", until the shortages would be over at Western Electric and I could go to work. My last tie to the United States Navy came in Mid-June when a post office truck pulled up with a package from the Navy containing a sea bag, mattress and hammock. It was my long lost navy gear which had been packed to the overflowing when I packed it, and now contained only a few items of clothing, and shoes. The only war souvenir to survive was my combat knife, but most of my clothing, my .45 gun, an enemy flag and Jap helmet souvenir items were gone. The hammock and mattress were not even mine; they had another name stenciled on them. The delivery man asked me to sign the receipt as received in good order, but I marked it as all personal effects missing. Eventually, I did receive a check based on the cost of a full issue of a regulation seabag. My final business with the United States Navy came when I received a check for the balance of my back pay, which the navy paymaster had withheld when they estimated my discharge pay. They had deducted ten percent in case of any error, in their favor not mine. At least some restitution had been made and I was through with the military except for a life insurance policy. Those years in the service between November 1942 and April 1946 were given in service to my country. The years ahead were now mine to live as I saw fit.

"The War Years", Serving aboard the USS Patrol Craft #606
From November - 1942 to April - 1946

The Commissioning crew of the USS PC-606

The sixty man crew, the five officers, and one Seadog by
The name of "Boats". (held by the captain above the life
preserver) Trained and ready for Anti-submarine warfare.
The author, is the third man in, on the left, front row.

The USS Patrol Craft - PC-606
Hard to believe, that sixty five men could live and work
on such a small ship, only 173 ft. long, and 25 ft. wide.

Post script to "Life and Times of Himself- The War Years"

Before ending my story of life aboard the USS PC-606 I want to honor all those who served aboard these small ships during the most difficult of times by sharing my personal observations and my post war research into what has been written about the men and their Patrol Craft and their part in the most destructive war ever endured by every land and country in the world, as follows:

As I look back on the years aboard ship we were a close knit crew with a common goal. Our uppermost thought were about winning the war and getting home to take up our lives again as civilians once again. Concerning my years on board the PC-606 I can only say I thank God for the men who shared my life aboard the ship during the perilous times we had to endure. Serving in wartime I cannot imagine a better set of circumstances than those I encountered as a crewman on the Patrol Craft 606. We had sailed over 20,000 miles of oceans and seas and visited continents. We lived on a ship only 173 feet in length and 25 feet wide sharing crowded quarters with sixty other men and officers for twenty eight months on end. We shared many hardships and dangers in enemy waters enduring food and water shortages where the threat of tropical diseases was a constant threat. We helped our nation achieve victory from the time when it seemed victory was just a dream up until to the final victory when the hope of peace and freedom for America became a reality. We also thank God for the courage of her people at home who suffered in our support for the victory. There were 600 SC's and 1100 PC's built in WW II and they all shared the same hardships and comradeship of that "Donald Duck Navy" as we did on the "606". There were a number of articles written during the war about the small anti-submarine vessels that served in the war at a time when the outlook wasn't very bright for America.

Here are some of those stories which told the story of the unknown fleet of ships which served as the David facing a Goliath during those times. Hundreds of Patrol Craft were built from 1942 on to fill the gap in protecting our merchant fleet from the destruction of our convoys by the U-boats. An article in National Defense magazine described the PC as the roughest thing afloat. Those little warships had a rugged reputation and at the same time, they were also one of the forgotten fighting ships of World War II. The great ships, battleships, carriers, cruisers, destroyers and destroyer escorts, grabbed the headlines and the glory, but the PC's and SC's fought in every war theater, chasing submarines, escorting the smaller convoys and helping shepherd landing craft toward enemy shores at the forefront of the invasion forces. They were the smallest of warships, but required to spend long periods at sea in all kinds of weather. Patrol Craft did much more than they were designed for and far more than what was expected of them and their crews. At the other extreme, they were among the largest of the navy craft deployed at the forefront of the invasion landing barges, sailing into waters that barely accepted their ten foot draft.

If Patrol Craft were the kid brothers of Destroyers, they have fought a common enemy the submarine. Early in the war Nazi submarines preyed upon the Atlantic convoys, destroying and damaging many of our cargo vessels even as they left safe harbor. Larger navy Destroyers were desperately needed on cross Atlantic convoys. That left the naval authorities with few escort vessels to protect American coastal water, where U-boats were roaming practically at will. At first the navy assembled the minute man force of world war one

Post script to "Life and Times of Himself–The War Years"

Eagle boats, and Converted Yachts, YP's, to fill the gap. Short on range and speed, they were little match for the enemy subs which slashed into convoys, sometimes within sight of land. To combat the undersea threat the navy began to build sub-chasers these were the SC's, patterned after those World War I, wooden hulled vessels for use in coastal waters. The first World War II SC's were all much improved both in speed, at 21 knots and firepower, but lacked the size, range and armament of the new steel hulled Patrol Craft, the PC's. the first SC-#453 and the first PC-461, launched on Dec. 23rd 1941, were grouped together as sub-chasers operating in Atlantic waters screening convoys. In 1943 the navy redefined sub-chasers as the SC and Patrol Craft, the PC. The SC was a 110 ft. Wooden vessel, which according to the dictionary of American fighting ships, operated in quantity during 1943-1944 and helped to curb the U-boat menace in the Atlantic and Caribbean. Their contribution was felt more in the deterrent effect they had on the enemy submarines prowling the Atlantic seaboard. Keeping them submerged for longer periods and away from coast convoys. Reducing their effectiveness, by forcing subs to exhaust their batteries and operate at reduced speeds.

....

During World War II, about 450 SC's were commissioned and over 1100 PC's. The Patrol Craft, by navy definition, was a 173 ft. Steel ship with a new hull design. Earlier versions of the PC, varied in size and armament, but the PC-461 class boats became the one most commonly built. The nameless little ships had hull numbers between 461 and 1603. National Defense magazine said of the PC's: one had to look closely to distinguish it from just another wave on the vast salty horizon. PC's weighed in about 450 tons, only 23 feet wide at their beam, they were skinny ships, powered by efficient twin 1600 horsepower diesel engines, they can bound through the waves at speeds up to 22 knots. A navy magazine had an article about PC's, stating: the PC is small and narrow and so continually hidden by flying spray that the need for extensive camouflage is practically nil. It had a draft of only 10 ft., similar to the boats plying our major rivers. The PC silhouette was indeed low. A main mast reached 53 feet topped by an inverted jar, radar dome, at its base was the super-structure amidships housing the bridge, chartroom, wardroom, radio and radar shack. The remaining silhouette of the guns and deck equipment were low to the deck, except for the forward main gun and the AA gun astern.

Another magazine of the day covered mass production methods of the PC's construction in a 1942 article: the larger and faster, hull #461 PC design, were first built at Defoe boat works in Bay City Michigan where the present day Patrol Craft Sailors Assn. Museum is located. PC's were ready made for mass producing taking four to five months to complete building a ship. PC hulls were fashioned in bow, stern, and amidships sections. Boat yard crews welded the sections together in an upside down position, rolling it over then launching it sideways. The hull was then towed to a fitting dock where the super-structure was put on in one piece. Patrol Craft were originally built as a stop gap to protect shipping until the heavier Destroyer and Destroyer escort ship building programs got into full production. Building a pc kept shipyards busy for over three years; they were built in places like Michigan, Connecticut, Wisconsin, Pittsburgh, Oregon, and Tennessee. The unpretentious PC's launchings attracted the families and friends of all the workers who built the small ships. Excitement was high when the ships struck water during the sideways launchings and the round bottomed ships heeled over almost 90 degrees.

The men, who later rode those ships in heavy seas, became quite familiar with this rough part of the PC's characteristics. A news story in a navy magazine called the little ships the bucking broncos of the sea. But after spending a week on board one the author called that a gross understatement. You can get off of a bronco, but you are stuck on board to endure the pounding and pitching that a Patrol Craft will go through, until you reach the safety of the calm harbor and the dock. That navy article, challenged claims that the English Corvette held the title of the most rugged escort vessel afloat. The PC is shorter and much narrower than a Corvette causing a PC to ride the crest of the waves, while a Corvette being much heavier slices through them. The difference in construction allows the PC more speed and maneuverability, with a shorter turning radius. For this necessary advantage though, a Patrol Craft had to endure Neptune's wrath. The Canadian navy considered sea service aboard a Corvette to be so much more hectic than life on aboard larger vessels, that Corvette sailors received a daily bonus of .25¢ a day for such duty. PC sailors would find that submariners pay rate would be more in keeping with PC duty, when you consider the excessive amount of time spent submerged under the surface rather than on top of it.

Another magazine article, written in March 1943, gave the PC sailors some well-deserved praise, stating: Uncle Sam has thousands of seamen on hundreds of Patrol Craft serving in convoy or escort duty in Atlantic and Pacific war areas. Yet these small ships are hardly known outside of the service, perhaps it is because the PC's are doing those hazardous and essential jobs which too often go unnoticed in wartime. They don't even have the dignity of names, they were given numbers. Perhaps, because of this anonymity that PC crews were close knit bunches. Salutes are seldom rendered or expected except at those formal functions like inspection. Informality was the norm as the crew went about their duties. A sharp contrast to the regulations found aboard the capital ships of the fleet. The effectiveness of this forgotten fleet against the Nazi undersea raiders, has been proven, in the fact that, as more and more of these tough little escort vessels became available, fewer and fewer of those convoy merchant vessels went to the bottom in the American War theater. Then after the sub menace subsided along the Atlantic coast, many Patrol Craft were diverted to Pacific waters to provide convoy and screening around the new bases and harbors which were liberated as our forces island hopped their way to the Japanese home islands. Late in the war many PC's were given to our allied navies for European duty. Navy records show that PC's had a part in the invasion of Europe on D-Day. The PC-1261 was blown out of the water by shore batteries as it led assault boats toward the shore.

· ·

For its size, the Patrol Craft was well armed. Its main battery was the three inch fifty gun on forward deck, with racks for contact depth charges, called mousetraps, on the bow. Three 20 millimeter

Anti-Aircraft guns bristled on the flying bridge. Two more 20MM AA guns at the quarter deck, with a twin 40 millimeter AA gun and its splinter shield aft of the quarter deck. For submarine combat two K-guns were on port and starboard amidships. Two depth charge racks were rigged at the stern. Also available were two portable 50 cal. Machine, guns to be mounted as needed. At the base of the mast in the chart room were two 45 caliber. Sub-machine guns, like the tommy guns of prohibition days. There were 45 caliber Side arms and rifles just in case. The PC silhouette was low on the horizon, the superstructure, about a third of the way aft of the bow, housed the bridge, chartroom, radio shack, yeoman's office, and radar room, aft of the chartroom was the wardroom. A steward's pantry was portside; a ship fitters shack was to starboard. Above that was the flying bridge with port and starboard signal lamps, and two rigid life rafts in their launch racks. Aft of the superstructure is the dummy smoke stack and a 16 foot, ship to shore, wherry boat, with its boom and davits. That was a PC's profile on the horizon, low on the water and almost invisible in the flying spray. Below decks, starting at the bow, the Bosun's triangle shaped Lazaret paint and material locker.

Next came the crews head or toilets, it had three seats, three washbasins and two showers for a crew of 60. It took quite a bit of planning to use the facilities. Water was rationed quite often, except while in port, where there was unlimited water available. The showers ran almost continuously. Next to the head were the forward crew's quarters with bunks lining the bulkheads three deep and additional bunks down the center of the compartment. Space not given over to bunks was used for lockers. With bunks down at night you had 18 inches from your nose to the bunk above unless he was a heavyweight, then it was even less. There was little deck space to pass between the bunks and lockers through the compartment on the way to the head, and very little head room due to the low overheads, as the navy refers to ceilings. Being a short person solved a few of the problems. There was storage space below decks in the wash room and crew's compartment, and the sonar equipment room as well. Amidships were chief and Officers' quarters, black gang compartment. The engine room, evaporators, electric generators and other machinery were below the quarter deck. The galley and crew mess hall, which was sick bay in between meals and social center at other times. The last of the compartments, in the stern, was the Lazaret. Used for storage for the deck crew etc.

....

On the ships bridge all of the PC's were equipped with submarine hunting units and navigational equipment. The Sonar Stack was mounted on the starboard side of the bridge and the Sonar operator sat on a swinging seat over the ladder to the chartroom, quite a feat, for a Sonarman to hang on to during heavy seas and still keep on pinging. On the port side plot table was the chemical recorder, a device which automatically traced contact range and bearings from the sonar gear. There was a Fathometer for depth readings and a magnetic compass at the helm, a gyro compass below decks, with two gyro repeaters. On each wing, port and starboard, of the bridge there was the Peloris, a gyro repeater calibrated to take shore bearings. PC's had no fire control capability to direct its guns; Radar and Sonar contact provided that necessary information. Near the chartroom was the one man Radar shack and inside the chartroom was the radio shack. Next to it, on the port side was the wardroom and officers galley, where the officers had their mess and the captain had his bunk while at sea, so he could be on the bridge each time a visual or sonar contact was made. Aft of the engine room stack amidships was the ships wherry boat, resting on its cradle between the vegetable lockers. The wherry could be hoisted on board, port or starboard side, using the ships boom. When in port at anchor that sturdy 16 foot wherry boat was the main ship to shore transportation for officers and crew.

Amidships at the 40 mm. Splinter shield, there was an engine room hatch, a blessing for the engine room gang, in the tropics on the equator, where the heat of tropic sun, the blistering decks and the high engine room temperatures were oppressive that hatch gave some relief. A 1944 Miami article said, a medal on the order of a purple heart, should be available for all those sailors with severe injuries inflicted by the unpredictable actions and gyrations of the rough riding Patrol Craft. Fractured digits, limbs, and skulls were often the end result of the pitching and rolling, as the PC's buffeted their way through heavy seas. The article pointed out that the rugged ships were designed so they seemed to swivel rather than knife through the waves with the resulting spray dousing the decks from bow to stern. Travels from forward compartments to the galley had to be made across the open deck, clinging to the available lifeline to help to remain standing. In the Miami news article the writer described the many difficulties of sleeping on board these small warships. To be lying in a chain supported bunk which leaves the occupant suspended in midair, as the ship rises and falls with the huge swells, isn't conducive to restful sleep or calm nerves. There is something very upsetting to wake up suddenly to discover yourself closer to the bunk mattress above you, than to your own. Other navy ships have their own claims to glory, serving well under all kinds of conditions, as they served their country around the globe. But PC sailors had a unique place in the final victory and not very many sailors who served in the PC fleet would have preferred service in other segments of the navy. The informality was more in keeping with citizen sailors, whose one dream was to bring the war to an end and head for home. Young officers had more opportunity for advancing in rank and achieve command of a naval vessel however small. For the crew, dress codes were reserved for port and cut-off shirts and dungarees were common.

A wartime history of USS PC-606, the USS Andrews from May of 1943 until Sept. 5th 1947 as outlined from the official war archives: from the United States Navy department and office of the Chief of Naval operations in the division of naval history, 0p-29, ship's histories section gives the history of the PC-606. The 606 was constructed by the Luders Marine Const. Co. Inc. Located at Stamford Connecticut. Her keel was laid on April 14th 1942 and she was launched on January 8th 1943. After ten weeks, beginning in May 1943, of pre-commissioning trials and shakedowns of engines and armament, PC-606 was placed in commission at the Brooklyn Navy yard in New York City on August 7th 1943 by Commander H.A. Sasse U.S.N. and placed under the command of Lieutenant D. F. Larkin. After outfitting was completed and after a brief shakedown training period in the waters off Miami Fla. The PC-606 then sailed for duty at Havana, Cuba, where she arrived on September 11th

1943 and reported to Commander Eastern Sea Frontier. The ship was then assigned to anti-submarine warfare, exercises and patrols in Cuban waters. She left Havana, bound for Miami where she joined a northbound convoy on September 27th 1943. Upon release from convoy duty off New York, she sailed to New York harbor and was moored at the U.S. Naval base, Tompkinsville, Staten Island. The PC-606 was assigned to anti-submarine patrol and convoy escort duties between the city of New York and Guantanamo bay, Cuba.

After period of Atlantic convoy duty, in early December 1943, the war against the U-boat in the Atlantic had lessened, she was ordered to the Pacific Theater of War. She transited the Panama Canal, and reported to Commander in Chief U.S. Pacific fleet for duty. Cinc/pac/flt commander in charge. Pacific fleet in turn, ordered PC-606 to proceed to Espirito Santos in the New Hebrides islands for anti-submarine and escort duties with elements of the Pacific fleet. As escort for a floating dry-dock towed by a seagoing tug across the Pacific. The PC-606 arrived at the New Hebrides base on January 31st 1944. Among her areas of operation were from 1944 to wars end in Aug. 1945, were the Solomon Islands, Tarawa, Eniwetok, Guam, Saipan, Tinian, and Iwo Jima. She continued her convoy escort and patrol duties for the duration of World War II, then on March 14th 1946, the ship left Guam, proceeding to Pearl Harbor then returned to the United States. PC-606 reached, San Pedro California, in May of 1946 and left the west coast on Oct. 21st was then ordered, via the Panama Canal, bound for Charleston, S.C. Upon her arrival there, on Nov. 21st 1946, the vessel was assigned to the 16th fleet. And shortly thereafter, began preparations for her de-activation. She ended her naval service and was placed out of commission, on March 24th 1947.

She had been launched at the height of the submarine war in American waters, and served until total victory over Japan, her total term of service lasted over four years. Pending de-activation she was berthed at Green Cove Springs, Florida and while still in reserve, the ship was given a name, the USS Andrews-PC-606", on February 15th 1947. They were named by the Secretary of the Navy to honor of two cities, Andrews, South Carolina and Andrews, Texas. It was an afterthought by Bureau of the Navy to give the little warships a name. But those who served on them proudly knew them by their numbers. She was struck from the navy list of warships; then de-commissioned on Sept 5th 1947 And was sold for scrap. A history of the hundreds of Destroyers, Destroyer Escorts, Patrol Craft and other wartime vessels waiting to be scrapped has been compiled by Robert Lally, and the Green Cove Springs historical group. It is a sad, but necessary end to the gallant ships that brought us to victory.

A list of Military Awards - Awarded to the crew of the PC-606.

American Theater ... Campaign Medal–Awarded to all personnel who served in the Atlantic waters during the period, from December 1941 to December 1945. The medal depicts a Plane, a Ship, and a sinking Submarine

Asiatic-Pacific Theater Campaign medal–With bronze battle star–Awarded to all navy personnel who served within the perimeter of the Japanese Expansion, from December 1941 until December 1945, in Asian and Pacific lands and waters–Depicting a Soldier, Marine and a Palm Tree.

Navy Occupation Service medal, With Asia clasp,–Awarded at the end of the conflict to naval ships and crews on duty in enemy occupied lands or enemy waters, serving from end of hostilities in 1945 until April 27th 1946, the official end of hostilities. – Depicting a mythical Neptune, with his trident, riding a seahorse in the sea.

World War II Victory Medal – Awarded to all those who served in the American armed forces during the war, from December 1941

until the end of hostilities. – Depicting the Lady Justice holding scrolls of peace.

Solomon Island Victory Medal – The Solomon Islands government issued this medal on the 50th anniversary of the Solomon's Island campaign to all members of the U.S. Marines, Army, Navy and Coast Guard armed forces and ships, which took part in the campaign for liberation of the Solomon Islands.

Commemorative Medals–Awarded by Congress for all those who served in the military during World War Two.

A list of Military Awards – Awarded to the crew of the PC-606.

"The War Years", Serving aboard the USS Patrol Craft #606
From November – 1942 to April – 1946

Military Awards – awarded to the crew of the PC- 606

Asiatic-Pacific Theater Campaign medal - With bronze battle star - Awarded to all navy personnel who served within the perimeter of the Japanese Expansion, from December 1941 until December 1945, in Asian and Pacific lands and waters - Depicting a Soldier, a Marine and a palm tree.

American Theater ... Campaign Medal - Awarded to all personnel who served in the Atlantic waters during the period, from December 1941 to December 1945. The medal Depicts a Plane, a ship, and a sinking Submarine.

Occupation Service medal, With Asia clasp. - Awarded at the end of the conflict to naval ships and crews on duty in enemy occupied lands or enemy waters, serving from end of hostilities in 1945 until April 27th 1946, the official end of hostilities. – Depicting a mythical Neptune, with his trident, riding a seahorse in the sea.

World War II Victory Medal – Awarded to all those who served in the American armed forces during the war, from December 1941 until the end of hostilities. – Depicting the Lady Justice holding scrolls of peace.

Personal Medals - Good Conduct, Naval Reserve, Combat action, and Disabled Veteran
The authors medals ... earned in addition to the military medals awarded to the crew.